D1719077

The Wisdom Of
VEDANTA

Books by S. Abhayananda

The Supreme Self

History Of Mysticism

Jnaneshvar: The Life And Works Of The Celebrated
Thirteenth Century Indian Mystic-Poet

Dattatreya: The Song Of The Avadhut

Thomas à Kempis: On The Love Of God

And do not be conformed to this world,
but be transformed by the renewing of your mind.
— Romans 12:2

The Wisdom Of
VEDANTA

Second *(Revised)* Edition

By S. ABHAYANANDA

ATMA BOOKS
OLYMPIA, WASH.

Atma Books
3430 Pacific Ave. S.E.
Suite A-6144
Olympia, WA 98501

Library of Congress Cataloging in Publication Data

Abhayananda, Swami, 1938–
  The wisdom of Vedanta / S. Abhayananda. -- 2nd (Rev.) ed
    p.   cm.
  ISBN 0-914557-06-8
  1. Vedanta.   I. Title.
BF132.V3A53   1994
181'.48--dc20

TABLE OF CONTENTS

PREFACE

The Wisdom Of Vedanta is the culmination of many years of efforts to express in comprehensible terms the reality of God and the means to know Him within as the ultimate nature of one's own Self, the ultimate Truth of one's own existence. This knowledge is not something new; it is the knowledge that has been put forth by the mystics of every tradition since the beginning of time. However, its earliest and best expression goes by the name of "Vedanta", the philosophy put forth in the ancient *Upanishads* of India.

Vedanta is the authentic teaching of those who have directly perceived the nature of God, the nature of Reality. This book, then, is an attempt to convey the teachings of Vedanta in an easily understandable and familiar manner to those who may have had no previous familiarity with the subject. It is composed entirely of individual lectures which I delivered over the past few years at the Vedanta Temple in Naples, Florida and in Lacey, Washington.

I have endeavored to arrange these lectures in something of a 'natural' order of progression so as to afford the best possible introduction of Vedanta to the initiate; but, as each lecture is complete in itself and capable of standing alone, the reader may feel free to roam at will through the various subjects according to interest. I have also made an effort to eliminate much of the inevitable repetition of thoughts and expressions, but there remains, naturally, some overlapping of themes and ideas. However, since the recurrance of essential themes serves to accentuate and reinforce important aspects of the message and wisdom of Vedanta, I think the reader may find this a beneficial feature of this collection.

Vedanta speaks of the bondage of those who live in ignorance of the eternal Self, and the liberation experienced by those who come to know that Self. But the great 13th century sage, Jnaneshvar, once said that, for the enlightened, "there is neither bondage nor liberation; there is nothing to be accomplished. There is only the pleasure of expounding."[1] Let no one imagine, therefore, that this collection of lectures is for the purpose of liberating anyone from their bondage. After all, no man may remove those imaginary bonds from another -- not even by the writing of a million books or by expounding words of wisdom from now till forever.

So why all this speaking? Why fling all these countless words of instruction at the ears of the deaf? It is simply for the pleasure of expounding. It's merely the way of Truth to express Itself in words; it's merely Joy's way to fling a bit of Itself about. Water exists whether the horses drink it or not. Likewise, the joy of expounding is Truth's pleasure and delight. Truth exults in the expression of Truth, as a tree exults in its fruit. The tree doesn't bother about who shall eat and enjoy its fruits; still, for those who can reach it, the fruit is sweet to the taste.

S. Abhayananda

INTRODUCTION TO VEDANTA

Vedanta is a religion as well as a philosophy, a religion based, not on the teachings of any one particular person, but on the common religious experience of countless souls since the beginning of time.

Vedanta means "the end of the Veda", and was originally intended to signify the collection of writings called the *Upanishads,* which were written nearly three thousand years ago by some anonymous Indian sages, and appended to the earlier *Vedas* as their final portion. But the word, *Veda,* simply means "knowledge", or "wisdom"; and so the real meaning of *Vedanta* is "the end of knowledge", "the ultimate wisdom". In this broader interpretation, Vedanta refers, not only to the Upanishads, but covers the whole body of literature which explains, elaborates and comments on the Upanishadic teachings from their conception to the present day. It is synonymous with "the perennial philosophy", that universal knowledge of Unity possessed by all the mystics and sages of past and present. In this sense, Vedanta is the culmination of all knowledge-seeking. It is the final philosophy, recurrently discovered by seekers of Truth in every age.

Because it is the highest knowledge possible to the intellect, the philosophy of Vedanta does not appeal to those without the courage and desire to ferret out the Truth for themselves. But those minds long-accustomed to enquiry and Truth-seeking will experience a thrilling surge of joy upon discovereing the philosophy of Vedanta. For it provides all the missing pieces to the puzzle of life and makes the total picture-puzzle at last intelligible and perfectly clear. What a moment it is for the long-searching intellect when it finally comes across the truths expressed in Vedanta! What excitement it feels on having all its doubts dispelled, like cobwebs swept from the newly-lighted corner of a room. How happy it feels on looking out upon a world perceived as for the first time bathed in clarity and light!

What is it then, about Vedanta that infuses the

mind with such delight and happiness? Reduced to its elements, the philosophy of Vedanta consists of three propositions: First, that man's real nature is Divine. Second, that the aim of human life is to realize this Divine nature. Third, that all genuine religious traditions are in agreement. For it is the teaching of all genuine religion that our separative ego, our vaunted individuality, is but a flimsy charade; and that who we really are beneath the ever-changing tide of thoughts and impressions which flood our minds, is that one, bright, undivided Consciousness whom men call "God". He is the one Self of all selves, "the One who has become many"; and the realization of our eternal and ever-joyful Self is the realization of the Truth that shall make us free.

It is the aim of Vedanta to show men the way to realize and become established in the awareness of their true, Divine, Self. A thousand years before Jesus asserted, "I and the Father are one," the Upanishads declared: *aham brahmasmi*, "I am Brahman"; and *tat tuam asi*, "That thou art." These assertions are not merely high-flown theories or mere suggestions to bolster the ego, but are the confident declarations of those who, in a moment of rare quietude and clarity, have "seen through the veil" of appearance and come face to face with their eternal Identity.

It is of utmost importance to understand that Vedanta is not a mere speculative theory about the nature of Reality; it is the account of Reality by those who have "seen" It and known It -- much more clearly than you see these words before you. It must be approached therefore as the sacred knowledge that it is. We must open ourselves to be taught, with an eagerness to look beyond the limitations of language and of our own conceptual framework, in order to understand what the seers of Truth have to say. If their words are true, they will not contradict our own intellectual judgement. If they are true, they will stir us to new heights of mental clarity and intellectual delight; and they will have the power to inspire us toward the realization of our own Divine Self.

Historical Origins

The *Vedas* may be thought of as 'The Old Testament' of Indian religion, insofar as they represent, for the most part, the views of an archaic Indian priesthood who had not the benefit of mystical vision, but who taught men rather to accept a conciliatory relationship to a pantheon of warring, jealous gods. The *Vedas*, which comprised the oral religious tradition imported into India at the time of the Aryan invasion (ca. 2000 B.C.), tended to hypostacize various natural elements and forces, attributing to them lurid personalities and histories, much as did the mythologies of ancient Greece. The *Upanishads*, on the other hand, were the esoteric writings of the *rishis*, the seers, the rare sages of ancient times, who had actually realized the Unitive Reality through their own contemplative experience.

The *Upanishads*, as well as the *Bhagavad Gita*, may be thought of, therefore, as comprising 'The New Testament' of the Indian religious tradition, which, while expanding upon the old Vedic writings, also supplants them by transcending the polytheism and anthropomorphism of the more elementary *Vedas*. However, neither the *Upanishads* nor the *Bhagavad Gita* should be thought of as the "authority" of Vedanta in the same sense as some take the Bible to be the authority of Christianity. The authority of Vedanta is one's own personal experience of enlightenment. But the *Upanishads* are the earliest and clearest expression of the mystical, or unitive, experience and of the knowledge resulting from such an experience; and for that reason, hold an honored place in the world of religious literature. They stand as testimony and proof of the common perennial knowledge available throughout the history of the world to all who earnestly seek to know their origin and their destination in this life; and all who have come to attain that knowledge have acknowledged the authenticity and purity of these ancient testaments.

Of the many recognized *Upanishads*, twelve are regarded as of primary importance and merit. In philosophical clarity and persuasiveness, these few represent what, for most of us, are to be considered the *Upani-*

shads. Their names are the *Isha, Kena, Katha, Prasna, Mundaka, Mandukya, Chandogya, Brihad-Aranyaka, Aitareya, Taitiriya, Svetasvatara,* and *Maitri Upanishads.* The authors and exact date of authorship of these separate spiritual treatises are unknown; we know only that they were written, by various anonymous sages who had realized that Truth of which they speak, sometime between 1200 B.C. and the first few centuries of the Christian era. While they vary in length and in style, their one common theme is the inner realization of the identity of the Self (*Atman*) and God (*Brahman*). We may seek to know God, or we may strive to know our Self; but, say the *Upanishads,* when you find the one, you will find the other as well -- for they are one. It is this inner discovery which constitutes enlightenment.

In its long history, Vedanta has had many enlightened sages, many holy saints, to serve as its glorious representatives. Indeed, it may be said that even those enlightened souls of other lands and other religious traditions -- such as the 3rd century Roman, Plotinus, or the 13th century Christian, Meister Eckhart, or the Sufi, Ibn Arabi -- may be regarded as representatives of Vedanta, insofar as their experiences and their teachings are wholly consistent with the philosophy of Vedanta. But, there is one historical figure who played a most prominent role in revitalizing Vedanta by his writings, his teachings and his very life: that man is the medieval Indian *acharya,* or teacher, known as Shankara.

Shankaracharya lived sometime between the 7th and 9th centuries, during a time when Vedanta had become almost forgotten and nearly supplanted throughout the Indian landscape by Buddhism. And even those who clung to the ancient ways tended, for the most part, to make of Vedanta nothing more than a priestly brahminism based primarily on the adherence to conventional Vedic ritual and the laws of behavior governing the various castes. It was Shankara who brought, through his single-handed efforts, a return to the unitive philosophy of the *Upanishads* and a re-awakening of the Indian spirit to its long-established heritage of spiritual wisdom.

Before his death in the Himalayas at the age of

thirty-two, Shankara authored many independent treatises as well as commentaries on ancient Vedantic texts; he re-established the monastic tradition on a firm footing; and he travelled the length and breadth of India on foot, teaching the truth which he had realized in himself, and which corroborated the teachings of the ancient rishis. He taught not only the metaphysics of Unity, but he taught also the means whereby one could realize, as he had done, that eternal Lord of the universe. Here are his own words:

"Gain experience directly. Realize God for yourself! Know the Self as the one indivisible Being, and become perfect. Free your mind from all unnecessary distractions and dwell in the consciousness of the Self.

"This is the final declaration of Vedanta: Brahman is everything; it is this universe and every creature. To be liberated (from ignorance) is to live in the continual awareness of Brahman, the undivided Reality." [1]

Shankara's philosophy, the philosophy of Vedanta, may be characterized by the use of a simple formula taken from his writings; it is this: *brahma satyam,* "God is the Reality"; *jagan mithya,* "the world is illusory"; *jivo brahmaiva napara,* "the soul, or self, is indeed, nothing but God". In the following sections, these three subjects: God, the world, and the Self, will be discussed in the light of the above statement.

God

The beginning student of Vedanta will have to become accustomed to many different names for God, as it has long been recognized in the Indian religious tradition that God cannot be limited to any particular name or form. It was stated in the *Vedas*: "Truth is one; men call It by many different names." The important thing to understand is that beneath the various names -- *Brahman, Purusha, Rama, Shiva, Hari* -- the Reality is one and the same for all.

The word most commonly used in the Upanishads for God is *Brahman*. By "Brahman" is meant the limitless Awareness, the universal Consciousness, that is experienced in the contemplative state. The *rishis,* who had experienced in their meditations this infinite Consciousness, gave it the name, "Brahman".   Of course, It is beyond names and unnameable, as It is That which exists prior to the manifestation of name and form; but, from another perspective, every name that can be uttered is God's name, as there is no name or form that is not His manifestation.

Brahman exists as both the subjective and the objective Reality, but He can only be *directly* known as the subjective Reality; i.e., from within as 'I'. The objective Reality is that which is perceived, either as subtle form (on the mental, or psychic, level), or as gross form (on the sensual level).   The subjective Reality is the perceiver, the Witness.   It is that very consciousness which we experience as our very own existence.   That is Brahman; and it is That which is to be known.   This is clearly explained in the *Upanishads*:

> What cannot be spoken with words, but That whereby words are spoken: know That alone to be Brahman and not what people here adore. What cannot be thought with the mind but That whereby the mind can think: know That alone to be Brahman and not what people here adore. What cannot be seen with the eye, but That whereby the eye can see: know That to be Brahman and not what people here adore.[2]
> ...It is not speech we should wish to know; we should know the speaker.   It is not the things that are seen which we should wish to know; we should know the seer.   It is not sounds which we should wish to know; we should know the listener.   It is not the thoughts which we should wish to know; we should know the thinker.[3]

The experience, or "revelation", of Brahman is an experience which changes forever the perceived identity of the experiencer.   For, having seen Brahman, he has seen his real, eternal, Self.   In that rare awakening, he experiences his own consciousness as the limitless Consciousness of the universe.   It is the background Reality to all that is manifest as universal phenomena. While immersed in that infinite Awareness, one is able to perceive that all the various worlds and galaxies of this vast universe are but the spreading rays of love expanding from one's own Self. All that we call "the world" is nothing but the mental projections of that one Consciousness, which expand to manifest as the evolving universe and then are withdrawn again, back into that unfathomable Consciousness. Like breaths alternating from inspiration to expiration, this creation-destruction cycle repeats itself eternally. Each "breath", though momentary from the perspective of that Awareness, contains the billions of ages required to evolve and then dissolve the myriad worlds presently evolving their destinies throughout space.

The ordinarily time-bound consciousness which experiences this glimpse into timeless Awareness is overwhelmed by this experience. While deeply immersed in it, he is God, he is eternal, he is alone -- without a second; and there is no limited consciousness to distract his atention by responses of awe and amazement. There is nothing but himself; and nothing could be clearer or more obviously true and natural. But after the absorption of the limited identity into the universal has waned, and the time-bound ego resurfaces, then the reflective mind is struck with bewilderment and awe. With breathless humility and gratitude, it realizes only gradually the immensity of the experience that has come to it. "I am all this!" it exclaims incredulously. "All this universe is only myself. I am the one Consciousness. There is no one but Me!"

Who is this one Self which includes all selves? What shall we call It? The ancient rishis of India who experienced It call It "Brahman". But because it is always experienced only as the subject, the I-consciousness, It is commonly referred to in the *Upanishads* also as the *Atman*, which means, "the Self". *Atman* and *Brahman* refer to the same One. In other words, Vedanta declares that God and the Self are one: God is who you are. Whether you know it or not, you are That; *tat tuam asi*. This is not merely a pleasant and convenient theory; it is the truth that has been experienced directly by countless souls since the beginning of time.

The World

The mystic who experiences Brahman, the unitive Reality, in the contemplative state experiences that Unity as himself. In fact, if he were something other than That, it would no longer be a Unity, but a duality. And while experiencing himself to be Brahman, the one pure Consciousness, he experiences also that all the manifested universe is but his own projection, much as a thought-form is the projection of an individual mind within itself. It is his own radiation, his own glory. No matter what words one uses to describe it -- whether as a "projection", "an imaging forth", a "superimposition", a "manifestation of Will" -- it cannot be adequately described, as we have nothing in our experience with which to compare it.

It is a unique and indescribable experience that the mystic confronts. He knows that he is the unchanging Ground, the Absolute, pure Consciousness; and yet simultaneously, he is exuding an inconceivably complex universe of evolving worlds in which he himself lives, as one lives within his own dream. This creative expansiveness is similar to the expansion of love which we, as humans, feel in the heart for all creatures, or like the emanation of a thought-image increased to an infinite degree of power and light. It is quite beyond telling, except to say that within the one Being these two complementary aspects exist: the one infinite and unchanging, an unblinking Consciousness, pure and clear, like the vast blue sky; the other, a Power of manifestation which creates the world in which all creatures and things exist. Seers have called these two aspects by many different names, such as "Godhead and Creator", "Theos and Logos", "Light and Darkness", Purusha and Prakrti", Shiva and Shakti"; Vedantists often refer to them as "Brahman and Maya".

One who has experienced this complementarity of aspects within the one Reality knows without a shadow of a doubt that the world is a projected Energy-manifestation of the universal Self. In other words, this world is nothing but God. Indeed, if a "world" is seen, that is an illusion -- because what is seen is nothing but God. To postulate a "world" as a second thing is to postulate an absolute duality. But duality is merely God's illusion; there is never anything but the One. The forms perceived by the senses, the forms perceived by the mind; the ideas, the images, the pleasures, the pains -- all God's. It is all His dream-like creation; nothing is separate from Him. All is God and nothing but God.

However, we must understand that, so long as we perceive a "world", there is an apparent duality: "apparent", because, while there is always One and One alone, there is the appearance of two-ness. Take, for example, the Sun and its rays: it appears to be two things, but, in fact, it is one thing. Or take the mind and its thoughts: they are apparently two. But no, there is only the mind. Shall we say then, that the rays are unreal, imaginary? Or that the thoughts are non-existent? No. Nor can we say they are real. They have no independent reality; that is to say, they do not exist independent of their source. It is like that also with God and the world. The world is a manifestation of God; and from that perspective, the two are one. But God is eternal, while the world has but an ephemeral, transient appearance, like a thought. Therefore, like a thought, the world is neither real nor unreal. Vedantists call it "Maya".

Maya is just another name for God's Power of manifestation, His Power of world-projection. That Power is inherent and co-eternal with God -- whether there's a creation or not. But "Maya" is both the (eternal) Cause and the (temporal) effect. Maya is God's Power (*shakti*); and it is also the world-illusion produced by that Power.

Anyone who has studied the analysis by modern-day physicists of the sub-atomic world of matter must have come to the realization that all this world of various forms is composed simply of "fields of force", or Energy; and that every form that exists is merely an "appearance" conjured by this mysterious chimera called "Energy". That Energy is God's Power of illusion; i.e., Maya. It is Maya that creates what we regard as the "objective" universe.

All experience of the world is dependent upon

there being both a subject and an object; in other words, a seer and a seen. It should be clear that if you have only the subject, the seer, nothing can be experienced unless you have also the object, the seen. Or, if you have only the object, the seen, but do not have a subject, a seer, still nothing is experienced. We have all heard the conundrum which asks, "If a tree falls in a forest, and no one sees it fall, did it really fall?" Modern physics has shown quite clearly that the subject, the seer, is an integral ingredient in the existence of an object, that which is seen. For example, the manner in which one observes a quantum particle determines its manner of existence; indeed, without the subject, the object cannot be said to exist at all. The one exists only so long as the other exists.

This is the view of Vedanta as well. There must be both the subject and the object; otherwise, there is only God, absolute, undivided. God has made Himself into both the subject and the object, the seer and the seen. This is how He has created all this drama within Himself. It is all Himself, of course; but, in order to make for any kind of experience at all, He had to provide out of Himself both sides; He had to become both the subject and the object. Now, keep in mind, there is really nothing else but God; He is playing both these parts. So you are That also. When you examine yourself, you find that, in your makeup, there are also these two sides, these two aspects: there is the subject, the "I"; and there is also that which is experienced through the senses as the body, and also as the thoughts, dreams, images that play before the subjective "I". These things are the objects of your experience. Of course, there is also the world outside of your body and mind; all that too is seen, experienced, as the "object". So you can see: everything has this (apparent) two-sided-ness. So long as there is a world, there will be "two"; in other words, an apparent duality. Only when we can merge the objective, thought-producing, mind back into God, are we able to realize directly the truth that there is ultimately only the One.

The Self

The Self is Brahman, the universal Consciousness. It is the one "I" that everyone experiences as the Self. In the *Upanishads*, the question is asked, "Who is the Self?" And the reply given is, "The Self is the witness of the mind." It is that inconspicuous Witness behind all of our various states of mind which is our true, everlasting Self, and not those various states of mind themselves, with which most of us identify. The Self is the only Reality; but, because we tend to identify with the separative mind and the transient body, we lose sight of our eternal nature as pure Consciousness. Yet It is always there, just behind our minds.

If we reflect, "Who am I? Am I the body? Am I the mind or the intellect?", we quickly realize that we are none of these; we are the pure Consciousness that is witnessing all these. For example, in the waking state, who is looking out from behind your eyes reading this? Who is witnessing all the forms around you? Is it only the senses? Only the mind? No. You cannot be the mind, because you are witnessing the activity of the mind. Is it not so? And, in the dream state, who watches the dreams and remembers them upon awaking? And, in the deep sleep state, if "you" were really asleep, who was it that experienced that blissful nothingness, and who knows that it was a sound and deep state of peace that was experienced? It is clear to the discriminating mind that, in all three states, there is an unchanging Consciousness which is not involved in the activities of those states, but who witnesses them, and who is the real "you", the real Self, independent of the mind and body. That is our true Identity.

There is a fourth state, which can be experienced in deep meditation. It occurs when the mind becomes entirely pure and still and merges into that universal Consciousness. Then, one becomes aware, "I am everything; all this universe is only myself! And yet, though all these things and beings are contained in Me, I am forever One and undifferentiated. I am Consciousness and Bliss." Such a state is not just

imaginary; it is not just a theory. Many people have
experienced such a state. It is the experience of
That which underlies all of the great philosophies
and religions of the world, and constitutes the wisdom
of all the saints. Listen to what the seers of the
Upanishads said:

When a man has seen the truth of the Spirit,
he is one with Him; the aim of his life is fulfilled, and he is ever beyond sorrow. [4]
When a man knows God, he is free; his
sorrows have an end, and birth and death are
no more. When in inner union he is beyond
the world of the body, then the world of the
Spirit is found where man possesses all -- for
he is one with the One. [5]
When a sage sees this great Unity, and
realizes his Self has become all beings, what
delusion and what sorrow could ever approach
him? [6] When awake to the vision of one's own
Self, when a man in truth can say: 'I am He',
what desires could lead him to grieve in fever
for the body? ... When a man sees the Atman,
his own Self, the one God, the Lord of what
was and of what shall be, he fears no more. [7]

In the Vedantic tradition, such an awareness is
said to be "Liberation". Jesus of Nazareth also
spoke of this freedom that is attained through knowledge of the Truth: "You shall know the Truth," he
said, "and the Truth shall make you free." Why
does the knowledge of Truth make you free? Because,
when you become aware that you are all-pervading,
you no longer suffer under the illusion that you are a
limited individual being. You will go on playing your
role as a father, mother, a wife, a doctor, a lawyer,
a beggar, or king; in fact, your enjoyment in playing
your role will be increased manifold. But you will
also be at rest within, in the joyful awareness of
your perfect Self, infinite and eternal -- like an
actor, who earnestly plays his role on stage, but who
remains conscious throughout the drama that he is
not the character whom he is playing. He remains
free within, happy and secure in the knowledge of
his true identity.

It is this truth that we must come to know and understand: Just as waves on the ocean are only water, just as golden ornaments are only gold, so all the various forms in the universe are only your Self. When you know this and make it a part of your understanding, you will begin to revel in that joy that had been missing in your life before. You will begin to drink the nectar of the love for which you had been thirsting before. And you will begin to take delight in simply being and living and acting in the world in a much more fulfilling way than you had been able to before. Indeed, the knowledge of the Self is the only means to real fulfillment, and enduring happiness. To know the Self is the aim and destiny of all human life.

The question then arises, "How can I attain it?" And the answer is, "It's already attained!" The Self has never left you; in fact, it can never go away. You are that eternal Self! The body will go; the mind will go. But you will always be. This is the truth. This is the liberating knowledge of all the wise seers and sages of every land of every time. It is found in the sacred scriptures of the Hindus, the Buddhists, the Jews, the Muslims, and in the teachings of Jesus. All say the same: 'You are the eternal Self, the Source and Witness of your thoughts. That is who you really are. But because you are not aware of it, you identify with the mental activity and the transient worldly forms, and forgetting your real Identity, you become swept away in the agitated currents of the mind. It is just this false identification which is the source of all your woes and troubles. And if you could become aware of your true, eternal, Self, the various thought-forms that arise would be powerless to affect you one way or the other.

Another question that may arise is that of the relationship of the individualized, transmigrating soul to the ultimate Self, the Divine Unity. This question is also resolved in the teachings of Vedanta. All the seers of the Self have acknowledged the existence of an individualized soul; but, they say, it has no permanent existence. The individualized soul is really nothing more than a congregation of mental tendencies which, while continuing throughout many lifetimes, must eventually come to an end when its real essence is realized.   Listen to what Shankaracharya had to say about it:

The Self is the Witness, beyond all attributes, beyond action. It can be directly realized as pure Consciousness and infinite Bliss. Its appearance as an individual soul is caused by the delusion of our understanding and has no reality. By its very nature, this appearance is unreal. When our delusion has been removed, it ceases to exist. [8]

This is why enlightenment is regarded as "liberation from the round of birth and death."   As Shankaracharya says:

The transmigrating soul is not different from the Lord.[9] ... Just as the light of the Sun and the Sun itself are not different, so also the soul and the supreme Self are not different.[10]

Because all souls are essentially not different, and their apparent difference is due only to ignorance of the Self, the individual soul, after having dispelled that ignorance by true knowledge of the Self, becomes one with the Self.[11]

This, indeed, is the teaching of all who have truly known the Self.   When the Self is experienced, they say, there is no soul.   All duality is swallowed up. The seeker and the sought, the seer and the seen, the "I" and the "Thou", are no longer two in the experience of Unity.   Only the Self experiences the Self.

It is this experience, this realization, of the eternal Self, which, according to Vedanta, constitutes salvation, or liberation.   We find this stated in every piece of Vedantic literature, including all the Upanishads.   It is not a very difficult concept to grasp: The Self is the Truth of the universe; It's the Truth of ourselves. It's who we really are.   There's truly no one here but you!   And to know, to really know, this Truth is the attainment of the final knowledge and the ultimate freedom.

What, then, is the means to attain this knowledge, according to Vedanta?   Those who have known the

Self say that there are basically two different paths
to the attainment of Self-knowledge: (1) The path of
identifying with the soul; also called the path of
Devotion; and (2) The path of identifying with the
Self; also called the path of Knowledge.

There are times when, as an individual soul, you
feel the necessity of approaching God as His child,
His devotee, His servant.   The love in your heart
bubbles up and expresses itself as devotion to the
Lord of the universe.   This is the noblest and highest
path for the soul, to focus on God within itself with
true humility and love in simple prayer and worship.
You will joy in the singing of His name, and in serving
Him in all His creatures, and in remembering His
presence at every moment in every place.

And there are other times, when you become
quiet, and your breathing becomes shallow and soft,
and you taste something of the certainty of your
eternal and limitless Selfhood.   Then you rest in that
quietude, that solitary joyfulness -- without thought,
without movement, aware only of your own infinite
presence.   This is meditation, a glorious practice.   It
enables one to become centered in the Self, to rise
above all the vicissitudes of life, and to remain established in peace and goodwill, attuned to the inner
joy, and seeing the one Divinity in all creation.

Both of these practises, the devotional and the
meditative, are perfectly valid; they are both firmly
based in Truth.   For remember, we are both distinguishable from, and at the same time, identical to,
the one Consciousness.   A ray of sunlight is both
distinguishable from and also identical with the sun;
a thought-image is both distinguishable from and yet
identical with the mind; a wave is at once distinguishable from and yet identical with the ocean.   We,
too, possess this complementarity in our identity.

Whether we turn, as a soul, to God, or turn, as
the Self, within to our own Identity; in both instances,
we are looking toward the one Light.   We should
come to understand ourselves so well that we can
worship God with heart-felt love at one moment, and
know Him as not different from our inner Self at
another moment, and not feel the slightest contradiction in so doing.   This whole world of creation is

God, and it is also God's.   If God in the form of
His creature lovingly worships God, the Creator, who
is going to object?   Remember, He, the One, is both
the subject and the object; He is both the worshipper
and That which is worshipped; He is the lover and
the Beloved; and He is the love as well.

It is only the ONE who has become many; and
there is nothing else but the ONE in the many.
Beneath the differences lies the Undifferntiated.   It
is that one Self who is spread out everywhere in all
these variegated forms -- in the drifting cotton-puffs
of clouds, and in the moist soil beneath our feet.   It
is our own Self who is the life-pulse in every form
of life -- in trees, crustaceans, amphibians, in every
weasel and woodchuck in its burrow.   Every yearning
human soul you see is you.   Every loving heart eager
for God is your own.   The crystal-clear eyes of
every illumined soul are bright with your love.   You
have cast yourself into the magical forms of man
and woman for the sake of delight, for the sake of
joy.   If we are to live in the Truth, we must learn
to expand our vision and our love to embrace all that
exists.   This is the teaching of Vedanta.   Listen,
now, to the words of the *Upanishads*:

> These three: the   soul,   the   world,   and   the
> Lord of all,
> Are nothing else but the one Brahman.
> It's Brahman alone who exists as everyone and
> everything;
> Beyond Brahman, the Self, there is nothing
> further to know.[12]

> That one conscious Self, the smallest of the
> small, the greatest of the great,
> Conceals Himself in everyone's heart.
> The wise, by the grace of God, become free
> When they see that majestic and desireless Self
> within.[13]

> When the Lord is known, then a man's soul is
> freed;
> He'll never know sorrow or birth again.
> Through devotion, he'll rise to the highest state,
> And rest forever in the bliss of God.[14]

To that effulgent Lord who's in fire and in seas,
Who lives as this world, who's in plants and in
trees,
To that Lord let us sing!   Give all glory to
Him!
To that Lord let us sing!   Give all glory to
Him! [15]

Reflection

The essence of Vedanta is "Surrender to God!"
The essence is "Cling to His feet!"   Vedanta means
"Remember Him constantly; lift yourself to Him by
the strength of your desire!"   How can one express
the essence of Vedanta?   It is a state of the soul
when it's buoyed up by grace.

Vedanta's essence is intimacy; "Be dissolved in
His Bliss!"   The offering of one's heart, mind and
body in service of God is the essence of Vedanta; it
is the wisdom of love.   It is unshaken confidence in
the strength of the soul; "Identify with Him -- be
as great and as good!"

There is one Life, one Mind, one infinite Ocean
of Truth.   He is manifest in souls, as the sea manifests waves.   Vedanta is the awakening of the wave
to its Truth; it is the joyful realization of the soul's
infinite Self.

*   *   *

THE PERENNIAL PHILOSOPHY

The viewpoint of the mystic -- one who has had a glimpse into the nature of reality -- is sometimes referred to as "The Perennial Philosophy", since it is one that is seen to resurface again and again throughout history. It is a worldview that is common to mystics of every conceivable religious tradition. It has been called, in the words of the *Vedas*, the *sanatana dharma*, "the eternal religion", as it is the foundation which underlies all the various sectarian "religions" and all mystical philosophy.

Vedanta is nothing but this perennial philosophy reduced to its most concise and succinct expression. Though the truths of the spiritual life were so clearly expressed in the *Upanishads* long ago, still, there have been many attempts since then to improve on their clarity and simplicity. It is only natural that the great sages of the past should attempt to give concise expression to their own realizations and to explain the spiritual path as they envisioned it. For example, recall the capsulization by Shankara of his philosophical message in the formula, "God is the reality; the world is illusory; and the soul is nothing but God." This he regarded as the simplest and best formulation of his philosophy, in order to best convey the truths of the *Upanishads* that the self of man is the Self of the universe; that *Atman* and *Brahman*, Self and God, are one.

How might we simplify in capsulized form the message of Jesus? Jesus, who had attained knowledge of his identity with God, taught the dualistic path of Devotion to his disciples, so that they too might become pure in heart and be blessed with the vision of God. At one time, in answer to a sceptic, he capsulized his message in this way: "Love the Lord, your God, with all your heart and with all your soul and with all your might and with all your mind. This is the greatest and the first commandment. And the second is like it: Love your neighbor as your Self." [1]

The first tenet, that we must give all our love to God, is primary and necessary before we can be

capable of doing the second, in the estimation of
Jesus; for he had realized the truth of man's eternal
Identity and his unity with all being.   From this, it
followed that to do unto others as though they were
one's own Self was clearly in accord with the truth.
But he knew also that, above all, one must strive to
draw near to God through devotion, so that one
might attain the realization of the eternal Truth,
which alone had the power to make a man free.
First, said Jesus, seek the kingdom of God; then all
the rest will be added unto you.

The Buddha, who lived long before Jesus, had a
quite different way of talking about the Truth and
the path to Its realization.   He taught the path of
Knowledge, the path of meditation.   He, like Jesus,
had experienced his identity with the Eternal, and he
realized that it is "the belief in a separate 'I' that
gives rise to all sorrows, binding us as with cords to
the world of sorrow."   This 'I', said the Buddha,
"does not exist, and the illusion of it conceals what
is truly the Permanent Reality."

He did not call this permanent reality "God",
but he asserted Its existence and the possibility of
Its realization in the following words:

> There is an Unborn, an Unoriginated, an
> Uncompounded.   Were this not so, there would
> be no escape from the world of the born, the
> originated, the compounded.[2]

Here is how the Buddha reduced his message to
a capsulized form as 'the four noble truths':

(1)   All beings experience suffering (This is
self-evident).

(2)   There is a cause of suffering (ignorance
of the "permanent Reality").

(3)   There is a release from suffering (the
extinguishing of the false ego and consequent
realization of the Unborn Self).

(4)   There is a path, or means, to the release
from suffering (meditation).

For the Buddha, this was the simplest and best
expression of the problem and the solution to the
problem.   For him, this comprised the essence of his

teaching.

There are, naturally, many different ways of capsulizing the perennial philosophy, or reducing the statement of the ultimate Unity to what appears to be its most concise and succinct formulation; and these are only a few such ways. Consider one more: this is a definition of the perennial philosophy, of Vedanta, if you will, which was offered by Christopher Isherwood in his splendid Introduction to a book called *Vedanta For The Western World*, published by Vedanta Press. It is this: "Reduced to its elements, Vedanta philosophy consists of three propositions. First, that man's real nature is Divine. Second, that the aim of human life is to realize this Divine nature. Third, that all religions are essentially in agreement." For me, this is one of the best of all such capsulizations, or reductions. Let's examine it:

The first proposition is that "Man's real nature is Divine." Not that there is a false or unreal nature which we experience as suffering or illusion, but simply that man's real nature is Divine. Notice too that there is no assertion that there is a 'God' out there somewhere; or that we can become one with that eternal Being; or that we need to worship or propitiate that God in some way; but simply that man's real nature is Divine, or in other words, is God -- for what else is Divine but the Divinity? There is no need here to explain that God is within us, or that the Transcendent is identical with the Immanent Divinity, for all that is already implicit in the statement that man's real nature is Divine. The idea that *Atman* and *Brahman* are one is also implicitly declared. And so, all of Shankara's formula is contained in this first proposition.

The second proposition is that the aim of human life is to realize this Divine nature. Who says this is the purpose of life? Is this decreed by God? How do we know this is the purpose of life? Well, if we grant that man's real nature is Divine, with all that this implies, i.e., that we are omnipresent as all existence, omniscient as the universal Consciousness underlying all that is, and all-blissful as the eternally unchanging Self of all, then who could deny that such a truth, being realizable, should be realized?

Truth is pursued, not for the sake of a reward, but simply for the sake of knowing. The instinct for knowing truth is inherent and self-evident; it needs no proof.

This proposition, that the realization of our real nature is the aim of human life, also has as its basis a profound and complex understanding of the evolution of the (transmigrating) soul, and of how it suffers in consequence of its ignorance of its real nature. It follows therefore that the realization of one's true nature is the means to be free of suffering -- just as the Buddha suggested. So, just as the precepts of Shankara were contained in our first proposition, so is all of the Buddha's preceptual formula contained in the second proposition, that the realization of our Divine nature is the aim and purpose of life.

Now, we come to the third proposition: that all religions are essentially in agreement. Implied in this is the tenet that all those who have experienced the Truth directly have described It and the path to Its realization in nearly identical terms. They are in agreement that the Truth, the Reality, the Eternal is one; i.e., is a unified, and indivisible, Field of existence, other than which nothing exists. But this is the understanding of the enlightened. What of the ignorant majority? They are unable to grasp this truth and assimilate it into their daily awareness.

You see, if men could agree that the first two propositions constituted the true understanding of life, the true religion, then all religions would certainly be in agreement. But the idea that man's real nature is Divine and that the purpose of life is to realize that Divine nature is not something to which all men can agree. Many, for example, think that the real nature of man is evil, is self-centeredness. Many others believe that the purpose of life is to obtain as much material wealth, power, and sense-pleasures as it is possible to attain in a lifetime. There are some who would turn Shankara's formula around to read: 'The world is real; God is illusion; and there is no such thing as a soul, but only a body which dies and that's the end of it.' But even those who are devoted to religious ideals often fail to see anything in common with other similarly devoted

souls if those others embrace another religious tradition, or follow a spiritual teacher other than the
one they follow.

So, it would seem that, despite our great hopes
for an enlightened society of integrated cultures, all
following the same ideal of realizing the Divine nature
of man, such a hope has little likelihood of being
realized in a world of extremely diversified levels of
understanding and soul-evolution. The unification of
world thought is a wonderful ideal, but, unfortunately,
it is not likely to become a reality in the foreseeable
future. It would be naive to expect the vast ignorant
masses of men to know the highest truth; for it
requires a deep and thoughtful mind to comprehend
the underlying unity of all religion, and great wisdom
to even seek to know the eternal Truth for oneself.

A great mystic of the 16th century, named
Dadu, expressed the idea very well when he said,
"Ask of those who have attained (the realization of)
God; all speak the same word. ... All the enlightened
have left one message; ... it is only those in the
midst of their journey who hold diverse opinions." [3]
And, of course, the great majority of the world's
people are in the midst of their spiritual journey,
and therefore, there are likely to be heard many
diverse opinions for many centuries to come.

While this third proposition, that all religions are
essentially in agreement, is a truth that has the
potential to unify world thought, it is one which we
need not concern ourselves overmuch about. It is
the first two propositions which should accupy all
our attention. Know that you are Divine. Make
that a part of your everyday awareness. Live in
that awareness; and immerse yourself in it during
your time of meditation. Strive toward the realization
of your true nature by whatever means are most
appealing to you. Be a *bhakta* (devotee); be a *jnani*
(person of intellectual discrimination); be a *karma-yogi*
(one who performs every action as worship); or a *raja-
yogi*, integrating all these paths into one broad and
royal highway. But never cease to endeavor to know,
to understand, to clarify your own mind, and to
become true to your real nature. Eventually, you
must come to realize all that is realizable. It is not

only the aim of human life, but it is the destiny of all human lives to realize the Truth.

Listen to some inspiring words from one who has attained that ultimate knowledge; these are verses from an ancient song, called *The Avadhut Gita:*

To some, the Self appears as 'other';
To me, the Self is 'I'.
Like undivided space, One alone exists.
How, then, could the subject and object of
   meditation be two? [4]

You are the ultimate Reality; have no doubt.
The Self is not something known by the mind;
The Self is the very one who knows!
How, then, could you think to know the Self? [5]

You are the one Purity! You have no body.
You are not the mind; you're the supreme
   Reality.
'I'm the Self, the supreme Reality!'
Say this without any hesitancy. [6]

Why do you weep, O mind? Why do you cry?
Take the attitude: 'I am the Self!'
O dear one, go beyond the many;
Drink the supreme nectar of Unity! [7]

Reflection

There is a summit of knowledge which has been reached by a few lone souls such as the Buddha, Jesus, Shankara, Ramakrishna, and others. This knowledge came to them by the grace of God, revealing the truth that all existence is forever One. This being so, there exists no separate beings such as the Buddha, Jesus, Shankara, etc., but only the One, knowing Himself in all these various forms.

It is, indeed, just this knowledge which constitutes the message of every seer of Truth: 'The One exists as you and me. Realize this Truth; know that you are the One, and be free of the pain of enmity.'

There is but one religion, not many. It is only the childish and the deluded who think otherwise. There is but one substance which is variously named as "water", "pani", "jal", "agua". But no matter what it is called, that same substance quenches the thirst of all.

There is but one Life, though it takes various forms, as tiger, serpent, and man; all breathe one air, all see one light. Understand too that one all-pervading Intelligence fills all minds, gives conscious Light to all that lives. He alone is, and lives and breathes as us. In knowing Him, all purposes of life are fulfilled. In shedding darkness from our minds, by rising high above the clouds of 'me' and 'mine', we come closer to this Light, and merge our souls in Him.

This is the tale which all have told who've seen the Truth. It is neither old nor new, but is an unchanging testament that neither time nor place on earth affects. Jesus, Buddha, Ramakrishna -- all have reached that same summit, and shown to us the way. Now, we must climb alone and find our way into the Truth which they enjoy, and make if finally our own.

*   *   *

THE SUPREME SELF

I'd like to talk a little about the convergence of the view of the modern physicists with that of the ancient mystics. This is a topic which has become a very popular one; and many books, both from the viewpoint of the physicist and from the viewpoint of the mystic, have been written to explain how these two fields, regarded for so long as irreconcilable, have now come to see things in very much the same way.

Much of what led to this convergence of views was begun in the early part of this century with the ideas of Albert Einstein and Neils Bohr. And what was formulated in merely a general way then, later became demonstrable through laboratory experiments, resulting in the use of atomic power and microtechnology; and, more significantly, in a radical revision of the scientific community's conception of the ultimate stuff of the universe. One of the more recent books about the convergence of the scientific and the mystical views summed up the conclusions of today's scientists by saying: "If there is any ultimate stuff of the universe, it is pure Energy." This, of course, is what mystical philosophy, including Vedanta, has been saying since the *Vedas*. For Vedantists, this universal Energy is called "*Shakti*".

It was Einstein, more than any other scientist, who brought home to us the fact that the universe is composed of energy -- incredibly powerful energy. Nearly everyone is familiar with Einstein's equation, $E=mc^2$; but few, I think, grasp the full significance of this equation. Translated into English, it says, "Energy is equivalent to the mass of a particle of matter multiplied by the speed of light squared." But think what that really means! The energy contained in a quantum of matter is equal to the mass of the quantum multiplied by an extraordinary large number: the speed of light squared. In other words, 1,119,480,000. This means that even the tiniest particle of matter has within it a tremendous amount of concentrated energy. This fact accounts, not only for the incredible devastation at the bombing of

Hiroshima, but it also accounts for the amazing recoup-
erative and healing powers of psychics, and the supernormal abilities and the tangible effulgence and
radiance emanating from master yogis who are able
to draw upon and control that energy within their
own being.

The world of science is rapidly merging into the
world of the mystic; indeed, this is exactly what
scientists are coming to understand: the world is not
divided; it is not constituted of multiple 'things' and
events, but is a unified whole.   It is becoming as
clear to physicists as it has always been to mystics
that there are never two things, but always only one
thing appearing in different forms.   Consider, for example, the two categories, "mass" and "energy",
which not long ago were regarded as two separate
and distinguishable qualities.   Since Einstein's General
Theory of Relativity, which was published in 1908,
however, matter and energy are no longer seen by
physicists to be two separate entities, but rather
simply two different forms, or states, of the same
thing.   In the language of physicists, these two words
are no longer even used separately; they speak only
of one thing: "mass-energy".   This is so commonly
understood among physicists that now the mass of
subatomic particles is routinely measured in units of
energy.   The old physics of Newton has become
revised.   For the word, "mass", as well as for the
word, "energy", we must now substitute the word,
"mass-energy".

For example, Newton's First Law of Thermodyn-
amics used to read: "The sum of the mass within a
closed-system remains constant."   Now, it is revised
to read: "The sum of the mass-energy within a closed
system remains constant."   In other words, in this
universe (which is the only existent closed-system),
there is a constant shifting or transformation of the
one stuff from mass to energy and back again.   This
is seen, for example, as sunlight, through the process
of photosynthesis, turns to plant-life, which eaten,
turns to animal tissue, which translates into work, or
energy.   However, as the law states, the sum, the
totality of the mass-energy within the universe,
remains constant.   The universe, as a whole, is un-

changing -- even though there appears to be a continuous changing of form, shapes, and activity, an unceasing flux. If we look at the universe from the viewpoint
of its content of mass-energy, we must acknowledge
that it is an undivided, undifferentiated, and always
constant, unit.

This is precisely what the mystic experiences. In
our normal state of awareness, we identify with a
part of this whole, and experience multiplicity. But
in the mystic's experience of Unity, there occurs a
shift of awareness from a limited part to the whole;
and he experiences within himself the one, unchanging,
eternally constant, Reality. He sees too that the
incessant change from mass to energy and energy to
mass goes on occurring -- everything goes on as
before. And yet everything has come to a stop.
There is only One, with no change, ever.

It is the oft-repeated verification by countless
people who have experienced It over the ages and
their unanimous testimony that Unity alone is, that
has kept the idea burning always in the mind of
humanity as a religious truth. Now, at last, we seem
to be entering a time when science, that is, empirical
knowledge, is catching up with gnosis, or intuited
knowledge; and the fact that there is One and only
that One is becoming truly inescapable. In course of
time, this knowledge will become universal, and will
become the underlying foundation of all our understanding about the world.

Thousands of years ago, a sage wrote in the
Upanishads: "What is here is also there, and what is
there is also here. He is deluded who sees any duality
here." And now, this is what scientists are rapidly
coming to understand: that the world is not divided,
that it is not constituted of multiple things and events,
but is a unified Whole. There are never two things,
but always only one. To truly know and understand
this is the foundation of all true knowledge and all
wisdom.

Neils Bohr, the father of quantum mechanics,
wrote that the new physics entails "the necessity of
a final renunciation of the classical ideal of causality,
and a radical revision of our attitude toward the
problem of physical reality." Let me try to explain

why: Scientists, like the mystics and yogis, are
coming to understand that, if everything is one "stuff",
then the breaking up of reality into subject and object,
cause and effect, or any other superimposed duality,
is just a conceptualization; i.e., a figment of our
imaginations.   It is we who create such divisions and
relationships; they don't in fact exist in any real
sense -- for there is only one substance.

Physicists now tell us that what we normally
regard as cause-effect relationships simply do not
exist.   Event A and event B are merely co-existent,
or if you like, synchronistic, events within the framework of the one Reality.   This is explained in a
remarkably lucid way by David Bohm, one of the
most highly regarded physicists of our time: 'The
world which we perceive', he says,

... cannot properly be analyzed into independently existent parts with fixed and determinate
dynamical relationships between each of the
parts.   Rather, the 'parts' are seen to be in
immediate connection, in which their dynamical
relationships depend, in an irreducible way, on
the state of the whole system (and indeed on
that of broader systems in which they are
contained, extending ultimately and in principle
to the entire universe).

Thus, one is led to a new notion of *unbroken
wholeness* which denies the classical idea of
analyzability of the world into separately and
independently existent parts.   We have reversed
the usual classical notion that the independent
'elementary parts' of the world are the fundamental reality, and that the various systems are
merely particular contingent forms and arrange-
ments of these parts.   Rather, we say that inseparable quantum interconnectedness of the
whole universe is the fundamental Reality, and
that relatively independently behaving parts are
merely particular and contingent forms with the
Whole.[1]

What this means is that local causes do not exist
in any real sense, since all relationships are contingent
on the condition of the Whole, and cannot be isolated

from the context of the Whole. The mystic, speaking from his viewpoint at the height of the unitive vision, says: "All things move together of one accord. Assent is given throughout the universe to every falling grain." And the scientists are now coming to a logical understanding of this. They are no longer able to rationalize the idea of local, individual causes, but are forced to admit that events are linked in a 'web of relationship'. As one scientific writer put it, "All that exists *by itself* is an unbroken wholeness that presents itself to us as webs of relations. Individual entities (and events) are idealizations only; they are correlations made by us. In short, the physical world, according to quantum mechanics, is ... not a structure built out of independently existing, unanalyzable entities, but rather a web of relationships between elements whose meanings arise wholly from their relationship to the Whole."

Since Einstein, not only do we no longer speak of mass and energy as distinct entities, we no longer speak of space and time as separate entities. We speak only of the "space-time continuum". They are entirely interdependent and inseparable, and hence synonymous. Think about it: Is what's happening happening in space or in time? You see, time is nothing but the sequence of events in space, and has no meaning outside of the sequence of events (even if they be mental events).

The interrelationship of time and space was given mathematical expression in the work of physicist and mathematician Herman Minkowski shortly after Einstein's General Theory was published. About his work, one scientific writer remarks, "Minkowski's mathematical explorations of space and time were both revolutionary and interesting. Out of them came a simple diagram of space-time showing the mathematical relationship of the past, present, and future. Of the wealth of information contained in this diagram, the most striking is that all of the past and all of the future, for each individual, meet, and always meet, at one single point: *now*. Furthermore, the now of each individual is specifically located, and will never be found in any other place than: *here* (i.e., where the subject is)." [2]

Physicists are now discovering truths about the universe which confirm the teachings of the mystics from thousands of years ago. We may think of these newly discovered truths as "the new-age wholistic view"; but the truth is, it is as ancient as man. It's just that some men take longer to grasp the nature of things than others. Today, we have what is called the "Quantum Field Theory". According to this Theory, particles of matter are simply the momentary manifestations of interacting energy fields which, intangible and insubstantial as they are, are the only real things in the universe. In short, as has been stated elsewhere, matter is not made of energy; it *is* energy!

The Quantum Field Theory states that "particles" (i.e., the most reduced elements of 'matter') are nothing but "excited states" of the featureless Ground state of the energy field. In other words, the "featureless Ground", the absolute Void, is manifesting as forms (or, at least, instrumental recordings of forms). Compare this phraseology with the words of Jnaneshvar, a 13th century Indian mystic, who said: "Although innumerable forms arise, it is one pure Consciousness which is the substance of all things."

Whether we call it "the featureless Ground", or "the Absolute", or "Brahman", it is the same One. And if we expand this Quantum Field Theory to include all of the cosmos, since ultimately everything is made of such "particles", and begin to see everything as one undifferentiated energy-field, we also begin to lose the old sense of cause-effect relationships. For, when space is time, and matter is energy, we can no longer find a clear distinction between what *is* and what *happens*, between the actor and the action. One scientific writer says, "At the subatomic level, and consequently at all levels, the dancer and the dance are one." In the Vedantic tradition, the world is regarded as the dance of Shiva, the expression of the Expressionless. Scientists have now understood and acknowledged what the mystics have known and experienced directly for thousands of years.

Now, let me say something about the advancement in the scientific community's understanding of the interrelationship, or rather, the oneness, of the subject and the object, the seer and the seen. The increase in understanding came when, many years ago, a problem arose concerning the misbehavior of light. Scientists discovered that, in the process of observing light in order to understand its nature, its nature seemed to be determined by the manner in which one observed it. With one kind of procedure, light turned out to have the properties of a wave; with another kind of procedure, it was shown unquestionably to be particular; that is to say, made up of particles. The new physics informs us, therefore, that an observer cannot observe without altering what he sees. One physicist expressed it this way: "The observer and the observed are interrelated in a real and fundamental sense. The exact nature of this interrelation is not clear, but there is a growing body of evidence that the distinction between the 'in here' and the 'out there' is illusion."

Since particle-lke behavior and wave-like behavior are the only properties we ascribe to light, and since these properties are now recognized to belong not to light itself, but to our interaction with light, then it appears that, independent of us, light has no properties. Now, this idea, that light depends on the observer for its existence, may be a difficult one for some; but that's only half of the equation. The other half is that, in a similar manner, without light, or, by implication, anything else to interact with, *we* do not exist! As the Quantum Mechanics pioneer, Neils Bohr, put it, "An independent reality, in the ordinary physical sense, can be ascribed neither to the phenomena nor to the agencies of observation." In other words, the observer and the observed, the seer and the seen, are interdependent complements, each of which cannot exist without the other.

In the philosophy of Vedanta, this interrelatedness between the observer and the observed, or the 'in here' and the 'out there', is fully discussed. According to Vedanta, the observer, or witness, in everyone is the Self, the one pure Consciousness, in Its limited form as the individualized soul, or *jiva*. The observed -- including our thoughts, sense-impressions, etc. -- is the projection of the Self; i.e., its "excited state". The Self vibrates into form and becomes the "extern-

al world". So, that one pure Consciousness which we
call the Self is *both* the observer and the observed,
both the subject and the object. And, without both,
neither can be. That is to say, neither one has an
independent reality. The subject and the object are
one; neither can exist without the other, as darkness
cannot exist without light.

In an ancient scripture of the Kashmir Shaivite
tradition, called *Vijnanabhairava*, it is said, "Awareness
of the perceiver and the perceived is common to all
beings. But with Yogis it is different. They are
aware of them as one." This is the true vision: to
see the world as not different from the Self. The
world is, indeed, the embodiment of God. The cause
is appearing as the effect.

Jnaneshvar, a great seer of the 13th century,
spoke of this truth from his own experience and his
own awareness. He said:

By His own nature, the Self *is* whatever He
sees. There is nothing else here but the Self.
Whether appearing as the seen or perceiving as
the seer, nothing else exists besides the Self.
... Just as water plays with itself by assuming
the forms of waves, the Self, the ultimate
Reality, plays happily with Himself. Though
there are multitudes of visible objects, and
wave upon wave of images, still, they are not
different from their witness. You may break
a lump of brown sugar into a million pieces,
still there is nothing but sugar. Likewise, the
unity of the Self is not lost, even though He
fills the whole universe. He is seeing only His
own Self -- like one who discovers various
countries in his own imagination, and goes
wandering through them all with great enjoyment.[3]

How does Jnaneshvar, a 13th century Indian
peasant, know this? He didn't come by this knowledge
the way that the scientist does, by rationality and
deduction; he saw it clearly in the mystical vision.
He realized his own Divine and eternal Self, the one
Reality. It is in the realization of one's Self that
all dualities become merged; night and day, happiness

and sorrow, birth and death, good and evil, and all
the multiple grades of judgement that can be made
about the world, all merge into the One which em-
braces all.   The distinctions of past and future are
also dissolved in that state.   All is contained in an
eternal present.   Life and death also lose their distinction from one another.   That one "Existence-Consciousness-Bliss" is continuous, and independent of
any individual form which comes and goes within It.
     In the experience of Unity, everything becomes
perfectly still -- and yet, everything continues.   How
can that be?   Absolute stillness, yet everything in
motion as before?   Remember Newton and his law?
The One, the Totality, is constant, while the contents
continue their fluctuation from one state to another.
The universe goes on for one in the state of Self-
realization, but it's experienced in the way the water
of the ocean would experience its own waves.   No
matter how turbulent the waves might become, from
the standpoint of the water, nothing is changed.
From the standpoint of the one Consciousness, so
many forms rise and subside, but, since everything is
Itself, nothing is changed.
     It is said in the scriptures that man is created
in the image of God.   And this is true, without any
doubt.   We, as individuals, are microcosmic reproduct-
ions of that macrocosmic Being.   Think of how,
within us, immensely dramatic upheavals and eruptions
of warfare are continually taking place, both in our
bodies and in our thought-processes.   And yet we
remain unmoved and unchanged in our identity, in
our self-hood.   It is the same with the absolute
Consciousness.   Within, all motion continues, but
nothing is changed.
     It is our own Self which, as Energy (*Shakti*),
creates, sustains and destroys all life.   In every form
of life, and even in inanimate matter, *you* exist.
You are the very life-pulse of all.   There is really
no other you than the one Self.   We call It God, or
Brahman.   It is He who is enacting every role, taking
on every form.   And everything is unfolding just as
He wills it to.   Be at peace; He is everything, and
He is doing everything.

Reflection

Who is God?   God is the magical Electricity out of which everything is formed.   He is the invisible Intelligence who disgorges from His vast riches of conscious Energy this universe of erupting stars and exploding galaxies.   He lives in His creation, as a dreamer lives in his dreams, imbuing them with his own intelligence and animating them with his own animate imagination.

He is the only Animator in all this wealth of manifold, magical forms.   It is He alone who lives as man and woman, bird and beast, cloud and shore. When we, His puny animated dream-images, imagine we have a life and being all our own, we selfishly imagine that we have some intelligence, some beauty, all our own; and we proudly boast of our talents and accomplishments, unaware that all is His doing.   But if we are able to comprehend His intelligence, His beauty, within us, then we may be able to turn within and know that One who is our life, our beauty, our intelligence, our joy.

And, with what marvel, what astonishment and delight, we -- first dimly, then with clearest light -- behold our own Infinity, unborn and deathless, wakeful throughout eternal morning!   He is the simple Self of all that lives and breathes; the only One who fills all space, and dances in His joy the dance of life.   "'Tis I", He sings within our hearts; "'Tis I", He laughs beneath our breasts; "'Tis I", we finally know; there is no other, but only I.

*   *   *

ONENESS

This world is called, in a Sanskrit phrase, *Chit-Shakti Vilas*, the play of Consciousness-Energy". This word, *Chit-Shakti*, is an interesting one, in that it stands for the one Reality, and yet it is made up of two words: "Consciousness" and "Energy". These are the two aspects of Reality with which we have become familiar as *Shiva-Shakti, Brahman-Maya, Purusha-Prakrti, Theos-Logos*, etc. *Chit*, or Consciousness, is the absolute and formless aspect, the transcendent Godhead; and *Shakti*, or Energy, is the creative aspect of that one Consciousness which manifests as the multiformed universe. They are one, but they are two. The two are but complementary aspects of the same one indivisible Truth.

Listen to how the 13th century sage, Jnaneshvar describes them:

> The Shakti cannot live without her Lord, and without her, He (Shiva, the absolute Consciousness) cannot exist. Since He appears because of Her, and She exists because of Her Lord, the two cannot be distinguished at all. Sugar and its sweetness cannot be told apart, nor camphor and its fragrance. If we have the flame, we have the fire as well; if we catch hold of Shakti, we have Shiva also. ... Shiva and Shakti are the same, like air and its motion, or gold and its lustre. Fragrance cannot be separated from the musk, nor heat from fire; neither can Shakti be separated from Shiva.[1]

The whole world of apparent phenomena is the manifestation of the Shakti of Shiva, or *Chit*. Shiva is our innermost consciousness, our very Self; and Shakti, therefore, is our own creative power, our power of will. By its very existence, an apparent duality is created in that which is one. From this original duality comes the duality of seer and seen, or subject and object. It is because of this apparent duality, this imaginary division in the One, that the world-appearance continues to exist. Nonetheless, the truth of the matter is that it is one Being who is playing all the roles; He is the Director, the stage Manager, the actors, and the scenery. He is the stage, and He is the audience of this play as well. There is nothing outside of God!

This is brought out in the story of the egoistic king who asked his Minister, "Who is greater, me or God?" And the wise Minister replied, "You are, O King! For you can banish anyone from your kingdom, but God cannot banish anyone from His kingdom."

It is not possible to leave God's kingdom. The only thing that really is is that one Being; He is both the unchanging Absolute, the Unity, and the world-appearance as well. He is both Shiva and Shakti. For, as we've seen, you can't have one without the other; they form an inseparable unit. And so the question, 'Who am I?' is readily answered: "I am the one Reality. I am *Chit-Shakti*, and all this is my play!" It is, of course, important to experience this truth; but it's perhaps just as important to understand it and to make this knowledge a part of one's being. This is not just philosophy or theorizing. It is very important to fully comprehend this; otherwise, who knows what you might imagine yourself to be? Some weak, insignificant creature, perhaps!

Because the final and ultimate Truth is unity, is oneness, all talk of duality is misleading. In our very good intentions of making the truth understandable to others, we like to describe the dual aspects of the One in order to explain the relationship between the Transcendent and the Immanent, the Absolute and the Relative, the Unity and the Diversity. And from there we go on to delineate all the limbs and subtle layers, and so forth; and before we know what has happened, we're immersed once again in the swamp of multiplicity.

The initial conceptual division of the One into two (Brahman-Maya, Shiva-Shakti, etc.) is the intellectually tempting pathway leading into this swamp. And almost every philosopher and teacher of metaphysics finds himself beguiled by the apparent usefulness of exploring this pathway. But, since the ultimate Truth is unity, and always unity, we are much better off adhering bulldoggedly to One and only One, without allowing for the slightest admission of duality or mention of even an apparent division in It. For this reason, the author of the Biblical book of Second Isaiah, as a counter to those who would dissect Reality into Good and evil, Jehovah and Satan, Light and Darkness, put these words in the mouth of God: "I am the one Lord; there is no other beside Me. I form the light and create the darkness; I make peace and create evil. I, the one Lord, do all these things."

Let's look for a moment, from the historical perspective, and see what happens when we begin dabbling with 'two-ness'. In the *Yajurveda*, we find the statement, "The One becomes the many by its own inherent power." This seems innocent enough. Everyone can see that "its own inherent power" is not an entity separate from the One; it is just an inherent quality. A little later, however, we find in the *Svetasvatara Upanishad*, "Brahman projects the universe through the power of His Maya. Then He becomes entangled in that universe of Maya. Know, then, that the world is Maya, and that the great God is the Lord of Maya."

Uh oh! Now, we have established a definite pair! Here, we have the Lord *and* His Maya. From the smallest seed, duality has sprung up as a full tree of contention. We have forgotten that "Maya" simply refers to His "inherent power" of manifestation, and we have begun to see "the Lord" and "His power" as two separate and distinct entities. Do you not see how craftily and insidiously this imaginary separation has taken place? Once you have a "Lord", you have a "servant" as well.

By the time of the *Bhagavad Gita,* this dualism has taken a firm hold on the mind. We hear Krishna saying, in the thirteenth chapter, to Arjuna: "He sees truly who sees that all actions are performed by Prakrti (i.e., Shakti, or Maya), and that the Purusha (Shiva or Brahman) is actionless." Now, this is a very useful concept for understanding that one's eternal Self remains constant, inactive, and unchanged, even while one's body and mind engages in actions; but a split is being established which will prove to be very difficult to patch up again.

The great Non-Dualist philosopher and sage, Shankaracharya, though quite aware of their underlying unity, describes "the two" in such a way as to widen the division between them. He says: "Maya ...is the power of the Lord. It is she who brings forth this universe. She is neither real nor unreal, nor partaking of both characteristics; neither the same as the Lord, nor different, nor both; neither composed of parts nor an indivisible whole nor both. She is most wonderful and cannot be described in words." [2]

Now, let's look at what's happened so far: The Lord emanates the universe by His inherent Power. And suddenly, we are saying that He is real, but the universe and the Lord's Power by which the universe exists are both unreal! Can we say that the Sun is real, but its rays are unreal? No; of course not. But, let's not be unfair to Shankaracharya; it should be perfectly clear that he was merely pointing out that the Godhead, the formless Absolute, is *eternally* real, while the manifestation known as 'the universe' is only *temporarily* real. And, to this, we all agree. But, can we say that the Lord's inherent "Power of manifestation" is also only temporarily real? No. His Power, His *Shakti*, His *Maya*, though it may indeed become inactive and dormant, is co-eternal with Shiva; it is inherent. It is never something separate or independent of the Lord, any more than wetness can be thought of as separate or independent of water, or any more than the power to think can be thought of as independent of mind. He, the Lord, and she, His Power, were never divided, were never two; and only confusion can result by allowing this mistaken impression to stand.

It was with just such an objection to Shankara's descriptive language that, in the 9th and 10th centuries, the authors of the literature of Kashmir Shaivism began to rephrase and reformulate the philosophy of Unity. As we shall see, however, there is really no satisfactory solution to the problem of expressing in language That which exceeds the capabilities of language. In every time, in every culture, the seers of the One have attempted to explain in a satisfactory way the fact that the universe is God, and yet

is not God; that He is eternal, and yet lives in the
temporal; that He is forever unchanging, and yet is
manifest as the ever-changing universe.

Jnaneshvar, in the 13th century, likewise felt
impelled to object to the language of Shankara, and
to attempt to do away with such concepts as "Maya"
and "superimposition". In his *Amritanubhav*, he says:

> When it is always only the one pure Conscious-
> ness seeing Itself, why postulate the necessity
> of a superimposition? ...By His very nature, He
> *is* whatever He sees.   Whatever form appears,
> appears because of Him.   There is nothing
> else here but the Self.   ... In the current of
> the river or the waves of the sea, there is
> nothing but water.   Similarly, in the universe,
> nothing else exists besides the Self. ... Therefore,
> whether He is the seer or the seen, it doesn't
> matter; there is only the Self vibrating every-
> where. [3]

Again, in his *Changadev Pasashti*, Jnaneshvar   says:
"Only Oneness is real.   All else is a dream!" [4] And
yet, we must ask the question, "What all else?"
And the answer can only be, "the appearance of
multiplicity!"   And this, of course, is precisely what
Shankara had said: "Only Brahman is real; the world
(the appearance of multiplicity) is illusory."   So, you
see, it is not possible to solve this question of how
to talk about the (apparent) duality in Unity.   This
is why, in India, there are so many authentic schools
of mystical thought.   There is the *Advaita*, the Non-
Dualism of Shankara; there is the *Dvaita*, or   Dualist,
school of Madhva; there is the *Vishishtadvaita,* or Qual-
ified Non-Dualism of Ramanuja.   All speak the truth,
and yet each sees the Truth a little bit differently.
But that's okay.   The built-in ambiguity of language
demands alternate expressions.   Still, the ultimate
Truth, the final Reality, known by the seers, is One
without a second.   All duality is apparent only.   We
can say that it is the "Play of Consciousness-Energy".

So much for correct understanding!   It is necessary
to pass beyond understanding if we are to experience
the joy of Unity, the bliss of God.   This Bliss is not
attained by engaging the mind in trying to comprehend

the nature of God -- though this has its place, of
course. The bliss of God is attained through devotion.
Devotion leaves the intellect far behind; in fact, it is
possible only through the abandonment of the pride
of intellect.   It is more akin to the longing of a
child for its mother than to the ratiocination of the
adult.   Devotion begins with the awareness of one's
utter dependency upon God for everything, and an
open upturning of one's mind and inner gaze to the
Source of all mind and all vision.

    We engage our minds so often in circuitous analysis
and repetitious thought-patterns.   Far better would
it be if we could build into our minds the thought-
pattern of calling on God for our succor and support.
He is capable of filling the mind and body with
ecstasy and light, and of setting our minds at peace
in perfect understanding.   All that is required is a
pure and innocent heart, and a simple and steady
regard to Him for all our satisfaction and reward.

    As the mind becomes steady and one-pointed on
God, all questions become answered automatically.
A mind at peace is a mind illumined by Truth.   Let
there be an apparent duality between you and your
Lord!   But keep on trying to close the gap through
love. Talk to Him. Pray to Him. Give all your life
and love to Him.   And the God within you will manifest the more as you become engrossed in Him.
You become what you meditate on; so meditate on
God.   Regard Him as the only Reality, and become
as a moth dancing about His flame.   Yearn to be
immersed in His perfect light, His perfect love, and
He will draw you into Himself and make you one
with Him.

Reflection

    The Latin phrase, *E Pluribus Unum*, is   the   motto
of our country.   It means "Of many, one."   But, it
would be closer to the truth to say, "Of One, many".
This simple formula explains everything we need to
know about the Reality in which we live.   For, just
as the one white light is refracted to appear as the
entire spectrum of colors in a rainbow, so does the
one undivided Existence appear as a multitude of
forms.   Just as a sunflower spreads itself out in its

many tender petals, so God spreads Himself out into this variously-formed creation. Just as the ocean raises up from itself a tossing surface of countless waves, so the ocean of Existence-Consciousness-Bliss raises up from Itself countless individual forms of life from shore to shore.

In every single form the One alone exists; it is He alone who lives in every life. However wise, however foolish, however attractive, however repulsive, the tiger and the scorpion, the spider and the snake, -- all is His life, playing in a million fantastic forms. And we, children of His mind, images projected from His light upon Himself, wander here and there upon His screen, playing out our roles, forgetful of the One in whose dance of Light we live. But when we turn within, behold! We discover as our very essence that One who lives as many, the heart and soul of all that lives, the joyful God whose life and breath we are.

*　　*　　*

MAYA: THE CREATIVE POWER OF GOD

In the final chapter of the *Bhagavad Gita*, Krishna says to Arjuna: "O Arjuna, the Lord dwells in the heart of all beings, while revolving them all on the wheel (of transmigration) by His mysterious power of *Maya*."[1] This word, "Maya", is one which we hear quite often in discussions of Vedanta, and, because it is a word that is so often misinterpreted, I'd like to see if I can clear up any misunderstanding about it.

We may well understand that Brahman (the God-head) is the absolute Consciousness, the eternal Mind, which mystics throughout history have experienced as the transcendent Source of all creation. It is said by those who have known It to be unmoving, unchanging, unqualified, beyond all form and beyond all activity. How then, the rational intellect questions, can such a quiescent Emptiness create a universe of myriad forms? The difficulty of explaining this satisfactorily is readily acknowledged by those who have experienced It directly. The truth of the one Reality is "seen" clearly in the mystical "vision", and yet to describe It is nearly impossible, because Its mode of existence is unique, and without parallel in the phenomenal world. There is nothing else with which It may be truly compared.

Those seers who do speak of It say that the one Reality has two distinct aspects: It is the absolutely pure Consciousness which remains as the eternal Ground, the immoveable Witness; and yet, at the same time, It possesses the power of projecting a manifold universe upon Its own Self. Frequently, the analogy is made of a mind and its power of projecting thoughts or images upon itself. These two aspects of our own immediate experience help us to grasp a little of what these two cosmic principles are like.

"Maya" is just another name for God's power of manifestation, His power of form-projection. However, the word, "Maya", is also used to signify the form-projection itself. It is God's Power of manifestation, which remains eternally with Him, whether there is a manifestation or not; and it is also the actual world of forms which results from that power. Maya, in other words, is both the cause and the effect, both the creator (or creatrix) and the creation.

This word, "Maya", is synonymous with all the other words used to represent the manifestory Power of God, such as "Shakti", "Prakrti", "Logos", etc. So many different words exist because every seer of every time and place has found it necessary to give a name to the creative power of God in order to distinguish the temporal from the eternal, the phenomenal appearance from the constant and unchanging Ground. "Maya", like so many of the other names for this "power", is a noun of the feminine gender. Just as the absolute Godhead is referred to as the figurative "Father", His Power of manifestation is commonly referred to as "Mother", as in "Mother Nature". Maya is the Creatrix, the Womb from which all are born, sometimes called the Will, or the effulgent Glory, of God.

Bear in mind that God's Power is not something other than God -- just as our own power of thought-production is not distinct from our minds to which that power belongs. However, we must bear in mind also that, just as the thoughts and images which are produced in our minds are mere ephemera which come and go, and once gone, have no claim to existence, so, likewise, the various forms in the universe are mere ephemera which come and go, and are therefore illusory, or unreal. The Power, Maya, exists eternally; but the world-illusion, Maya, has a beginning and an end.

Those who have experienced God, through contemplation, have "seen" the creation of the world-illusion, its flourishing, and its dissolution, in a recurrent cycle. It is somewhat like the recurrent cycle of breath which we, as creatures, experience. In something similar to an exhalation, the Lord manifests and plays out the drama of the universe; and, in something similar to an inhalation, He draws it all back into Himself once again. In just one breath, the whole universe is created, evolved, and dissolved. From the perspective of God, it is but a breath; from our temporal perspective, it is an immensity of time. Perhaps our own breath, which seems to us but a moment, is an eternity to certain sub-atomic particles, whose life-span is measured in millionths of a second. See how relative is our concept of time and space!

Maya creates the illusion of time. It distorts our experience so that years pass which are but moments from another perspective -- just like in a dream. Let me tell you a story which illustrates this:

Once, the legendary sage, Narada, was out walking with Krishna, who is, of course, representative, in literature, of God. In the course of their conversation, Narada asked God to explain to him the mystery of His Maya. And the Lord said, "Alright -- but before I do, since my throat is a little dry, please fetch me a drink of water." So, Narada ran off to find some water for the Lord. Soon, he came to a pleasant little hut, where he stopped to get directions to the nearest water, but when the door to the hut was opened, there stood a most beautiful young maiden with whom Narada was immediately smitten. As she invited him inside, Narada forgot all about his mission to fetch some water to his Lord; and, as the days passed very pleasantly, Narada fell more and more in love with his beautiful hostess, and soon they were wed.

The blissful couple soon had children, and Narada toiled in the field to grow food for his growing family. He was extremely happy with his new family, and thought himself to be surely the most fortunate of men to have such a beautiful wife and such fine children. But, one day, a great monsoon rain fell. The river-banks overflowed, and the little hut was filled with water. Narada climbed, with his family, to the top of the hut, clinging with one hand to the roof, and with the other to his wife and children. But the rains continued, and the hut began to collapse from the flooding waters. First one child, then another, was swept away in the raging torrent; and finally, Narada felt his darling wife slip away from his grasp as well. Then, he too was swept away in the flood, crying out in the darkness for his wife and children.

At last, nearly unconscious, and completely exhausted, Narada found himself washed up on a wreckage-strewn shore. And, as he lay there desparately lamenting the loss of his family, suddenly he looked up to see the feet of Krishna at his head. Quickly, he struggled to his feet, and Krishna, with an ironic smile, asked, "Where have you been, Narada? I sent you for water nearly ten minutes ago!" It was in this way that the Lord showed to Narada His power of Maya. Indeed, this life *is* like a dream, in which we become entirely involved and embroiled, forgetful of our real purpose, only to wake to find it was all unreal, a mere play of thought.

"All this," said the insightful sage, Shankaracharya, "from the intellect to the gross physical body, is the effect of Maya. Understand that all these and Maya itself are not the absolute Self, and are therefore unreal, like a mirage in the desert."[2]   "Real", for Shankaracharya, meant "eternal", that which never ceases to be. This phenomenal universe obviously does not fit this definition of "real", and is therefore "unreal" -- like a mirage. It is only God's imagination -- similar in some ways to a dream.

Do you remember the song: "Row, row, row your boat, gently down the stream. Merrily, merrily, merrily, merrily; life is but a dream"? That song conveys the idea of Maya. And this is a great understanding to have of the world. But, of much more significance is the understanding that we are, ultimately, the Dreamer of the dream. Then, whatever nightmarish conditions manifest before us, we will always remain fearless and unmoved, confident that we are above and beyond the conditions of the dream. The realization of God, the realization of the eternal Self, is an experience very similar to awaking from a dream. Indeed, such realization is often referred to as an "awakening". It is similar in the sense that one who has awakened to the Self can then re-enter the dream and enjoy the play fearlessly and with great enjoyment.

When I was a child, I remember I would sometimes have disturbing dreams in which some creature of my imagination would chase me and would be just at the point of gobbling me up, when I would pinch myself in the dream, and wake myself, thus escaping the beast by withdrawing suddenly from the dream to my warm and safe bed. Once I discovered this handy trick, I would taunt the villains in my dreams, secure in the knowledge that, just at the critical moment, when they had me cornered with no apparent exit, I could pinch myself, and disappear from their clutches just like that.

The same kind of confidence belongs to the one who has realized the Self, through contemplation. Just as, when a dream-character awakes, he realizes he is the dreamer, likewise, when we, who are God's imagination, awake from this dream of a world, we realize that we are the Imaginer, the pure Consciousness from whom all this imagined universe sprang. We realize that we are, and have always been, the one Self; that we have always been safe and secure as the eternal One.

When we awake to the Self, then we can enter back into the dream, and share our knowledge with everyone else in the dream. This is what the mystic does; he returns to the dream, the world, and tells everyone, "Hey! This is just a dream. Each of us is really that one Dreamer; He is the Self of all of us. And, if you really want to enjoy the dream in the best possible way, and at the same time know that you're free from the dream, then wake up and realize who you really are!"

This reminds me of the parable told by Socrates, called 'The Analogy of The Cave'.[3]   Socrates, who was an enlightened man, attempted to explain his own state by asking his listeners to imagine that there were some people chained in a cave far underground, with their backs to a fire before which some other people were parading back and forth. The people chained are facing toward a cave-wall on which the images of the people parading in front of the fire are cast as shadows. The images on the wall are all that they can see, and so they take that to be the reality. Then, one day, one man escapes from his chains. He discovers the fire and the figures marching in front of it, and realizes how mistaken he had been in regarding only the shadows as the reality. Then, he discovers a way out of the cave, and he climbs up, out of the cave, into the sunlight, and discovers the real source of light in the world. He is overjoyed, and elated, and he returns to the cave, telling everyone, "Look, this is only shadows, illusions! Break your bonds; come up out of the cave, and see the reality!" The problem, of course, is that no one believes him. They think him mad; they curse him and stone him, and ostracize him from their company.

That was Socrates' way of explaining the idea of Maya. But, just as the unchained man in his story was brutally treated by his brothers, so was Socrates. When he tried to explain the Truth that he had seen to the people of Athens, they scorned him and condemned him to death, and eventually murdered him. Jesus also, like Socrates, was simply trying to show the people the way out of the cave, out of Maya's snare of illusion, so that they too could know the Truth and be free.

In the 7th chapter of the *Bhagavad Gita*, Krishna says, "The whole world is under the delusion of my Maya; for this Maya of mine is very difficult to penetrate. Only those who take refuge in Me go beyond it." [4] In other words, it is only by intense devotion and the grace of God that we are released from the delusive power of Maya. If we think of this release as the awakening from a dream, we can easily understand that it is not just the person within the dream who must awake, but the dreamer must become awake. There must be a complicity, or grace, extending from the Dreamer to the dreamed. It's not as though one can awake from the cosmic dream simply by pinching oneself. But, through a strong desire for liberation, with a focused mind intent on God, with an all-consuming will and devotion, it is possible to draw that complicity, that grace, and bring about an "awakening". Then you will be free -- even though you still live within the cosmic dream.

Though everything in the world will remain the same, it will be quite different; for your vision of it will be very different. You will carry with you the awareness of your eternal Self, and you will view all this dream-like world as your own glorious play. Maya will no longer bind you in any way, for you'll know that you are, in truth, the Lord of Maya. As the great Shankaracharya said, "Maya is destroyed by

the realization of the One without a second."   The
revelation of your true nature, the one, and only
Reality, destroys all previous notions of your identity,
just as awaking from a dream destroys the illusory
reality of the dream.

Swami Vidyaranya, another great Vedantic sage,
wrote, "Maya is called 'the wish-fulfilling cow'.   It
yields milk in the form of duality.   Drink as much
of it as you like; but the Truth is non-duality." [5]
Final release from all duality, including life and
death, is obtained only through (the awakening called)
knowledge of the Self.   One does not come to the
end of dreaming until one awakes.

All the Self-realized sages agree: the knowledge
of the Self is the only means to transcend the ignorance in which we are enmeshed due to the veiling
power of Maya.   Once one has awakened from a
dream, he may enter back into the dream, but he is
never troubled by the occurances within the dream
again. He is aware that he is everything that appears
before him, that everything that happens is a mere
imagination, and that he can never be threatened or
be destroyed.   All is himself; and, at the same time,
he is quite free and safe, beyond all this phantasmagoria of things and events.

Then, he will say: "I am the Absolute, completely
independent, ever-pure, eternal and free.   I pervade
everything; I am everlasting, undefiled, pure Existence,
beyond Maya, without cause or limitation.   I alone
am. I am eternal Consciousness."

Reflection

Thou art my world; I have no other world but
Thee.   One face with many masks confronts my
daily gaze; 'tis Thee alone who fills my vision, both
within and without.

How then shall I find enmity in crowds, or single
out the good from bad, the friend from foe?   Behind
each mask -- however dark -- Thou alone art shining
brightly still.

Lord, Thy masquerade enchants me and distracts
me often to the point that I forget the Oneness of
it all, mistaking, as it were, the forest for the trees.

But, again and again, I blink away the fog of multiplicity to see that every tree is but a member of
Thy endless forest, and is none else but Thee.

O Lord, each glimmering form is Thine: Thou art
my world, and -- wonder of all wonders -- Thou art
this 'me' who sees, and marvels at the sight, and
thus creates a 'me' and 'Thee' where only One
exists.

*   *   *

THE QUEST FOR JOY

Everyone in the world is seeking joy. We may
call it by different names, like happiness, fulfillment,
satisfaction, bliss, perfection, etc.; but, whatever the
name, it's that joy we're seeking. Whether in eating,
drinking, sleeping, playing, or working: in everything
we do, we're looking to find some joy. But, how
many, I wonder, find that ideal, that ultimate state?
We may have a wonderful wife or husband, a success-
ful career, good health, a nice home to live in, in
beautiful suroundings, with plenty of good food to
eat; and still, we're unfulfilled, unsatisfied, restless
for something more. It's that joy we lack. And we
continue to look for it in all our activities and occupations, all our relationships, and all our pleasure-
seeking.

But, alas, at the end of the day we have found
no joy. And, with what relish we turn at last to
our beds, where we can find some respite, some
rest, from all the day's busyness and toil, from all
our futile searching. We know that here, at least,
in the oblivion of nothingness experienced in sleep,
we shall find a little of that joy we sought so vigor-
ously during the day. In sleep, we don't gather with
a group of friends and drink cocktails; we don't
witness any extravagant floor-shows, or listen to any
rock and roll bands; rather, we enter deep into ourselves, and it's there that we find the joy of peace,
of silence. Then, when we awake, we feel refreshed
and renewed, and ready to enter into the clamorous
din of activity in search of joy all over again.

The truth is, the joy we seek is there within us
all the time. Have you heard the story of the musk-
deer, who runs madly about in search of the source
of the wonderful fragrance which it has sensed, only
to discover, as it lies down in exhaustion, that the
fragrance which it so eagerly sought, emanates from
its own navel? Well, we are in a similar predicament.
We, too, seek in the world outside that which lies in
its fullness within us. That joy is our true nature.
In fact, the reason we search for joy with such
unflagging determination is that we have the memory

of our true nature. We remember in the dim recesses of our being that we are heirs to a tremendous joy; that, in fact, we *are* that joy.

As we grow up, we nurture the desire to become great, to live as gods; no one ever desired to become little and poor. No one ever prayed to God for suffering, not even in a dream. It is joy we seek. And why? Because joy is our nature, our heritage. Joy is another name for the Self, for God -- the one and only Reality of our being.

There is a story in the *Taittiriya Upanishad* which tells of a boy named Bhrigu and of how he came to understand his true nature as joy: One day, according to the story, Bhrigu Varuni went to his father, Varuna, and said, "Father, please explain to me the mystery of Brahman." Then his father spoke to him about the food of the earth, the vital breath, the mind, and so forth; and then he said to his son: "Seek to know Him from whom all beings have come, by whom they all live, and unto whom they all return. He is Brahman."

So Bhrigu concentrated all his energy on knowing the Truth; and he came to the conclusion that Brahman was the food of the earth, since all beings have come from food, they live by food, and unto the earth they return. But this did not satisfy him. So again he went to his father, Varuna, and said: "Father, explain further to me the mystery of Brahman." And his father replied as before, and added: "Seek to know Brahman by prayer, because Brahman is prayer."

So Bhrigu concentrated all his energy again in order to know the Truth, and he came to the conclusion that Brahman was life; for from life all beings have come, by life they all live, and unto life they all return. But this too he found unsatisfactory. Again and again he returned to his father, and again and again he came to unsatisfactory conclusions, until finally he realized that Brahman was joy; for from joy all beings have come, by joy they all live, and unto joy they all return.

Upon realizing this, Bhrigu exclaimed, "Oh, the wonder of joy! I am the food of life, and I am he who eats the food of life. I am the 'two-in-One'.

I am the self-born Truth!   I was before the gods,
and I am the source of immortality.   The light of
the sun is my light; but I am beyond this universe!" [1]
This was the vision of Bhrigu Varuni which came
from the Highest; those who experience this vision
live in the Highest.   This is why it is said in the
Vijnana Bhairava that, "if one experiences, even for
a fraction of a moment, the upsurging of joy, that is
a glimpse of God."   For, according to those who
have known the Truth, all joy that we experience --
even that joy we associate with sensual pleasure --
is a taste of the joy of God.   When we meet a friend
after a long time, and we feel a wonderful joy on
embracing him -- that is the joy of God.   When we
taste a sweet fruit, that sweetness is God.   All the
wonderful delight we experience in this world is just
a little taste of the perfect and completely full joy
that resides in us as God's Bliss -- that which Vedantists refer to as *Ananda.*
Naturally, the more we are in touch with our
inner Self, the more we are in touch with *Ananda,*
our own natural blissful state.   Those who experience
in the depths of contemplation their identity with
God know the fullness of that joy.   This is declared
by the author of the *Maitri Upanishad,* who says: "Words
cannot describe the joy of the soul whose impurities
are cleansed in deep contemplation, who is one with
the Self.   Only those who feel this joy know what it
is." [2]   This is the declaration of all the great sages
and wise men of all time; real happiness, real fulfillment, comes only when you discover the Self.
Listen to a passage from a 14th century Vedantic
work, called *Panchadashi,* which was written by a
Self-realized sage named Swami Vidyaranya; this is
what he says:

> The knower of Brahman has the feeling of
> absolute self-satisfaction.   He feels that he has
> done all that was to be done, and, meditating
> continually on Brahman, he enjoys supreme bliss
> all the time.   Having achieved all that was to
> be achieved, and having done all that was to be
> done, the illumined man rests in complete con-
> tentment, and the thoughts engaging his mind
> are such as these:

I am blessed. I am blessed. I am ever-
merged in the direct cognition of Brahman.
The bliss of Brahman is directly and clearly
evident to me. I am blessed; I am blessed.
The worldly woes (which others seem to
suffer) have no meaning for me. My ignorance of the Self has fled, I know not where.
I am blessed; I am blessed. I have no further
duties to perform; I have achieved the highest
that one could wish for.

I am supremely blessed. There is no
earthly joy to compare with my great bliss.
I have acquired the greatest merit, and my
good deeds have brought me their richest
fruit. O how blessed am I! How great are
the Vedantic scriptures! How merciful is
my teacher! How wonderful is my enlightenment! How great my bliss, my infinite
bliss. [3]

Such is the state, says Vidyaranya, of one who
is continually conscious of the Self. 'But is such
a thing really possible?' we must wonder. It is
one thing to write such exuberant statements during
the brief moment while one is most clearly aware
of the Self, and quite another thing to actually
live one's life through in all its various aspects,
through all its highs and lows, in such a state.
Surely, we need not believe that those who have
realized the Self are continually in the same ecstatic state all the time. But, just as surely, we can
easily understand that there is a steady underlying
certainty and calm that supports and sustains one
who has known the Self. While it would be an
exaggeration for one to claim that he or she is in
the same state of bliss all the time, it is not an
exaggeration to say that one who has known the
Divine Self is ever-aware that the Self is an always-
present support that is only a remembrance away.

A trapeze artist who knows that the net is
there below him doesn't have to think about the
net all the time. Just knowing it's there gives
him a sense of security, and he can go about his
business, concentrating on his performance, with an
underlying confidence that he is secure and safe.

It's the same way with Self-knowledge; it serves as
a safety net to the knower of God.   It is always
there, just underneath.   He is always safely in the
hands of God.   And when his worldly tasks are out
of the way, then he is able to sit quietly in meditation, and come closer to the actual experience of
God's complete freedom and joy.   Then, he may
become directly aware of his true nature as *Ananda*.

Somehow, we must learn to face in the direction
of the Self, while at the same time facing in the
direction of the world about us.   God within us, the
Absolute, the transcendent Self, is always at rest,
always blissful.   Then, there is the very fact of life
in the world which stares us in the face, demanding
that we pay attention to what is going on before us,
in caring for ourselves and in caring for others who
are dear to us.   We find these two centers of focus
vying with one another; one the theocentric view, the
other, the anthropocentric view.

We may find one or another of these centers of
focus accentuated in the religious traditions to which
we belong.   There are those religious traditions which
are predominantly theocentric, and those which are
predominantly anthropocentric.   The theocentric are
those that take God, the Divine Source, as their
central focus.   The anthropocentric are those which
center their efforts around the material and spiritual
welfare of man.   All religious organizations, of course
contain a little of each in them, but generally, they
are predominantly one or the other.

Western Christianity, for example, is very much
influenced by Western materialism, and is predominantly anthropocentric.   In the Western churches,
there is almost never any mention of meditation or
prayer, but instead a great concern with "serving our
brethren" or "serving the world".   Too often, such
anthropocentrism forgets that, unless it replenishes
itself in the waters of contemplation, unless it becomes
illumined through contact with the Divine Light, it
will have nothing of any value to give, and no way
to dispel the darkness of the world.

We can also find fault with the exclusively theocentric attitude.   Look at those countries where the
contemplation of God is the sole focus, such as

India; what do we see? We see everywhere a great emphasis on prayer, meditation, and the realization of the identity of the Self and God; and very little emphasis on providing the basic necessities of life for the millions of starving souls. Don't get me wrong. I've seen Indian peasants whom we would regard as poorer than poor, who had practically nothing of worldly goods, who were much more content, more blissful, than most of the people in our country whom we regard as rich. Indeed, the so-called "rich" in our country are so very often the most effective representatives of the spiritual poverty of the anthropocentric attitude. My point is that both attitudes are not only correct, but necessary, if we would not only experience, but manifest, our innate bliss, our joy.

Joy is a two-way street. It is being man turned to God; and it is being God, turned to mankind. The soul, turned to God, becomes irradiated with Divinity, simply by becoming transparent to that Divine Light which is its Source. And that Divine Light shines through the soul, illumining all who come in contact with it. Recall that Jesus held this very same position, confirming the dictum adopted by the Hebrews, that not one thing, but two things were necessary: first, love God with all your heart and all your soul; and secondly love man as yourself. "First," he said, "seek the kingdom of God"; in other words, you cannot really do much for others or shed any light in the world, until first you find that light within yourself. The light itself will do what is necessary for mankind; our only task is to rid ourselves of all that tends to obscure that light -- in other words, our ignorance, our selfish attachment to our own make-believe world of self-gratification, our inner darkness.

Joy is God, and that joy is in ourselves; but joy demands, for its fulfillment, that it be shared. It is the nature of light to shine outwardly. As Jesus said, a light on a hill cannot be hidden, or covered over with a basket; it must shine. And, likewise, joy, which is the light of God, cannot be only experienced within in solitary indulgence. It must go outward to all creation. That is its very nature.

Many times, throughout my life, I've been reminded from within of this very truth. Once, when I had been giving much thought to how I might explain to others what had been revealed to me, a voice from within taught me with these words: "Take no thought of others, how they might be shown the way to Me; for, if I would teach others through you, I will do so only after you have subdued yourself, so that I might shine freely from your eyes as a beacon for all. I am Love, and am best taught by loving."

And this has been for me a great and enduring lesson -- one which I am still attempting to put into practice: that it was not me, that is, my little ego-self, that had any light; but that light was God's own, and it was He who would do whatever was to be done. The more I, with my own interests and ideas of personal values, got in the way, the less of that light would shine through. And so, my only task in this life is to remain turned to God, to that Source of light and joy within -- that is my theocentric focus; and He will do all that is necessary in the way of fulfilling the anthropocentric focus. It is His Love and His Love alone which has the power to do good to the world.

Neither the theocentric nor the anthropocentric attitude is complete in itself; these two, opposed 180 degrees, are truly complementary aspects of God's joy. Our task is to seek it and find it within ourselves; when it is found, that joy itself demands to radiate outwardly to all creation. There is a saying by one of my favorite saints, Jnaneshvar, which underlines this truth. He said, "For the enlightened, there is neither bondage nor liberation; there is nothing to be accomplished. There is only the pleasure of expounding (the truth)." In other words, now that he had known the eternal joy of the Self, his greatest pleasure was in expressing that joy in the form of knowledge to others. When you know God, the world becomes, not an obstacle to God-vision, but rather the image and expression of God. The truth is that there is nothing that is not God. It is this very realization that constitutes worldly joy.

The sage, Vidyaranya, whom I quoted a moment ago, said: "Whatever (worldly) happiness is experienced is a reflection of the bliss of Brahman." What, then, of the bliss of earthly loves? Can you impose true vision upon the world, and see that your beloved is the very form of God? Can you begin to see that all beings share that very nature? Is this not God's own joy? The realization of God does not exclude the world from one's enjoyment; rather, it spiritualizes the world, and adds a new and much more satisfactory dimension to the enjoyment of the world.

I hasten to add the warning that one musn't take this to mean that one has free license to become a sensualist, an unbridled degenerate, under the guise of spirituality. No. To be able to see the world as God, and to integrate the enjoyment of worldly pleasures into one's unitive awareness, is a very high state -- is, in fact, the final integration and the ultimate attainment of freedom. But, it should be said, the enjoyment of the senses of one still bound to ego-attachments, who is without intellectual discrimination or mental control, is a much lesser thing; and, for the person striving for God-realization, is best left alone, as one is, at that stage, in great need of one-pointedness of the mind, and will find sense enjoyments extremely distracting to that attainment.

For those who are firmly established in the awareness of the Self, however, sense-objects pose no threat. Nonetheless, those who understand that the Self is the Source of all joy, are not very tempted by sense enjoyments, for the simple fact that they have little to offer in the way of increase of the innate joy that exists in its fullness within. For that reason, the Self-realized of every age, while they do not make a great point of avoiding sense pleasures, do not make any effort to seek them out either. More often than not, the great knowers of God have lived out their lives in simplicity, and with a reliance on very little in the way of creature-comforts or sense pleasures. There are many wonderfully radiant, and joy-filled, saints whom I could cite as examples, but to the wise, I have said enough.

Reflection

Joy is ever-present in my life, because I am nothing else but a manifestation of the Joy that is God. That Joy is my core, my essence; and therefore can never be absent from my life. I am the Life in all life; I am the wakefulness of all conscious beings, clear and flawless, like the infinite blue sky.

Whenever my mind produces clouds of thought to obscure that clear sky of Joy, I turn those thoughts to worship of that Joy from which they sprang -- and thus return to Joy. And whenever this body raises unpleasant sensations to disturb the serenity of my Joy, I turn my attention to the Watcher, the Listener within me who witnesses all sensations and thoughts undisturbed; for that is my permanent Self, my eternal Being, the never-changing Joy that is ever-present as my life.

THE WISDOM OF THE SVETASVATARA UPANISHAD

The *Svetasvatara Upanishad* is a very great song in praise of God. It is truly a work of great beauty and wisdom, containing such sublime knowledge and such pure-souled love, that I cannot think of any other scripture with which to compare it. Written in six parts, it reveals the nature of the soul, its one goal, and the means to attain that goal. It is a complete scripture in itself, containing all the knowledge to give satisfaction to the soul and raise it to the awareness of God.

About its author, Svetasvatara, we know nothing -- not even the age in which he lived, although scholars guess he lived shortly before or after the time of Jesus. Regardless of the uncertainty surrounding the time during which he flourished, it is certain that he was a great visionary, for his song of Divine love has well endured the test of time, and continues to inspire many hearts with devotion to the Lord. It begins with a Prologue which sets the stage for Svetasvatara's paean in praise of God:

Hari Om. The ancient seekers of Brahman enquired:
What is the Cause of the universe? Is it Brahman?
Why are we born? What upholds our lives?
And where do we go after life on earth?
O knower of Brahman, what compels us to this life of joy and sorrow in this world?

Is it Time, or Nature, or Fate, or Chance?
Is it the Elements? Or perhaps the soul is itself the Cause!
All these others exist only for the sake of the soul;
And the soul, which is under the sway of joys and sorrows, also cannot be an independent Cause!

*   *   *

Then, through the practice of meditation, they
   realized
That the power of God (*Devatma-shakti*) is
   the Cause
Who is hidden by, and exists within, His own
   effects.
It is He, the Lord, who alone rules all those
   other sources
Such as Time and the individual soul.

... Within the Cycle (of existence), in which
   all live and seek rest,
The swan-like soul wanders restlessly;
It thinks it's separate and far from God,
But, by His Grace, it awakes to its identity
   with Him.[1]

Then Svetasvatara begins the first part of his
Song, which is based entirely on his own experience.
He does not present a "religious philosophy"; rather,
he speaks of his own vision and attempts to express
the Truth as he experienced It in the mystical vision
of Unity. His recurrent theme is that by experiencing God, the absolute Self, the individual soul becomes
freed from its limited identification, and knows itself
to be, in fact, the one Soul of all. Thus, it becomes
free from all fears attending individual existence,
and no longer mistakenly identifies with any imaginary
separate identity.

I sing of Brahman: the subject, the object, the
   Lord of all!
He's the immutable Foundation of all that
   exists;
Those souls who realize Him as their very own
   Self,
Are freed forever from the need for rebirth.

The Lord is the Foundation of both aspects of
   reality:
He is both the Imperishable and the perishable,
   the Cause and the effect.
He takes the form of the limited soul, appearing to be bound;
But, in fact, He is forever free.

Brahman appears as Creator, and also as the
    limited soul;
He is also the Power that creates the appear-
    ance of the world.
Yet He remains unlimited and unaffected by
    these appearances;
When one knows that Brahman, then that soul
    becomes free.

The forms of the world change, like clouds in
    the sky;
But Brahman, the Lord, remains One and un-
    changed.
He is the Ruler of all worlds and all souls;
Through meditation on Him, and communion
    with Him,
He becomes known as the Self, and from
    illusion one is freed. [2]

It is only the One who becomes the many; and in
the many, there is nothing but the One.   Beneath
the differences, lies the Undifferentiated.   It is that
One who is spread out everywhere in all these variegated forms.   For one continually identified with the
Self, the universe goes on, of course, but it is experienced in the way the water in the ocean would
experience its own waves.   From the standpoint of
the water, the waves could be turbulent or calm;
nothing has changed.   From the standpoint of Consciousness, so many forms rise and subside, but,
since everything is Itself, nothing is changed.   The
whole of creation is manifested from Consciousness;
it is nothing but Consciousness during its existence,
and nothing but Consciousness at its end.   All is the
glorious play of the Self.

When that Lord who pervades all the worlds
    everywhere,
Gave birth to the first motion, He manifested
    Himself as creation.
It's He alone who is born in this world.
He lives in all beings; it's only Him everywhere.

... Those who have known Him say that,
While He manifests all worlds by His Power,

He remains ever One and unchanged.
He lives as the one Self of everyone;
He's the Creator and Protector to whom all
    beings return. [3]

Svetasvatara wishes us to understand that the Self
of the universe is the only Self. It is our Self. And
everything we see is the manifestation of our own
effulgence: the drifting clouds, the moist soil beneath
our feet, every form of life; the trees, crustaceans,
amphibians, every weasel in its burrow -- we are the
life-pulse in every one. All these magical forms of
man and woman: we have cast ourselves into these
molds for the sake of enjoyment, for the sake of
play. Says Svetasvatara, every yearning soul you see
is you. Every loving heart eager for God is your
own. The crystal-clear eyes of every illumined soul
are bright with your love.

He has eyes everywhere and mouths everywhere;
Everywhere are His arms and His feet.
The wings of all birds, and all men's arms are
    His own;
Both heaven and earth belong to Him.

Though He has no senses of His own, all senses
    are His;
He tastes all the pleasures of life through
    their use.
He's the Lord and Ruler of all that exists;
To all beings that live, He's the one and only
    Refuge.

The Self is the Swan who rules the whole
    universe
Of all that is sentient or insentient;
But when He confines Himself as the spirit in
    man,
He flies through the senses to sense-objects
    outside. [4]

It is all His play; He is the subject who enjoys,
and He is the object of enjoyment. It is all Himself;
He has become the Enjoyer and the object of enjoyment in order to experience the world. But, the
truth is, it is all a charade; from the standpoint of

the Self, nothing is happening. It is a mirage, a
world of dreams. All the pleasures depend on that
which is ephemeral, perishable. The beautiful body
decays. The gourmet food decays. The beautiful
children decay. This very life slips away, and, eventually one must learn to see that a life given to
these pursuits was a life in pursuit of clouds --
wispy little clouds that dissolve away into nothingness.
   "What a cheat!" we exclaim; "What a dirty trick
to play on us!" But it is all really Himself. Nothing
is lost; nothing dies. And, after all, each of us is
free to choose what we desire. God is not concealing
His Bliss. His hands are open. It is we who choose
from His bounty according to our desires; and, by
choosing, create our own heaven or hell. We can go
on grabbing at dreams, and struggling to possess and
squeeze what pleasure we can out of mere clouds,
and tasting their emptiness; or, we can see the dreams
for what they are, and thereby remain free, Self-ful-
fulled, exulting in our own imperishable, and blissful
Soul.

> He is greater than the world; He is beyond
>   what is perceived.
> Though He lives within man, the Lord has no
>   limits or bounds.
> When a man realizes that Lord who pervades
>   everything,
> He knows, in that moment, his own deathless
>   Self.

> I know that one Self who shines like the Sun,
> Through all the deep folds of the darkness
>   within.
> This knowledge give freedom from death and
>   from fear;
> It is the sole means to the attainment of
>   life's highest goal. [5]

How does one attain that knowledge, according to
Svetasvatara?   He prescribes the path of devotion
and meditation. It is the path of love for God which
he reveals as his own path; and he asks us also to
follow that way, in order that we might also attain
that experience of Self-revelation, and know the

freedom inherent in the knowledge of unity. "You shall know the Truth," said Jesus, "and the Truth shall make you free." It's true; the knowledge of the Self is liberating. Knowing your own infinite and eternal Self, how could you ever be overwhelmed with worldly care or anxiety? Knowing that you are everything, your only care must be to love everything. Knowing your Self, how could you fear? Fearlessness is the mark of such knowledge.

> O man, serve God during the hours of the day;
> Serve Him who engendered this whole universe.
> Then, in deep meditation, become one with
>   Him;
> You'll no longer be bound by the fruits of
> your works.
>
> A wise man should sit with his body erect;
> With his head, neck and shoulders aligned.
> He should turn both his mind and his senses
>   within;
> Then, by God's trusty boat, he'll cross over
> this world.
>
> A yogi should see that his Prana is controlled;
> His breath should flow softly and evenly.
> It is then that the mind may be held and
>   made calm,
> As one controls a wild horse by holding the
> reins.
>
> With His blessings, and by His light,
> We'll join our hearts and our minds to God.
> We'll surely reach to the highest state
> By earnest effort and faithful meditation.
>
> Just as gold which is contained in the ore,
> Becomes manifest when the dross is burned
>   away,
> A yogi, in whom God is revealed,
> Knows that he's one with the Self, and he
> sorrows no more. [6]

It is a theme that is repeated in subsequent verses of Svetasvatara's song: God manifests the world and

all souls, yet remains transcendent to all; the soul
imagines that it's separate from God, but when its
true nature is revealed, it realizes that it is nothing
but the one Soul of all. It is this realization that
sets a man free from ignorance and the suffering
that results from the false identification with the
body and the mind:

> Though producing the whole universe, He re-
>   mains unaffected;
> He never changes, but remains as He was.
> Without revealing His purposes, He continually
>   creates,
> And then withdraws it all again.
> May that effulgent Self enlighten our minds!

> He is fire, He is the Sun; He is wind, He is
>   the moon!
> He is the stars, and the mountains, the rivers
>   and seas!
> Thou art woman and man!   Thou art the old
>   and the young!
> It is Thou alone, Lord, who hast taken all
>   these forms!

> Thou art the blue bee; Thou art the green
>   parrot.
> Thou art the dark clouds, the four seasons,
>   the seas.
> Thou art the birthless and limitless God
> Who hast given birth to all worlds and all
>   souls.

> Unborn Nature (*Prakrti*), with her qualities
>   (*gunas*), gives birth to all forms;
> Countless unborn souls seek pleasure in Nature's
>   array.
> But the unborn Self, who projects both Nature
>   and souls,
> Lives apart from Its creations, in eternal Free-
>   dom and Bliss.

> The Self and the soul are like two birds, though
>   one;
> They have the same name, and they're in the

same tree.
But, while the soul tastes and enjoys the sweet
   fruits,
The other eats not; He's the Witness, the
   Self.
The soul, through enjoyment, forgets it's the
   Self;
And, feeling bewildered and helpless, it moans.
But when it beholds that its own Self is the
   glorious Lord all adore,
Then, it forgets all its grief.

... As cream is in milk, that one Self is in all;
Subtle and hidden, He pervades everything.
One who knows that radiant God who is Bliss,
Becomes released from all the bonds of this
   world.

When His light dispells the darkness of man's
   ignorance,
Both existence and non-existence vanish; both
   day and night disappear.
Brahman, and Brahman alone, is all that remains.
From His light comes the Sun and the wisdom
   of man.

... By knowing that One who exists as the
   world --
That One in whom everyone is born, and in
   whom everyone dies --
By knowing that Lord, the Bestower of grace,
   the adorable God,
One attains the supreme peace.[7]

Reflection

Our Father, who art purely Consciousness and Joy,
beyond this phenomenal universe, may Thy Name be
ever revered in my heart.

May the great awakening into the realm of Thy
indivisible Consciousness come to my eager soul; and
may Thy will of Love be expressed through me, as it
is expressed through those great souls who have
reached Thy subtle, heavenly realm in nearer proximity

to the fountainhead of Thy Light.

Father, sustain us, Thy children on earth, with the simple nourishment of our daily bread so we may continue to give our minds, not to bodily concerns, but to Thy Love and Thy service.

And forgive us our past thoughts and acts which were not in accord with Thy will of Love, as we forgive those who have thought or acted unlovingly toward us.

And lead us not into temptation in this, Thy delusive world of desire; but deliver us from the ignorance that overpowers the soul deluded by Thy glamorous world.

For Thine is the one transcendent Consciousness in which all souls and all objects exist, and Thine is the Power which produces and sustains all forms, and Thine, O Lord, is the glory of all that is, forever. Amen.

* * *

THE WISDOM OF THE SVETASVATARA UPANISHAD
PART II

When I spoke to you last, I borrowed some passages from the *Svetasvatara Upanishad* to   illustrate   the teachings of Vedanta.   I'd like to continue in that same vein today, and, once again, borrowing from the *Svetasvatara Upanishad*, see if I can explain   some key concepts in the philosophy of Vedanta.

In the Vedantic philosophy, much is said regarding the universal *Atman*, or Self; but what about the individual *jiva*, or soul?   How   does   that   fit   into   the Vedantic position?

Vedanta   deals   with   the   directs   knowledge,   the "realization", of the ultimate Reality, our Divine and eternal   Self   --   that   which   has   been   called   God, Lord,   Father,   the   Truth,   and   many   other   names. "Self"   is   in   many   regards   the   best   name   for   us   to use   in   talking   about   our   true   nature,   because   it brings   home   to   us   most   forcefully   that   the   "God"   we wish   to   know   is   not   something   *other*   than   ourselves; it is our very own essential being.   It is who we are!

This   proposition,   that   we   are   all   essentially   one Self,   and   not   many   individual   "souls",   flies   in   the face   of   the   popular   belief   in   a   multiplicity   of   souls separate   from   God,   and   also   opposes   our   stubborn belief   in   our   own   unique   individuality.   Since   the beginning   of   time,   men   have   discussed   the   nature   of the   soul   and   its   existence   after   death   of   the   body. Theologians and ministers eulogize the soul.   Psychics communicate   with   the   ghostly   presence   of   souls   on the   "astral"   planes.   Astrologers,   when   they   discuss the   personality   portrayed   in   the   birth-chart,   describe the   soul.   Furthermore,   many   normal   people   like   you and   me   have   told   of   experiences   of   soul-travel   during what   are   called   "near-death   experiences".   Many others   have   reported   having   memories   of   previous lives   in   other   times,   implying   the   continuity   of   the soul.   And perhaps hundreds of thousands have declared that   they   have   been   visited   in   their   dreams   or   in visions   by   loved   ones   who   are   no   longer   in   the   body. All   of   these   are   phenomenal   realities.   It   is   true: the *jiva*, or soul, has a phenomenal reality; but it is not the permanent Reality. The soul, like the body, exists in the phenomenal, that is to say, the spatio-temporal, reality; it is part of the created universe. But the essence, and true identity, of every soul is the Uncreated, the absolute Reality, the Unchanging, the eternal Self.

Most of us are aware of ourselves throughout our lifetimes as separate individual identities, or souls; yet, in the experience known as "enlightenment", one's true nature is directly perceived, and it is realized that there is no separate thing such as a "soul". The soul is then seen to be a mirage, an illusion, an imaginary identity resulting from the subject-object dichotomy that occurs with the emanation of the phenomenal universe of form. This is not difficult to understand. Just think about it: God expands Himself into a universe of multiple forms; each form, possessing Consciousness, relates to the rest of the universe as a subject to an object; i.e., "I am the seer. That which I see is the seen". So you have countless subjects and objects where, in fact, there is only the one expansive Self.

Each subject, or experiencing entity, is what we call a "soul". But, of course, all souls are nothing but the radiance of God, the one Self. His outflowing Love manifests as countless souls, each with its own desires to fulfill, its own tasks to accomplish, its own evolutionary history. The one Consciousness has extended Itself, as it were, from Its eternal Pure-Mind state to appear as countless individual living forms in a temporal universe of forms. These conscious forms, in the process of being imaged forth, have lost the memory and awareness of their original state, and identify with the separate characteristics they possess. They regard themselves as separate competitive entities with specific goals and desires. They have the power to direct their activities through thought and will, though not the absolute power they once had; and so they construct an identity unique to themselves which is really nothing more than a conglomerate of acquired habits and reactions to environmental conditions.

But the truth is that all souls are, after all, God's expression, His multiformed, multi-experiencing,

Self; and eventually must awake to their true, Divine
nature. Amazing and impossible as it sounds, that is
the truth of our identity -- a truth that would never
occur to anyone in a million years if there had not
been the many seers throughout history who have
been granted a glimpse into the reality of their
Divine identity, and who have told of it to others.
Over and over this truth has been told in many different languages, in many different ways; and in each
age it is forgotten, and has to be restated in a new
way in order to guide all those souls lost in ignorance
back to the Truth.

Here is what Svetasvatara said of it:

Each soul is impelled to act by the power of
    Nature;
It sows actions, and reaps the fruits of those
    actions.
Thus, it goes on assuming new forms and new
    qualities,
And wanders widely over the pathways of life.

The soul is small, but it shines like the Sun;
It possesses a will and a sense of 'I'.
It is because of its identification with the
    limited intellect,
That the perfect Self appears to be separate,
    weak, and of little worth.

That wandering soul may be compared
To a hair divided a hundred times,
Then again divided by a hundred more;
And yet, in fact, it's the infinite Self.

It is not female; it is not male;
Nor is it something in between these two.
The soul simply becomes identified with
Whatever body it dwells within.

Desiring fruits, the embodied soul
Attains its goals, and becomes attached to the
    fruits;
But, through pain of loss, it learns, and in this
    way grows,

As a body grows by taking food and drink.

The embodied soul, by virtue of its various
    actions,
Adopts new forms, either gross or subtle;
And, according to the knowledge and desires it
    posseses,
It assumes a new body to enjoy the world.

This is the doctrine of the transmigration and evolution
of souls. But what is the destination of that evolution?
Here is what Svetasvara says:

Once it knows the infinite Lord,
The Creator and Pervader of all life's forms
Who remains unmoved, while all the universe is
    in motion,
Then that soul is released from all its bonds.

Those souls who know that effulgent Lord,
The One who is realized by the pure of heart,
The Creator, Destroyer, the Cause of all,
Those souls are freed from embodied life. [1]

This excellent summary of the soul's relationship
to the Self is the essence of Vedanta; not only that,
it is a true expression of the knowledge obtained by
all the mystics in the experience of Unity, which has
been endlessly repeated throughout the ages.   Put
briefly, it is this: The "soul" has a unique kind of
existence which is neither "real" nor "unreal".   Ultimately, there are no souls; there is only the one
Self, the one pure Consciousness, God, who manifests
as all souls.   The soul, then, is a sort of thought-form,
or aggregate of tendencies, which exists in a filmy,
tenuous sort of way, but is really simply a mis-reading
of its true Identity.   Though it is ultimately false
and illusory, it is real enough to become re-embodied
numerous times in order to play out whatever desires
it wishes to fulfill, to pay off its debts incurred in
its previous embodiments, and to evolve in understanding of the truth.
    However, when it has evolved in understanding
enough to recognize the ephemeral nature of worldly
enjoyments, and having tired of these unsatisfactory
activities, becomes cognizant to some degree of its

real Identity which is always perfect, always satisfied, always God, then it begins to make progress in the spiritual life toward clarity of mind, toward universal loving-kindness, and toward infinite knowledge and peace. At some point along this path of progress, the soul is granted a "vision", a revelation, of its true, infinite and eternal nature; and then everything becomes clear, and the soul realizes that it has always been nothing else but the one Self, though caught up, by desire, in the masquerade of a soul.

All the mystics who have ever lived have experienced this same truth, and realized the oneness of all souls, despite their apparent variety.   Listen, for example, to what the great mystic-sage of 3rd century Rome, Plotinus, had to say regarding the nature of the soul:

> There is one identical soul, every separate manifestation being that soul complete.   The differentiated souls issue from the Unity and strike out here and there, but are united at the Source, much as a light is a divided thing on earth, shining in this house and that, while yet remaining one.   One Soul is the Source of all souls; it is at once divided and yet undivided.
> ... Diversity within the One depends not upon an actual spatial separation, but is a result of the differentiation of qualities.   All Existence, despite this (apparent) plurality, is a Unity still.   ... The souls are apart, but are not separated.   They are no more hedged off by boundaries than are the multiple items of knowledge in one mind.   The one Soul so exists as to include all souls. [2]

This is almost identical to what was said by the great Vedantist sage of 8th century India, Shankara-charya, on the same subject:

> The Self is the Witness, beyond all attrib-utes, beyond actions.   It can be directly realized as pure Consciousness and infinite Bliss.   Its apppearance as an individual soul is caused by the delusion of our understanding, and has no reality.   By its very nature, this appearance is unreal.   When our delusion has been removed, it ceases to exist. [3]

And again, on the same subject, he says:

Because all souls are essentially non-different, and their apparent difference is due to
ignorance (*avidya*) only, the individual soul,
after having dispelled ignorance by true knowledge, passes into Unity with the supreme
Self.

... The transmigrating soul is not different
from the Lord. ... Just as the light of the
Sun and the Sun itself are not absolutely different, so also the soul and the supreme Self are
not different.[4]

Shankaracharya speaks here, not as a theorist, but
as one who has experienced it, "seen" it, in the
mystical "vision".   All who have thus known the
Truth have testified that, in that experience of absolute Unity, there is no soul.   All duality is swallowed
up in that Oneness, including the duality that exists
on the relative plane between the soul and God, or
'I' and 'Thou'.   Here, there is only one; only the
Self experiences the Self.   And such experience is
not the experience of an object by a subject; there
is no "vision" in the ordinary sense.   Rather, it is an
expansion of (one's own) awareness, which experiences
itself as the ultimate Ground, the primal Source and
Godhead of all being.   It is an experience of the
consciousness, not the eye; and in it, there is no
distinction whatever between the experiencing mind
and the one Mind of the universe; all is experienced
as Identity.

Listen to what the 13th century German Prior,
Meister Eckhart, said about this experience:

If the soul sees form (in this vision), whether
she see the form of an angel or her own
form, it is an imperfection in her.   But when
all forms are detached from the soul and she
sees nothing but the One alone, then the naked
essence of the soul finds the naked formless
Essence of the Divine Unity, the superessential
Being, passive, reposing in Itself.

... Some simple people think that they will
see God as if He were standing there and
they here.   It is not so.   God and I, we are

one. ... The eye by which I see God is the
same as the eye by which God sees me.   My
eye and God's eye are one and the same --
one in seeing, one in knowing, and one in
loving. [5]

The visionary experience, which many men and
women have told of, such as the visualization of
prophets, saviors, heavenly landscapes, and even lights
of various colors, are no doubt significant experiences
of the mind or psyche, revealing subtle realms of
phenomena; but they are somewhat less than the
"vision of God", and must be categorized as psychic
experiences rather than mystical ones.   In the mystical
experience of Unity, one "sees" all, from the vantagepoint of God, as one's Self.   It is the final destination
of all knowledge-seeking; and there is no necessity
to question whether or not it is the final knowledge,
for that Unity, wherein all is one's Self, is the perfectly evident end of all one's seeking.   And it is
this realization of the eternal Self which is, from
the viewpoint of Vedanta, the ultimate salvation, or
liberation, from the bondage of ignorance.
        We find this idea of ultimate "liberation" in
every piece of Vedantic literature; it is the corner-
stone of the Vedanta philosophy as originally expressed
in the Upanishads.   And it is not a very difficult
concept to grasp.   The Self is the Truth of the
universe; it is the Truth of ourselves; it is who we
are!   There's really only One here!   All appearance
of multiplicity is a dream, an illusion -- conjured up
by the one Self for the purpose of multiplying Its
enjoyment.   To have experienced this Self directly,
to know with complete and absolute certainty that
there is really no one here but you -- this is the
real freedom, the ultimate fulfillment and satisfaction
of all man's thirst for truth, the final salvation.
        Here is what Shankaracharya says about it:

Of all spiritual disciplines, knowledge of
the Self is the only real means for Liberation,
just as fire is the only real means for cooking.
Liberation cannot be attained without knowledge
of the Self. [6]

And again:

Let people quote the scriptures and sacrifice
to the gods; let them perform rituals and
worship the deities, but there is no Liberation
without the realization of one's identity with
the Self; no, not even in the lifetimes of a
hundred Brahmas put together.

... Neither by yoga, nor by philosophy, nor
by work, nor by learning, but only by the
realization of one's identity with Brahman is
liberation possible, and by no other means. [7]

Once again, on this subject, we shall let Svetasvatara have the last word:

The Light of the Lord is undivided,
Though He dwells as the Self in all creatures
    and things.
He is the One who impels all to action, and
    witnesses all;
Though all-pervading, He remains unqualified
    and absolute.

He controls everyone as their inner Self;
He is the one Seed from which all these innum-
    erable forms have grown.
Only those who see Him within themselves
Obtain the gift of eternal Bliss.

He is the Eternal within the temporal, the
    Infinite within form;
He's the One within many, who grants all
    desires.
Only those who see Him within themselves
Obtain the gift of eternal Peace.

... There is nothing in this universe but the
    Self, the 'I AM';
Like a flame, He lives in the hearts of all.
The only way to pass beyond death is to know
    Him;
There's no other means, and there's no other
    End. [8]

'And so,' we might well ask, 'how is one to

attain this realization of the one Self? To whom
must we turn in order to acquire this supreme knowledge?' To the Self, of course; to God. Very humbly,
to the Lord of the universe.

> He is the sole support of the soul and the
>   world;
> He is the sole Cause of bondage, and the sole
>   Cause of liberation.
> He is the Creator, the Knower, the Self of all
>   things;
> All good comes from Him; He's the omniscient
>   Lord.
>
> He is the Controller of everything in the world;
> Bondage and Liberation are dealt by His hand.
> He, the immortal Protector of everyone,
> Is the Ruler of all. To whom else might you
>   turn?
>
> As one who seeks Liberation, I take refuge in
>   Him
> Who is the Revealer of the Self, the Giver of
>   all knowledge,
> The Creator of the Creator, who, at the begin-
>   ning of time,
> Gave expression to the truth, and shared it
>   with men.
>
> When man shall be able to roll up the sky like
>   a rug,
> Then suffering will end without attaining know-
>   ledge of Him.
> But till then, the knowledge of that undivided
>   and unchanging Lord
> Is the one and only Bridge to cross over the
>   ocean of life. ⁹

Reflection

To see God, to become one with Him in this life, is impossible for man. But, for Him it is possible. He, who has transformed His own radiance into this many-splendored universe, He who has become manifest as these myriads of souls and lives as each one -- is He not able to lift the veil which He has placed before His own eyes?

When the soul refuses to go on with this pretense, and has no other desire but to waken, then, turning inward to its true, eternal Self, it pleads with a beaten and surrendered heart for mercy. It is then, and only then, that the Lord, with His tender glance, releases the covering veil of darkness, and wakes the soul to the truth of its deathless Being.

'Tis not the soul who brings about this parting of the veil, but He who placed it there. 'Tis not the soul who sees, but He, who is the soul's substratum and existence -- He sees. And it is Himself He sees: one all-inclusive, undivided, independent, pure, unending Consciousness, who *is* all that He sees.

For man, it is impossible to see God, to become one with Him in this life. But, for Him, it isn't difficult at all.

*   *   *

VEDANTA -- CHRISTIAN STYLE

Vedanta, as we have said, is both a religion and a philosophy; and yet it must also be said that it is beyond both philosophy and religion. Truly speaking, Vedanta is a description of and commentary on the nature of Reality as directly experienced in "the mystical vision". Only those who have actually experienced the Truth directly are able to speak authoritatively about Vedanta. And, the fact is, there have been many wise and pure-hearted men and women of every nationality and every religious affiliation who have experienced the Truth. There are Christians who have experienced It, and Jews, and Muslims, and Hindus, and Buddhists, and so on. And so, we must include as part of the Vedantic heritage the teachings and writings of all those of various traditions who have directly realized the Truth.

Let us consider, for example, some of those Christians who taught the philosophy of Vedanta. They are the seers, the mystics of the Church, who taught the path to God-realization, and who proclaimed the identity of the soul and God, and the indivisibility of the one absolute Reality. First among these, of course, is Jesus of Nazareth, called 'the annointed one', or *Christos*, in the language of the Greeks. It is of his own mystical experience that Jesus spoke, a mystical experience which transcends all doctrines and all traditions, and which is identical for Christians, Muslims, Jews, and Vedantists alike. It is an experience of absolute Unity -- a Unity in which the soul merges into its Divine Source, and knows, "I and the Father are one."

This knowledge is unacceptable in all religious traditions, however; and so, those, like Jesus, al Hallaj, Eckhart, Spinoza, and many others who have experienced the Truth, are inevitably rejected by the religious traditions to which they belong. The religious tradition which arose around the teachings of Jesus, in its turn, ironically, rejects its mystics as well. Nonetheless, down through the centuries, a few of the followers of Jesus also experienced this Unity, by the grace of God, and spoke of It for posterity. Here, for example,

is what the famous Christian mystic of the 13th
century, Meister Eckhart, had to say about his own
experience:

> As the soul becomes more pure and bare
> and poor, and possesses less of created things,
> and is emptied of all things that are not God,
> it receives God more purely, and is more
> completely in Him; and it truly becomes one
> with God, and it looks into God and God into
> it, face to face as it were; two images trans-
> formed into one. ... Some simple people think
> that they will see God as if He were standing
> there and they here. It is not so. God and I,
> we are one.[1] ... I am converted into Him in
> such a way that He makes me one Being with
> Himself -- not (simply) a similar being. By
> the living God, it is true that there is no
> distinction![2]

Or this, by the 15th century Christian Bishop,
Nicholas of Cusa:

> Thou dost ravish me above myself that I
> may foresee the glorious place whereunto Thou
> callest me. Thou grantest me to behold the
> treasury of riches, of life, of joy, of beauty.
> Thou keepest nothing secret.[3]
> I behold Thee, O Lord my God, in a kind
> of mental trance,[4] ... and when I behold Thee,
> nothing is seen other than Thyself; for Thou
> art Thyself the object of Thyself, for Thou
> seest, and art That which is seen, and art the
> sight as well.[5]
> Hence, in Thee, who are love, the lover is
> not one thing and the beloved another, and
> the bond between them a third, but they are
> one and the same: Thou, Thyself, my God.
> For there is nothing in Thee that is not Thy
> very essence.[6]
> Nothing exists outside Thee, and all things
> in Thee are not other than Thee.[7]

Or listen to this, by the 16th century Christian
monk, St. John of the Cross:

What God communicates to the soul in this
intimate union is totally beyond words.　In
this transformation, the two become one.[8]
... The soul thereby becomes Divine, becomes
God, through participation, insofar as is possible
in this life.　... The union wrought between
the two natures, and the communication of the
Divine to the human in this state is such that
even though neither changes their being, both
appear to be God.[9]
... Having been made one with God, the
soul is somehow God through participation.[10]

This is the truth revealed in "the mystical vision",
the truth that Vedanta speaks of as "Non-Duality".
The central teaching of Vedanta, and of all genuine
religious teachers, is that the inner Self (*Atman*) and
God (*Brahman*) are one.　This is expressed in the
Upanishadic dictum: *tat tuam asi*, "That　thou　art!"
It is this very knowledge, experienced in a moment
of clarity in contemplation or prayer, which prompted
Jesus of Nazareth to explain to his disciples who he
was, and who they were, eternally:

If you knew who *I* am,　you　would　also
know the Father.　Knowing me, you know
Him; seeing me, you see Him.　... Do you not
understand that I am in the Father and the
Father is in me?　... It is the Father who
dwells in me doing His own work.　Understand
me when I say that I am in the Father and
the Father is in me.[11]

There are many other Vedantic teachings which
one can find in the utterances of Jesus, and his
followers.　For example, it follows from the teaching
of Non-Duality -- that is to say, the teaching that
all beings are manifestations of the one Divinity,
that we should therefore treat all beings as our own
Self, as they most truly are.　We find this teaching
very prominent among the teachings of Jesus.　In his
Sermon On The Mount, he says:

Ye have heard that it has been said, thou
shalt love thy neighbor, and hate thine enemy;
but I say unto you, love your enemies (also),

bless them that curse you, do good to them
that hate you, and pray for them which despite-
fully use you, and persecute you; that you
may be the children of your Father which is
in heaven; for He maketh His sun to rise on
the evil and on the good, and sendeth rain on
the just and on the unjust. Be ye therefore
perfect, even as you Father which is in heaven
is perfect.[12]

This is the message of equality-consciousness, of
seeing God (one's eternal Self) in all beings, and of
thinking and acting for the benefit of all. It is this
kind of reformation of our minds and hearts that is
called for if we are to assume our true identity, and
experience the perfection of our eternal Self. It is,
of course, our own minds which must be transformed
so that we are capable of ridding ourselves of the
false notion of a separate and distinct identity apart
from the one eternal Identity. It is the mind which
must be made single, one-pointed, and eventually
identified with the eternal Self.

To this end, Jesus spoke to his disciples of the
necessity of releasing their minds from concerns for
the welfare of their separate personalities and worldly
holdings in order to lift them up to God through
meditation and prayer. "How," he asked them, "can
you have your mind on God and at the same time
have it occupied with the things of this world?" He
pointed out to them that their hearts would be with
that which they valued most. One's attention could
not be focused on God and on one's worldly concerns
at the same time, for, as he said, a city divided
against itself must fall. He advised them frequently
to let God be the sole focus of their attention, and
to let God be the sole master whom they served.
"No man can serve two masters," he said;

for either he will hate the one, and love the
other, or else he will hold to the one, and
despise the other. Ye cannot serve both God
and Mammon (the flesh). Therefore, I say
unto you: take no thought for your life, what
ye shall eat, or what ye shall drink; nor yet
for your body, what ye shall put on. For your

heavenly Father knoweth that ye have need of
all these things. But seek ye first the kingdom
of God, and His righteousness; and all these
things shall be added unto you. [13]

Naturally this is a hard saying to those who harbor
many hopes and dreams of individual worldly wealth
and attainments. You'll recall what Jesus said to
the sincerely spiritual man who, nonetheless, was yet
attached to his worldly wealth; "It would be easier
for a camel to go through the eye of a needle," he
said, "than for such a man to experience the kingdom
of God." The necessity for renouncing the preoccupation of the mind with worldly things if one is to
occupy the mind with thoughts of God, is a teaching
that is found, not only in Vedanta and Christianity,
but in all true religion. It is certainly a consistently
recognized fact within the long tradition of Christian
mysticism. Listen, in this regard, to the words of
the 5th century Christian mystic who called himself
Dionysius the Areopagite:

> While God possesses all the positive attrib-
> utes of the universe, yet, in a more strict
> sense, he does not possess them, since He
> transcends them all. [14] ... The all-perfect and
> unique Cause of all things transcends all, (and)
> is free from every limitation and beyond them
> all. [15]
> Therefore, do thou, in the dilligent exercise
> of mystical contemplation, leave behind the
> senses and the operations of the intellect, and
> all things sensible and intellectual, and all
> things in the world of being and non-being,
> that thou mayest arise by unknowing towards
> the union, as far as is attainable, with Him
> who transcends all being and all knowledge.
> For by the unceasing and absolute renunciation
> of thyself and of all things, thou mayest be
> born on high, through pure and entire self-
> abnegation, into the superessential radiance of
> the Divine. [16]

We are accustomed, perhaps, to associating the
word, "renunciation" with the Vedantic tradition of

India, and most especially as it is used in the *Bhaga-vad Gita*; but renunciation of the false individual self is a prerequisite to God-consciousness, regardless of one's nationality or religious affiliation.   It is a word which occurs frequently among the writings of the great Christian mystics of the past.   Listen, for example, to the 16th century Spanish monk, St. John of the Cross:

> The road and ascent to God necessarily demands a habitual effort to renounce and mortify the appetites; and the sooner this mortification is achieved, the sooner the soul reaches the summit.   But until the appetites are eliminated, a person will not arrive, no matter how much virtue he practices.   For he will fail to acquire perfect virtue, which lies in keeping the soul empty, naked, and purified of every appetite.[17]
> Until slumber comes to the appetites through the mortification of sensuality, and until this very sensuality is stilled in such a way that the appetites do not war against the Spirit, the soul will not walk out to genuine freedom, to the enjoyment of union with its Beloved.[18]

Now, I would like for you to hear one more Christ-ian seer on this same theme: Thomas à Kempis was a German monk of the 15th century who, above all other mystics, Christian or Vedantic, had a great influence upon me for the beauty of his expression and the pure sincerity of his longing for God.   Here is just a little of what he had to say:

> You may in no manner be satisfied with temporal goods, for you are not created to rest yourself in them.   For if you alone might have all the goods that ever were created and made, you might not therefore be happy and blessed; but your blessedness and your full felicity stands only in God who has made all things.   And that is not such felicity as is commended by the foolish lovers of the world, but such as good men and women hope to have in the bliss of God, and as some spiritual persons, clean and pure in heart, sometimes do

taste here in this present life, whose conversation is in heaven. All worldly solace and all
man's comfort is vain and short, but that
comfort is blessed and reliable that is perceived
by the soul inwardly in the heart.

Await, my soul, await the promise of God,
and you shall have abundance of all goodness
in Him. If you inordinately covet goods present,
you shall lose the Goodness eternal. Have
therefore goods present in use and Goodness
eternal in desire.[19]

Here, again, from the same author:

Many desire to have the gift of contemplation, but they will not use such things as are
required for contemplation. And one great
hindrance of contemplation is that we stand so
long in outward signs and in material things,
and take no heed of the perfect mortifying of
our body to the Spirit. I know not how it is,
nor with what spirit we are led, nor what we
pretend, we who are called spiritual persons,
that we take greater labor and study for transitory things than we do to know the inward
state of our own soul. But, alas for sorrow,
as soon as we have made a little recollection
to God, we run forth to outward things and do
not search our own conscience with due examination, as we should, nor heed where our affection rests, nor sorrow that our deeds are so
evil and so unclean as they are.[20]

... You shall much profit in grace if you
keep yourself free from all temporal cares,
and it shall hinder you greatly if you set value
on any temporal thing. Therefore, let nothing
be in your sight high, nothing great, nothing
pleasing nor acceptable to you, unless it be
purely God, or of God. Think all comforts
vain that come to you by any creature. He
who loves God, and his own soul for God,
despises all other love; for he sees well that
God alone, who is eternal and incomprehensible,
and fulfills all things with His goodness, is the
whole solace and comfort of the soul; and

that He is the very true gladness of heart, and none other but only He.[21]

This grace is a light from heaven and a spiritual gift of God. It is the proper mark and token of elect people and a guarantee of the everlasting life. It lifts a man from love of earthly things to the love of heavenly things, and makes a carnal man to be a man of God. And the more that nature is oppressed and overcome, the more grace is given, and the soul through new gracious visitations is daily shaped anew and formed more and more to the image of God.[22]

Thus, as we have seen, the true religion, the true understanding, is always the same. The teachings of the saints who have known their true nature as Divine have always declared the same path of one-pointed devotion as the means to experience and become united with the Divine Self. And so we find, in the words of the mystics of Christianity, Islam, Buddhism, and of every true religious tradition, the authentic teachings of Vedanta.

Reflection

Father, grant me new eyes with which to see Thee -- both in the stillness of my heart and in the world of Thy creation. Lift from my mind the inclination to chase after images and forms which divert my attention from awareness of Thee.

Lord, when I sit for meditation, let me rise on thrilling waves of bliss toward Thee above. Let me enter into Thy kingdom of silence, where Thy all-pervading Light surrounds me with love.

O Father, grant me the freedom to look away from all else that tempts and distracts my inner eye from Thy clarity and splendor; for Thou alone art my true and everlasting joy.

Thou art my foundation and my support, my gift and my reward, my seeking and the treasure sought. Thou art the Sun of my striving and the moon of my salvation. Therefore, do keep me, O my Father, in Thy watchful care; lead me, O my Mother, by Thy kind and gentle hand: return me safely to my home in Thee.

NON-DUALISM IN THE TEACHINGS OF JESUS

I think it is important to stress the fact that the saints and sages of India have no deed to the Truth over and above the devotees of other lands and other religious traditions. Every religious tradition worth its salt recognizes the same eternal Truth; and all great religious teachers have taught according to their own intimate experience of God, their "mystical vision" -- whether it is called "samadhi", "nirvana", "fana", or "union with God". Since there is but one ultimate Reality, which all share, each one who has experienced the Truth has experienced that same ultimate Reality. Naturally, therefore, their teachings about it, and about how one can experience It for oneself, are bound to be identical.

The languages and cultures of the various teachers who have lived throughout history are, no doubt, different from one another. Their personalities and life-styles are different. But their vision is one, and the path they teach to it is one. In the mystical experience, which transcends all religious traditions and cultures and languages, the Christian and the Vedantist alike come to the same realization: They realize the oneness of their own soul and God, the Soul of the universe. It is this very experience which prompted Jesus, the originator of Christianity, to explain at various times to his disciples that he had known the great Unity in which he and the Father of the universe were one.

"If you knew who I am," he said,

you would also know the Father. Knowing me, you know Him; seeing me, you see Him. Do you not understand that I am in the Father and the Father is in me? It is the Father who dwells in me doing His own work. Understand me when I say that I am in the Father and the Father is in me.[1]

This is the truth that Vedanta speaks of as "Non-Dualism". The term, "Unity", is, of course, the same in meaning; but it seems that the declaration, "Not-two" is more powerfully emphatic than a mere

assertion of oneness.   Indeed, the word, "Unity" is
often used by religionists who apply it to God, but
who have not even considered the thought that they
themselves are included in an absolute Unity, philo-
sophically speaking.   Non-Dualism, the philosophy of
absolute Unity, is the central teaching, not only of
Vedanta, but of all genuine seers of Truth.   This
position is embodied in the Vedantic assertion, *tat
tuam asi*, "That thou art".

Once we begin to look at the teachings of Jesus
in the light of his "mystical" experience of Unity,
we begin to have a much clearer perspective on all
the aspects of the life and teaching of the man.   His
teachings, like those of the various Vedantic sages
who've taught throughout the ages, is that the soul
of man is none other than the one Divinity, none
other than God; and that this Divine Identity can be
experienced and known through the revelation that
occurs inwardly, by the grace of God, to those who
prepare and purify their minds and hearts to receive
it.   The words of Jesus are so well-known to us from
our childhood that, perhaps, they have lost their
meaning through our over-familiarity with them.   He
attempted to explain to us, with the words, "I and
the Father are one", that the "I", our own inner
awareness of self, is none other than the one Self,
the one Existence, the Lord and Father of all.

Why, then, are we so unable to see It?   Why
should it be so hard for us to attain to that purity
of heart which Jesus declared so essential to Its
vision?   Probably because we have not really tried --
not the way Jesus did, going off into the wilderness,
jeapordizing everything else in his life for this one
aim, focusing completely and entirely on attaining
the vision of God.   Not the way the Buddha did.
Not the way all those who have experienced God
have done.   Perhaps we're not ready for such a concentrated effort just yet.   Perhaps we have other
desires yet to dispense with before we will be free
enough to seek so high a goal.   For us, perhaps,
there is yet much to be done to soften the heart, so
that we are pure enough to hear the call of Divine
Grace.   It is to such as us, for whom much yet needs
to be accomplished toward the attainment of a "pure

heart", that Jesus spoke.

All of what Jesus taught to his disciples was by way of explaining to them that his real nature, and that of all men, is Divine; and that the reality of this could be realized directly.   Furthermore, he taught them the path, or method, to follow in order to attain this direct realization.   Let us look to his own words to corroborate this: In the Gospel book of John, he laments to God, "O righteous Father, the world has not known Thee.   But I have known Thee".[2] And, as he sat among the orthodox religionists in the Jewish temple, he said, "You say that He is your God, yet you have not known Him.   But I have known Him."[3]   Jesus had "known" God directly during a time of deep prayer, following his initiation by his "guru", probably during his time in the wilderness; and that experience had separated him and effectively isolated him from his brothers, because he alone seemed to possess this rare knowledge of the truth of all existence.

This is the difficult plight of all those who have been graced with "the vision of God".   It is the greatest of gifts, it is the greatest of all possible visions; and yet, because the knowledge so received is completely contrary to what all men believe regarding God and the soul, it is a terribly alienating knowledge which brings upon its possessor the scorn and derision of all mankind.   History is replete with examples of others who, having attained this saving knowledge, found the world unwilling to accept it, and ready to defend its ignorance agressively.   This circumstance is little changed today.

Because the "vision" of God is so difficult to convey to those who had not experienced it, Jesus spoke often by way of analogy or metaphor in order to make his meaning clear.   He spoke of the experience of "seeing" God as an entering into a realm beyond this world, a realm where only God is.   In his own Aramaic language, he called this realm *malkutha*. In the Greek translation, this is *basileia*.   In English, it is usually rendered as "the kingdom of God."

> His disciples asked him, "When will the kingdom come?"   Jesus said, "It will not come by waiting for it.   It will not be a matter of

saying, 'Here it is!' or 'There it is!' Rather, the kingdom of the Father is [already] spread out upon the earth, and [yet] men do not see it.[4] ... Indeed, what you look forward to has already come, but you do not recognize it."[5]

The Pharisees asked him, "When will the kingdom of God come?" He said, "You cannot tell by signs [i.e., by observations] when the kingdom of God will come. There will be no saying, 'Look, here it is!' or 'There it is!' For, in fact, the kingdom of God is [experienced] within you."[6]

Jesus said, "If those who lead you say to you, 'See, the kingdom is in the sky', then the birds of the sky will have preceded you. If they say to you, 'It is in the sea', then the fish will precede you. Rather the kingdom is inside of you, and it is outside of you [as well]. When you come to know your Self, then you [i.e., your true nature] will be known, and you will realize that it is you who are the sons of the living Father. But if you will not know your Self, you live in poverty [of understanding], and you are that poverty [i.e., you are what you think you are]."[7]

Another of Jesus' metaphors utilized the terms, "Light" and "darkness" to represent the Divinity and the inherent delusion of man, respectively:

Jesus said, "The world's images are manifest to man, but the Light in them remains concealed; within the image is the Light of the Father. He becomes manifest as the images, but, as the Light, He is concealed."[8]

He said to them, "There is a Light within a man of Light, and It lights up the whole world. If it does not shine, he is in darkness."[9]

These are terms which have been used since time immemorial to represent the Divine Consciousness in man and the hazy ignorance which obscures It. In the very first paragraph of the book of John, we find an excellent explanation of these two principles, and their Greek synonyms, *Theos* and *Logos*:

In the beginning was the Logos, and the Logos was with God, and the Logos was God. He [or It] was with God in the beginning. All things were made by Him; without Him nothing was made. Within Him was Life, and the Life was the Light of man. And the Light shown in the darkness, but the darkness comprehended It not. [10]

A word of explanation is necessary: These two terms, "Light" and "darkness" are also indicative of the cosmic aspects of Reality; in other words, they are not only the Divine Consciousness in man and the darkness of unknowing, but they are, at a higher level, the very Godhead and Its Power of manifestation. They are those same two principles we have so often run into, called "Brahman and Maya", "Purusha and Prakrti", "Shiva and Shakti". It is the Godhead in us which provides the Light in us; it is the manifestory principle which, in the process of creating a body, brain, and nervous system, provides us with all the obscuration necessary to keep us in the dark as to our true Identity.

Jesus said, "If they ask you, 'Where did you come from?' say to them, 'We came from the Light, the place where the Light came into being of Its own accord and established Itself and became manifest through our image.' If they ask you, 'Are you It?' say 'We are Its children, and we are the elect of the living Father.' If they ask you, 'What is the sign of your Father in you?' say to them, 'It is movement and repose'." [11]

Jesus said, "I am the Light; I am above all that is manifest. Everything came forth from me, and everything returns to me. Split a piece of wood, and I am there. Lift a stone, and you will find me there. [12]

Here, Jesus identifies with the Eternal Light; but he seems never to have intended to imply that he was uniquely and exclusively identical with It; it should be clear that his intention was always to convey the truth that all men are, in essence, the transcendent Consciousness, manifest in form:

Ye *are* the Light of the world.   Let your Light so shine before men, that they may see your good works, and glorify your Father which is in heaven. [13]

Frequently he declared to his followers that they too would come to the same realization that he had experienced:

"I tell you this," he said to them; "there are some of those standing here who will not taste death before they have seen the kingdom of God already come in full power." [14]

"The heavens and the earth will be rolled up in your presence.   And the one who lives from the living ONE will not see death.   Have I not said: 'whoever finds his Self is superior to the world'?" [15]

"Take heed of the living ONE while you are alive, lest you die and seek to see Him and be unable to do so." [16]

"That which you have will save you if you bring It forth from yourselves.   That which you do not have within you will destroy you." [17]

"That which you have" is, of course, the Truth, the Light, the Divinity who manifest as you.   "That which you do not have" refers to the false identity of separate individuality, which is simply a lie.   It is wrong understanding of who you are that limits you, and which prevents you from experiencing the Eternal.
    The teaching, common to all true "mystics" who have realized the Highest, is "You *are* the Light of the world!   You are That!   Identify with the Light, the Truth, for That is who you really are!"   And yet Jesus did not wish that this should remain a mere matter of faith with his disciples; he wished them to realize this truth for themselves.   And he taught them the method by which he had come to know God.   Like all great seers, he knew both the means and the end, he knew both the One and the

many. Thus we hear in the message of Jesus, an
apparent ambiguity which is necessitated by the
paradoxical nature of the Reality.

In the One, the two -- soul and God -- play
their love-game of devotion. At one moment, the
soul speaks of God, its "Father"; at another moment,
it is identified with God, and speaks of "I". Likewise,
in the words of Jesus to his disciples, we see this
same complementarity: At one moment, he speaks
of dualistic devotion in the form of prayer ("Our
Father, who art in heaven ..."); and at another moment he asserts his oneness, his identity, with God
("Lift the stone and I am there..."). But he cautioned
his disciples against offending others with this attitude
("If they ask you, 'Are you It?' say 'We are Its
children...").

At times, identifying with the One, he asserts
that he has the power to grant the experience of
Unity ("I shall give you what no eye has seen and
what no ear has heard and what no hand has touched
and what has never occurred to the human mind").[18]
And at other times, identifying with the human soul,
he gives all credit to God, the Father ("Why do you
call me good? There is no one good but the ONE,
that is God."[19]).

There is an interesting story that appears in both
Matthew and Luke which illustrates the knowledge,
from the standpoint of the individual soul, that the
realization of God comes, not by any deed of one's
own, but solely by the grace of God: Jesus had just
commented upon how difficult it would be for a
young man, otherwise spiritually inclined, who was
attached to his worldly wealth and occupations, to
realize God; and his disciples, who were gathered
around, were somewhat disturbed by this, and asked,
"Then, who *can* attain salvation?" And Jesus answered,
"For man it is impossible; but for God it is possible."

And Peter, understanding that Jesus is denying
that any man, by his own efforts, can bring about
that experience, but only God, by His grace, gives
this awakening, objected: "But we here have left our
belongings to become your followers!" And Jesus,
wishing to assure them that any effort toward God-
realization will bear its fruits in this life and in lives

to come, said to them: "I tell you this; there is no one who has given up home, or wife, brothers, parents or children, for the sake of the kingdom of God, who will not be repaid many times over in this time, and in the time to come know eternal Life."[20] He could guarantee to no one the knowledge of God; that was in the hands of God. But Jesus knew that whatever efforts one makes toward God must bear their fruits in this life, and in the lives to come.

And so, throughout the teachings of Jesus, one finds these two, apparently contradictory, attitudes intermingled: the attitude of the *jnani* ("I am the Light; I am above all that is manifest"); and the attitude of the *bhakta* ("Father, father, why hast Thou forsaken me?"). They are the two voices of the illumined man, for he is both, the transcendent Unity and the imaged soul; he has "seen" this unity in the "mystical experience".

Jesus had experienced the ultimate Truth; he had clearly seen and known It beyond any doubt; and he knew that the consciousness that lived as him was the one Consciousness of all. He knew that he was the living Awareness from which this entire universe is born. This was the certain, indubitable, truth; and yet Jesus found but few who could even comprehend it. For the most part, those to whom he spoke were well-meaning religionists who were incapable of accepting the profound meaning of his words. The religious orthodoxy of his time, like all such orthodoxies, fostered a self-serving lip-service to spiritual ideals, and observed all sorts of symbolic rituals, but was entirely ignorant of the fact that the ultimate Reality could be directly known by a pure and devout soul, and that this was the real purpose of all religious practice.

Jesus realized, of course, that despite the overwhelming influence of the orthodox religionists, still, in his own Judaic tradition, there had been other seers of God, who had known and taught this truth. "I come," said Jesus, "not to destroy the law [of the Prophets], but to fulfill it."[21] He knew also that any person who announced the fact that they had seen and known God would be persecuted and belittled, and regarded as an infidel and a liar. In the *Gospel of Thomas,* Jesus is reported to have said, "He who knows the Father (the transcendent Absolute) and the Mother (the creative Principle) will be called a son-of-a-bitch!" [22] It seems he was making a pun on the fact that one who does *not* know his father and mother is usually referred to in this fashion; but, in his case, he had known the Father of the universe, and knew the Power [of Mother Nature] behind the entire creation, and still he was called this derisive name.

It is the common experience of all the great seers, from Lao Tze to Socrates and Heraclitus, from Plotinus and al-Hallaj to Meister Eckhart and St. John of the Cross. All were cruelly tortured and persecuted for their goodness and wisdom. Jesus too found the world of men wanting in understanding; he said:

> I took my place in the midst of the world, and I went among the people. I found all of them intoxicated [with pride and ignorance]; I found none of them thirsty [for Truth]. And my soul became sorrowful for the sons of men, because they are blind in their hearts and do not have vision. Empty they came into the world, and empty they wish to leave the world. But, for the moment, they are intoxicated; when they shake off their wine, then they will repent. [23]

Reflection

Dear Father, grant me the Grace to lift my mind ever upward to Thee! I have much need of Thy Grace if I am to live as Thy child and servant and find my way into Thy Kingdom. Lord, grant me the Grace to cling to Thee, and rise above all fantacies and images that now have power to distract me from Thy service.

Let the oil of Thy Grace anoint my head, and lubricate all the parts of my body with its nourishing balm. Thy Grace, Lord, is nectar to my body and to my mind, and lifts me up in rapture beyond myself, beyond weariness and care, beyond the world and its ignorance.

Lord, what else shall I look to but Thy Grace to restore my heart and erase my errors? Where else shall I find the cool and gentle breeze of peace and joy but in Thy merciful Grace?

Do, Father, forgive me what is past; remember my efforts and let them not be in vain. Restore me, Father, to my place in the light of Thy Feet, and shed on me, Thy foolish child, the loving Grace that shall make me whole again.

*   *   *

PRACTICAL VEDANTA

Everyone needs to feel that they are improving, that they are progressing toward their goals. However, as soon as we attain one worldly goal, we realize that the attainment of that goal held very little satisfaction; and so we go on changing our goals, continuing to seek some satisfaction, until eventually, we set our sights on the ultimate goal, the ultimate satisfaction: the knowledge of ultimate Reality. That goal may initially take the form of wanting to understand the ultimate Reality. Then, as we make some efforts in that direction, we discover that it is not like all our other goals of acquisition; it is not subject to understanding. It cannot be attained in the same manner as all previous kinds of knowledge; it requires an entirely new approach.

That ultimate Reality which we long to grasp is nothing but our own Self, our own Identity; and to realize It, we learn, requires a turning of the mind from its normal outward course inward upon itself. We must become introspective; i.e., we must look into ourselves. This is such a radical change from the way we are accustomed to acquiring knowledge that it takes a bit of getting used to. In fact, it can be extremely unsettling, not to mention threatening, to the habit-bound ego. We were very willing to go along with the idea of improving upon ourselves; we had hoped to go on adding to our understanding, our capabilities, possessions, and enjoyments indefinitely, until we became the greatest ego on earth. But the notion that the Self is already perfect, if only we would get out of the way, is a realization that can be very upsetting to the ego.

We come to learn that the Self, our real Self, cannot be improved upon; it is identical to the absolute Reality, to God. Rather, it is the limitations we have placed on our Self by our false ideas of who we are and what is in our best interest that must be removed. All those limitations are, of course, mere dreams, insubstantial clouds of ignorance, which prevent the inherent radiance and clarity of our immortal Self to shine forth. The light of Consciousness, the Self, is pure Light, clear and all-illuminating; but we cannot experience it for the dark clouds of false belief. So, as it has been said by the ancients, we must get rid of what we haven't got, and let shine the glory which we have always possessed.

Consider, as an illustration, a fruit, such as the orange; there is sweet juice there within the orange; but it is covered by a bitter rind. If you try to eat the rind, you will get a very bad taste in your mouth. We all know that in order to get at the sweet meat within, we must remove the rind. It is the same with ourselves. There is the sweet nectar of love, peace and wisdom within, but we must peel away the bitter, outer coating of wrong thinking, wrong understanding and wrong behavior. Then we can enjoy the nectar. But if we are content to eat nothing but the outer rind of life, we must not be surprised if we are left with a very bitter taste in our mouths.

And yet, O how we cling to that bitter rind! How tenaciously we hold onto it, refusing to give it up, sucking away at that peel and tasting nothing but acrid bitterness. What is this rind? It is the false ego, the belief in a personal selfhood, an independent existence, which keeps us from tasting and enjoying the sweetness of the Self. Because of this false belief, we trade away the inner nectar of the Self for all the transient externals of life that serve to bolster our sense of individuality. Thus we give more attention to our personal loves, personal pleasures, than we do the purification of our hearts, without which we shall not enter into "the kingdom of God", the nectar of the Self.

Don't get me wrong; I have nothing against the enjoyment of life. Life is God; it is nothing but enjoyment -- so long as we can retain the awareness, through the eyes of God, that all about us is nothing but God. "All this is my Self!" should be our constant awareness, instead of "All this is the field of battle where I must either conquer and plunder or be conquered." Implicit in such a thought is the assumption of the false identity. All this is your own manifestation; it is only the ego, the limited identity, that feels threatened and willfully demands the fulfillment of its desires.

The enlightened soul, the purified ego, wishes only to do God's will. To commune with God, to maintain that communion, to become one with Him, becoming the instrument of His will and surrendering completely to His love: that is the only real 'self-improvement' that counts in life. Whatever else seems to be self-improvement is mere delusion. That self-improvement which leads to the soul's surrender to God, to the Self, to Love, is not only practical Vedanta; it is practical religion, practical life.

Did you know that "religion" is a word stemming from the Latin, *religare*, which means to re-tie, or to re-bind? It is the re-uniting of the consciousness of the individual soul with its origin and source that the word, "religion" is intended to signify. The word, "yoga", has a similar meaning; it comes from the Sanskrit root which gives us the word, "yoke", as in "Yoke the oxen to the wagon!" It means to unite the individual consciousness and the universal Consciousness. Religion, like yoga, is universal. There are not many different religions, but one many-named religion -- which is the re-uniting of the soul to God. Perhaps it is more concise to say that it is the awakening of the soul to its eternal unity with the Divine. In either case, the path of religion, like the path of yoga, requires a purification of the individual consciousness, a purification of the heart, in order for the individual to realize his Divine Self, to know the kingdom of God.

Listen to the recommendations of a great sage of the 3rd century, the Roman, Plotinus. He belonged to no religious sect; he was neither Christian nor Jew nor Vedantist, but a man who had realized the truth of his own Self. This is what he advised to those who would follow in his footsteps:

Withdraw into yourself and look. And if you do not find yourself beautiful yet, act as does the creator of a statue that is to be made more beautiful; he cuts away here, he smoothes there; he makes this line lighter, this other purer, until a lovely face has grown upon his work. So do you also; cut away all that is excessive, straighten all that is crooked, bring to light all that is in shadow; labor to make all one glow of beauty and never cease chiseling your statue until there shall shine out on you from it the Godlike splendor of virtue, until you shall see the perfect Goodness established in the stainless shrine.[1]

This instruction of Plotinus is the first order of business if we would know God: "Withdraw into yourself and look!" The "perfect Goodness" is always there in its perfection; it is the shrine -- i.e., the body and the mind -- that must be made stainless, transparent, so that the perfect Goodness can shine through.

Let's understand well what it is that is to be purified. We are easily able to understand the idea that we are not the body, that the body is eventually discarded like a suit of old clothes, being merely the vehicle through which we operate on the phenomenal plane. But it is much more difficult for us to understand that we are not the mind either. "The mind?" you say; "How can I not be the mind? And, if I'm not, what am I?" The answer, of course, is "You are the Self. You are the pure Consciousness that is the witness of the mind." It is just as the great Shankaracharya said:

The fool thinks, 'I am the body'; the intelligent man thinks, 'I am an individual soul united with the body'. But the wise man, in the greatness of his knowledge and spiritual discrimination, sees the Self as the only reality, and thinks, 'I am Brahman'.[2]

If you examine yourself carefully, you'll discover that the thoughts and images produced within, and which flit by on the screen of your own consciousness, cannot be you -- because you are perceiving the thoughts. They are produced out of consciousness by your own thought-producing power, but they are not who you are. You are the ocean of Consciousness; you project the thoughts on yourself in order to experience the subject-object relationship without which there could be no experience, or knowledge, or enjoyment at all.

"But how, then", you may ask, "can the Self witness

Itself? How can the Knower know Itself?" Only by
allowing the production of thoughts and images to
subside, to become still, without thought, becoming
aware of yourself as pure Being.   You alone are.
You are Existence. Consciousness. Bliss. But, instead,
what happens: We become swept away by the thought-
producing mind!   Old habits, old passions, desires, our
very nature, seems to pull us into ways of behaving
which go against our most strongly held intentions.
We may even come to the conclusion that the religious
life is impracticable, that one would have to be a
reclusive monk living on some faraway mountaintop in
order to live the spiritual life, the life Vedanta speaks
of.
     Many have wondered this very thought; "Is Vedanta
practicable in this world while living a normal life?
And the answer is "Yes!" It is practicable, without a
doubt.   The Truth would not be of very much use if
you couldn't live in accordance with It!   That is not
to say that it is easy to do so in a world where truth
is regarded as falsehood.   There is some effort involved,
to be sure.   It is only because we have so deeply
established ignorance into our patterns of thinking and
behaving over so many lifetimes that effort is now
required to alter those false and destructive ways of
thinking and acting.
     How did we get into such a fix?   Were we cursed
by God to such a fate?   Some religious traditions
hold such a view; but Vedanta does not agree that
the reason for our being out of accord with our own
Divinity is some past indiscretions on the part of our
ancestors for which all succeeding generations have
been accursed to a life of weariness and pain by a
vengeful and wrathful God.   No.   This doctrine of
"original sin" is the invention of minds unwilling to
accept the fact of evolution. It is a wrong and hurtful
notion and is responsible for turning many away from
religion because of its obvious stupidity.
     Vedanta offers an alternative theory to account
for the presence of animal passions, negativities, psych-
ological perversities, in our nature.   It teaches us that
we, as evolving souls, passing through all the stages of
life--from vegetable to lower animal, to vertebrate
animal forms, and finally to the highest, human form--

have within our very cell-structures all the old habit-patterns of those past lives relating to the need for survival, procreation, security, etc.   And, to a greater or lesser degree, all of us are motivated by these primitive instincts according to how firmly we identify with the "nature" aspect of our being; i.e., our bodies, minds, and stored personal impressions.   These inherited instincts become less imperative, less all-consuming, when we come to realize that we are not the manifested phenomena -- the bodies, the habits -- , but we are the one Life, the Spirit.   Then, we must pass through the long and arduous process of disengaging our minds from the old familiar urgings and cravings that were so much a part of our evolving consciousness in past incarnations, in order to free our Consciousness to know Itself as the Unlimited, the Transcendent, the Ever-Free.

This theory of the evolution of the soul is much more in keeping with the scientific approach to our spiritual life than is the arbitrary postulation of a curse which we have inherited from our remote ancestors -- and which, if you believe the doctrine of the Christians, was rescinded by the sacrifice of God's only begotten son, Jesus of Nazareth, to the exclusive benefit of those who believe, or profess to believe, this nonsense.   The theory of soul-evolution is a theory which is backed up by common sense, by various forms of clear evidence, and by occasional instances of actual memory-recall of past lives.   It is a theory which relieves us of the necessity to believe in absurdities.   It is a theory which is reinforced as well by the experiences of the mystics who have transcended the soul, to know the one Existence.

The endeavor to clarify the soul, to purify the heart, so as to live in the awareness of the Divine Joy which you are, is easier or more difficult in accordance with our own past efforts and understanding, and according to our willingness to be taught and uplifted by the Grace that is always around us. That Grace is always there, and always seeking ways and opportunities to lift us up in consciousness. That Grace is the Grace of our own inner Self, and so it has no trouble reaching us -- so long as we are open and receptive to it.

The necessary thing is, we must look to God incessantly. His compassion is well-known. Why should He not be compassionate to one who is a manifestation of Himself? Have absolute faith in that truth: you are a manifestation of the highest Lord. Continually commune inwardly with Him. Beg Him to draw you nearer and nearer in likeness to Him, to lift up your soul into His Light. Have no other thought for as long as you can sustain it. Focus your attention so deliberately, so entreatingly, that He cannot resist the urgency of your call. Show Him your tears and your bare heart. He will caress you with His tender touch.

Concentrate on the thought that this very body in which you sit is the Light-body of God. It is only a quivering mass of Energy after all, vibrating at frequencies which give the appearance of form. What is this Energy? It is that one Light. He alone fills all this universe. Know that you are nothing else but That. What else, indeed, could you be? There is but one Reality! So be filled with Divine Joy; never cease your prayer that you may live and act as His instrument on earth. Prayer is the tender thread by which you retain contact with that highest Self; it is nothing else but a concentrated focus of Consciousness upon Itself. As much as you are able, keep that contact alive by calling inwardly His Name during the course of your active life. This will keep awake your awareness of His eternal presence.

And, of course, when you are able to cease your involvement in worldly affairs, then leave everything else aside, and be free to give your whole mind to Him. Keep as your special time for communing freely with your Self at least a half-hour to an hour in the morning; and at night also, break away from your recreation, and sit in your special and private place, so you can return to the peace and silence of your Self; or, at least, so you can examine how you have behaved during that day and resolve to live in the awareness of God on the following day.

It is here, in your meditations and prayers, that you will find your rest, your invigoration, your inspiration, your solace, your strength, your greatest joy. And it will carry over into all your life and all your

relationships and all your activities in the world.   It
is not true that such a life is impracticable; it *is*
practicable.   If you tell yourself that you cannot do
it, you are lying to yourself; you are copping out.
You are giving in to the old, comfortable, habits of
indolence.   You have come to drink, but you will not
pick up the cup.   You have been given the recipe,
but you refuse to bake the cake.   It's up to you.
But do not say that the spiritual life as declared by
Vedanta is impracticable. It's not.

Reflection

There are many answers to the question, "What is
the purpose of life?"   One might say, "The purpose
of life is simply ... life"   Or another might say, "The
purpose of life is to become fully conscious."   Or
yet another might say, "There is no purpose.   It is a
tale told by an idiot, full of sound and fury, signify-
ing nothing."

But consider the viewpoint of all the great sages
and visionaries throughout time, which says, "You
are, in your innermost essence, none else but the one
Consciousness of the universe.   You have become, by
your manifestory Power, enmeshed in ignorance of
your true nature; you have become ensnared in the
web of the false ego.   And your task, your purpose
at present, is to free yourself from this mentally-
constructed prison of delusion; and regain your awareness of infinitude, of omniscience, of unshakeable
wholeness and perfection and absolute freedom."

Perhaps it is true that the purpose of life is
simply life; but you are the eternal Mind from Whom
all life originates, and your purpose is to awake to
the knowledge that you transcend life, just as a
thinker transcends his thought.

Life is the stage upon which you enact all the
parts in this cosmic drama.   But it is only a play.
You are the Author of the play, the actors, the
stage, and the unfolding drama as well.   It is all
your play.   And as you created it, you will also
withdraw it, just as a thought is dissolved in the
mind of the thinker.   For you are the pure Mind,
the infinite Consciousness behind the play, and upon

which all this play is projected.   You are the nectarean
Joy that is the sole source and goal and purpose of
it all.

*   *   *

BEYOND LEARNED IGNORANCE

When we learn about the truth of Unity and our identity with the One, the Absolute, so often we imagine that this understanding that we have acquired is the height and summit of attainment. But no; this understanding, this knowledge *about* Truth, is not the experience of Self-realization, but merely the setting of the foot on the path to Self-realization. If we were to say that Self-realization was simply a matter of increased understanding, it would be a gross misrepresentation of that knowledge. "Understanding" is a word which we use to denote the mind's ability to recognize the significance of a specific concept, thing, or event, and to assimilate that information into our store-house of knowledge. But the word is woefully inadequate to represent that "realization" which is neither of a concept, thing, or event, but rather of the very Source of all concepts, things, and events.

The realization of the Self is a directly perceived knowledge, more on the order of "seeing" than understanding. "Understanding" refers to indirect knowledge; "Self-realization" refers to *direct knowledge*: a distinction that is brought out in a 14th century work on Vedanta, called *Panchadashi*:

> The knowledge arising from enquiry and reflection is of two kinds, indirect and direct. Enquiry ends on the achievement of the direct knowledge of the Self. The indirect knowledge is 'Brahman is'; the direct knowledge is 'I am Brahman'. [1]

The direct knowledge dissolves the distinction between knower and known; it is an experience of absolute Unity, in which the knower is aware of everything as himself.

The consciousness by which we experience knowledge is the screen on which we project thought. Therefore, no amount of thought, of whatever quality, which is projected on that inner screen will reveal or portray the Self to you. For the Self is the screen, the very Consciousness, on which the thoughts are project-

ed.   This is why it has so often been emphasized by
the knowers of the Self that no amount of thought
can reveal Him.   He is the Thinker.   He is the Source
of that consciousness which you experience as you.
And it is in His power to reveal Himself, when He
so wishes it, and not otherwise.

Listen to what the sages of the Upanishads had
to say:

> He is known by those who know Him beyond
> thought.   ...If you think, 'I know Him well',
> you do not know the Truth.   You only perceive
> that appearance of Brahman produced by the
> inner senses.   Continue to meditate. [2]

> What cannot be thought with the mind, but
> That whereby the mind thinks: know that
> alone to be Brahman. [3] ... It is not what is
> thought what we should wish to know; we
> should know the thinker.   'He is my Self':
> this one should know.   'He is my Self': this
> one should know. [4]

The activity of the intellect, which is to say, the
reasoning faculty, must be left far behind in the
ascent to God, to the Self.   Of course, it is by the
means of this active intellect that we come to accept
the fact of Unity, the fact of a transcendent Mind
from which all minds devolve and to which they
evolve again.   But that is the extent of its function;
to gather information and reach the proper conclusion.
Once it has done so and has established the need
for the mind's devotion to its Source, for the inversion
of its gaze from outward to inward, then it has
fulfilled its function.   And then it is time for one's
practice to begin: the turning of the mind to quiet
reflection, meditation.

To many, this word, "meditation", means the
swirling around in one's mind of one or another
concept or idea, as one might swirl a sip of wine in
one's mouth to garner its taste to the full.   But
meditation proper, is not the dwelling on thoughts
and ideas, but rather the alert and expectant search
of the inner horizon for absolute clarity of vision,
much as a lover might eagerly scan the horizon for a
sign of her returning beloved.   There is no room for

reasoning here; indeed, in this state, thought, other
than a direct call to the Beloved, is a distraction,
like weeds cropping up to obscure the distant view.
It is the Infinite we wish to see; it is God's thrilling
caress we wish to feel; it is the unveiling and delimit-
ation of our consciousness that we wish to experience.

It is not reasoning or cunning that brings us to
that vision of Truth; rather, it is prayer, it is longing,
it is purity of heart, and naked humility of soul
which brings His mercy; it is a likeness of motive and
will, conforming to His, which brings the soul into
the necessary transparency for merging into the Absolute. Again, hear the words of the Upanishads:

> Not even through deep knowledge can the
> Self be reached, unless evil ways are abandoned,
> and there is rest in the senses, concentration in
> the mind, and peace in one's heart. [5]

> He is seen by a pure heart and by a mind
> whose thoughts are pure. ... Not through much
> learning is the Self reached, nor through the
> intellect and the memorizing of the sacred
> teachings. The Self is reached by those whom
> He chooses; to His chosen the Self reveals His
> glory. [6]

However, let us not imagine that the exercise of
the intellect in Self-enquiry and reflection is a dead-
end street. It is definitely not Self-realization, but it
is a path to Self-realization. "But," you may object,
"if the Self is beyond mind, thought, and speech, how
can thought, speech, or the mind enable one to reach
the Self? Is not the intellect completely useless in
acquiring Self-knowledge?"

And the answer is, "No. It is not useless." It is
in fact most useful and necessary in bringing the soul
to Self-realization. For, as the intellect focuses more
and more on the Self, it becomes refined itself.
Ultimately, the intellect *becomes* pure Consciousness,
and disappears as intellect. To comprehend this, we
may think of the analogy of a flame produced by
burning camphor. When the flame burns up the camphor, the flame is extinguished as well. The flame is
the means to dissolve the camphor, and in the process
it dissolves itself as well. Likewise, intellectual know-

ledge is used to burn up ignorance; and as it does so, it uses itself up as well, and becomes silence.   As thought becomes more and more clear and refined, it leads us, beyond thought, to the silence of pure Consciousness.   Then, only the pure stillness of absolute Consciousness remains, beyond the contraries of knowledge and ignorance.

The intellect, after all, is nothing but a contracted form of the one universal Intelligence.   Its light is but a dim reduction of the universal Light of Consciousness.   And, because it is nothing else but the one Intelligence, it is capable of expanding to its original state.   It is a little like the expansion of the aperture of a lens; when it is narrowed, only a little pinpoint of light enters it; but when it is widened, its scope is greatly expanded, and the light streams in its fullness.   Likewise, the small aperture through which we presently experience Consciousness can be expanded.

This Intelligence, this Consciousness, which we *are* is the only means we have of experiencing.   Therefore, yes, the universal Consciousness is experienced, in a sense, through the intellect.   But to say this may easily be misleading.   For, it is not the activity of the intellect which is capable of revealing the Self; but rather the intellect, itself *is* that universal Consciousness in contracted form.   And when the Self is realized, it is known as that very Intelligence by which you have always thought and wondered and known.   It is the "you" who has always been you.

The term, "learned ignorance", which I have used in the title of this talk, is the title of a book by a 15th century Cardinal of the Catholic Church, named Nicholas of Cusa, who was extremely interested in addressing this question of whether the intellect was capable of knowing God.   In Nicholas' time, the learned Doctors of the Church were much occupied with discussing theology and dialectics, with the thought that such intellectual busyness was the holiest of activities.   Nicholas wrote his book, *de docta ignorantia*, "On Learned Ignorance", to convince these learned scholars that no amount of reasoning, no amount of intellectual effort, could reveal That which was beyond the reach of words and intellect.

His theme was that all the metaphysical haranguing

and theological bickering of such learned fellows was, in fact, nothing more than ignorance, "learned ignorance"; and that the highest state to which all their learning could possibly bring them was to the knowledge that they didn't know the ultimate Truth. It was this highest state possible through learning which he termed, "learned ignorance". And, it was this state which Nicholas regarded as the starting point from which one could then truly embark on the spiritual journey to true knowledge, *direct* knowledge, of God.

Here is a passage from his book in which he explains that the reasoning of the intellect cannot reach to God:

> Reason strives for knowledge, and yet this natural striving is not adequate to the knowledge of the essence of God, but only to the knowledge that God ... is beyond all conception and knowledge. [7]

He goes on to say:

> The Reality, which is the Truth of all beings, is unattainable in its purity [through learning]; all philosophers have sought it, and none has found it, as it is; and the more profoundly learned in this ignorance [we are], the more we shall approach Truth itself. [8]

And in another book, called *de sapientia*, "On Wisdom", he describes his method of approach to Truth itself:

> Wisdom [or 'the one Intelligence'], shining in all things, invites us, with a certain foretaste of Its effects, to be borne to It with a wonderful desire. For life itself is an intelligent Spirit, having in itself a certain innate foretaste through which it searches with great desire for the very Font of its own life. Without that foretaste, it could neither seek after It nor know when it had acquired It. It is due to this that it is moved toward It as its proper life. Every spirit finds it sweet to ascend continually to the very Principle of life, even though this appears inaccessible. For a persistent and continued ascent to (the Principle and Source of) life is the

constituent element of increased happiness.[9]

... This Wisdom [or supreme Intelligence] is
not to be found in the art of oratory, or in
great books, but in a withdrawal from these
sensible things and in a turning to the most
simple and infinite reality.   You will learn how
to receive it into a temple purged from all
vice, and by fervent love to cling to it until
you may taste it and see how sweet That is
which is all sweetness.   Once this has been
tasted, all things which you now consider as
important will appear as vile, and you will be
so humbled that no arrogance or other vice will
remain in you.   Once having tasted this Wisdom,
you will inseparably adhere to it with chaste
and pure heart.   You will choose rather to
forsake this world and all else that is not of
this Wisdom, and, living with unspeakable happiness, you will die.   After death you will rest
eternally in that fond embrace which the eternally blessed wisdom of God Himself vouchsafed to
grant both to you and to me. [10]

In closing, let me say that learning and the knowledge reflected in the intellect are wonderful indeed.
Let us not disparage learning or intelligent discussion.
It is the clarification of ideas through reasoning
which is the means by which the mind assimilates
knowledge to itself, and centers in on the Truth.
However, the greatest wisdom, such as that acquired
by Socrates, is the acquisition of the knowledge that
one doesn't know, and cannot by any intellectual
means know, the ultimate Reality.   The innate desire
to know It can only be fulfilled and satisfied by direct
revelation, and not by any amount of study or thought.
It is at this stage of wisdom, as Nicholas of Cusa
insists, that we are ready and able to embark on our
sadhana, our search for God.   This wisdom leads us
beyond thought, beyond reasoning, to a simplicity
attainable only by the wise fools of this world.   It is
the simple, child-like, humility before our Lord and
Father, by which we purify our hearts for the reception
of His mercy and grace.   In that grace we shall find
the knowledge and freedom and perfect happiness

which we seek.

Let us then give up this discussion, these wordy ideas, and turn to the simple regard of God, who is ever-present to us within.

Reflection

There is a Knowledge beyond knowledge, won only by the brave, who soar on wings of love, beyond the knowing mind. The penetrating laser-light of intellect is able to comprehend the spoken truth -- but it cannot know the source of its own light. It can form myriads of concepts about the knower, but it cannot turn its light on itself and thereby know the knower.

To know that knowing Self, we must set out blindly, without words, without images; even that shining intellect which is our pride and joy must be left behind. With no borrowed or reflected light, with no idea-projecting faculty to cast images on the cave-wall of the conscious mind, we must enter naked, empty-handed, and alone into that dark light.

Without intellect, without a preconceived identity or even existence; unknowing, unseeing, guided only by a faith in Truth and the longing of a pure heart, we may enter into the silence of that all-knowing Light. There, no questions rise to separate the knower from the known. There, the Knower is alone -- with a Knowledge beyond knowledge, won only by the brave, who soar on wings of love, beyond the knowing mind.

*   *   *

HOW TO MEDITATE ON THE SELF

First, we must ask ourselves what is this Self on which we are going to meditate? The answer to this question which we find in the Upanishads is, "The Self is the Witness of the mind. ... It is not the thought, but the Thinker one must know. It is not what is seen that should be known, but it is the Seer which must be known." This, of course, is why the Self is so hard to get a handle on; we are used to tackling the task of "knowing" by focusing on the object to be known, but, in this case, it is the knowing Subject which we are attempting to know. It is the Ground, the very Consciousness which is the background of knowing, the Screen, as it were, on which the thought-images appear.

To make matters even more difficult, this Self has no qualities, no characteristics whatsoever by which one can describe It. It is as empty and as character-less as the vastness of the sky. It is the Source of everything that exists, but It is, Itself, nothing -- void. It is called by the Vedantists: "Sat-Chit-Ananda". It does not exist; It *is* Existence (*Sat*). It is pure Consciousness (*Chit*), unstained, unwavering, eternal. It is perfect, unchallenged, Freedom, since It alone is; and for that reason It is Bliss (*Ananda*). We, who are manifestations of that Satchidananda, are not different from It. Our body, our physical existence, is That; we can experience our oneness with the universal Energy. We can know It as Consciousness -- the very consciousness which is our self-awareness, the silent Witness of all our various states of mind. When we come to realize that we are That, that we are none other than the one, undivided, Reality, then we experience the infinite, carefree, Freedom that is devoid of any obstacle, or any 'other'. Then we experience the Bliss.

Another way of understanding the Self is by examining the physical, the mental, and the spiritual aspects of our own reality. We possess a body, we experience a mind, and we are spirit -- i.e., the Self. And we identify sometimes with one aspect of our being, and at other times with another aspect of our being.

This is clearly illustrated in a story which appears in the famous Indian epic, called the *Ramayana*. In it, a character, Rama, who represents the eternal Self, has a monkey-servant, named Hanuman, who represents the mind or intellect. At one point, Rama asks Hanuman, "How do you regard me?" And Hanuman replies, "When I regard myself as the body, I'm your servant; when I regard myself as a soul, I'm a part of you; but when I regard myself as the universeal Self, then I am one with you."

Now, a great truth is pointed out in this saying of Hanuman's: namely that our relationship to God, and our spiritual practice as well, is entirely dependent upon how we regard ourselves, upon what we believe ourselves to be. Because there are these different ways of thinking of oneself, there are also differences in the way one might approach God, the eternal Self. Notice that, in the first two ways in which Hanuman identifies himself, there is a separation between the subject and the object of reverence. Whether identifying himself with the body or the soul, Hanuman regards himself as having a separate identity from Rama: in the one case, he relates to Rama as a servant, and in the second, he relates to Rama as a part to a whole. But in the third case, there is no separation, no relationship; Hanuman sees himself as not different from Rama.

And so, as we have seen, there are these three different attitudes regarding not only God, but one's own identity as well. Basically, however, there are only the two different approaches to God: (1) as an individualized identity separate from the supreme Identity, or God; and (2) as pure Consciousness, identical with God, the supreme Self. Let's look more closely at these two approaches, or methods, for they are found to be the methods adhered to in every single religious tradition: some adhering to the one, some adhering to the other, accounting for the apparent incompatibility of the various religious traditions.

The subtle world of the soul, and the gross world of physical phenomena, are both emanations, or projections, of the one Self. The forms of the physical world, of course, are continually changing; each lasts

but for a short time, and the physical Energy of
which they are constituted continues, in its kaleido-
scopic way, to take on ever-new forms.   On the
subtle level of phenomena, souls take form, and live
for a relatively longer time than physical bodies; and
therefore, each soul, in its lifetime, requires a number
of bodies through which to manifest.

The relationship of the soul to God is as the
relationship of a thought to the mind from which it
sprang, or as the relationship of a wave to the ocean
from which it rises.   The wave wishes to be dissolved
back into the oneness of the Ocean; the thought
wishes to be dissolved back into the one mind; the
ray wishes to be reabsorbed back into the pure source
of all light.   These are some of the metaphors used
to describe the relationship of the soul to God.   And
in each of these cases, there is a distinction between
the part and the whole.   The ray experiences its
separateness from the Sun; the thought feels isolated
from the mind; the wave wonders, 'Where is my
father, the ocean?'   None of these is really separate
from its source, of course; but the sense of separation is there.   Each *feels* separate and apart from its
originating principle, and will not be satisfied until it
becomes fully aware of its oneness with its source.

We, as souls, are in the same fix.   We are not
truly separate from our Self; but, so long as we are
not aware of our infinite and eternal Identity, we
suffer, and go on seeking ways to become aware of
our Source, our real Self.   Until we do, we cannot
feel complete and fulfilled.   Even though, ultimately,
this separation of the soul from its source is purely
imaginary, still, it is real so long as we suffer the
pains and anxieties accompanying this imaginary
plight.

So, what to do?   The soul turns all its attention
to the Self.   It loves the Self as a child loves its
father or mother.   It longs for the embrace of the
Self as a lover longs for her beloved.   It offers all
its thoughts and actions in the service of the Self,
as a devoted servant offers himself to his master.
What are some of the ways a soul endeavors to close
the gap between itself and its God?   It sets aside
times to think lovingly on the Self.   To wash away

all other distracting thoughts, it continually sings in
its heart its mantra: the name of the beloved Self.
It sings songs of love, it prays, it meditates, it lan-
guishes, it agonizes, it becomes pathetic.   At last,
all the clouds of ego, or error, are dispersed, and
the bright light of the Sun shines through; the Self
reveals Itself resplendently in the consciousness-sky
of the soul; and the soul cries out: "O my God!   I
am you and you are me!   All along, there has only
been this one Mind, playing the game of 'I' and
'Thou'."   The ray realizes it is only sunlight, and
has never been apart from its true self, the Sun; the
thought-image realizes it is nothing but mind, and
has never been separate from mind; the wave realizes
it is only ocean, and has never been separate from
the ocean.

   That is the way of the soul, the way of *bhakti*,
or "devotion".   It is also called the way of duality,
because, in this path, there are two: the soul and
the Self -- until, of course, the soul realizes its
oneness with the Self, and knows that there has
always been only one.

   There is another pathway, however: that way
mentioned by Hanuman when he said, "When I identify
with you, then you and I are one."   This is the way
of non-duality, or unity.   It is also referred to as
the path of *jnan*, or "knowledge".   This path takes
as its starting-point the knowledge that the soul is
none other than the Self, that nothing else exists but
that One, and the meditation on the Self is therefore
devoid of any relationship such as exists on the path
of *bhakti*, or devotion.   There is no babbling of the
soul crying out, "O Lord, O Lord!   Pity me, Thy
poorest and most worthless servant!"   No, not at all.
Non-dual meditation is the absolutely silent awareness
by the Self of Itself.

   But how, you may wonder, is it possible to experience the Self by the Self?   What is one to do with
the exuberantly effusive mind?   Does one continually
repeat in one's mind, "I am the Self!   I am the
Self!"?   No.   The method of mantra repetition is
helpful, and even necessary, in the early stages of
devotional practice; but, in the path of non-dual
meditation, it is not helpful.   Certainly, repetition of

a mantra is the way to occupy the mind and force it to pay attention to one single thought to the exclusion of all else, but non-dual meditation is intended to go beyond the process of thought.

The Self is pure Consciousness, absolute Awareness; does it make sense then for one who wishes to experience this awareness to give it a name and call out to it?   This is like painting the word, "wall" on a wall in order to reveal the wall; or like using black paint to color a house white.   The active thought-producing mind is exactly that which stands in the way of your awareness of the Self.   To use it to produce even more thought-forms is not the way to become aware of the Self.   It is like flashing more and more words on a screen instructing you to look only at the screen, and thereby so completely obscuring the screen with words that the screen cannot be seen at all.

How, then, does one meditate in the non-dual path, the path of *jnan*?   In this path, the awareness is not focused on some 'other', such as God, or some Divine form or mental image, but rather on one's own being.   It is an inturning of the awareness, so that it is not asking, "Where are you, O Lord?", but "Who am I?"

If we turn our attention for just a moment to the question, "Who am I?", the mind becomes absolutely still, does it not?   When we enquire within in this way, Consciousness immediately sits up and takes notice of itself.   Thoughts are nowhere to be seen. That is the state of a mind in meditation on its Self. The Shaivite scripture, *Vijnana Bhairava* says, "Meditation is not concentrating on a form.   True meditation consists of uninterrupted awareness, without any image or support."

Here is an exercise for meditation: Watch for the emergence from within yourself of mental images or thoughts.   Do not attempt to wage war with your mind, but rather take the Self's rightful place above the mind.   God's place is above nature; likewise, that pure Self has its place above the chatter of the mind.   You'll discover that, so long as you maintain conscious attention in this way to whatever might turn up, nothing at all turns up.   This is because once you've made this separation between you, the Witness, and the active mind, the mind is deprived of the fuel of consciousness and ceases of its own accord. Like a fire without fuel, the fire of thought goes out when your attention is on the witnessing Self. Hold it there. Don't give in to fueling the wandering mind. You'll find this a difficult task, like walking a tightrope; one which requires some effort. But we cannot reach that state of "uninterrupted awareness" without the effort of concentration, without intense aspiration.

Aspiration, whether it is the longing for God, or for the realization of the Self, lifts the consciousness above the ego-involved mind. Just as, on a mountain-top, the air becomes thinner and purer, so, as the mind focuses its intent upward toward the supreme Consciousness, it transcends the hill-country of deliberate thought, and enters the high atmosphere of pure Spirit, where reigns the silence of the clear blue sky of sweetness, peace, and light.

There, no world, no thoughts, exist; from the top of the mountain, the gaze is fixed upward, into the silver, silent sky of God, or the Self. That is meditation. And if, from there, we are drawn inside His mystery, above that sky, to know His perfect identity in ourself, then that is His most wonderful Grace. If not, we nonetheless absorb from that sky some of the radiance of His Light, some of the nectar of Self-awareness, to keep in our minds and hearts; and we offer thanks to Him, and pray for His continued presence in our conscious life.

By repeated practice, we learn to identify more and more with the witnessing Self, and less and less with the thought-activity of the mind; and the various habitual traits of the mind have less and less power to uproot us from our natural peace. Meditation is not meant only for those times when one is formally "sitting"; meditation is really a state of awareness that can be stretched to include all of one's time, during all of one's activities.

During the time of sitting, the mind is filled with the blissful awareness of the Self; this is the practice of Truth. As that practice permeates our awareness more and more, it will be carried into more and

more of our active life as well. Listen to what the
great 13th century mystic, Jnaneshvar, who had wholly
incorporated Self-awareness into his life, had to say
about this:

> One who has drunk of the nectar of Self-
> awareness may say whatever he likes; his
> silent contemplation remains undisturbed.   His
> state of actionlessness remains unaffected --
> even though he performs countless actions.[1]
> Whether he walks in the crowded streets or
> remains sitting in his room, he is always at
> home. His 'rule of conduct' is his own sweet
> will. His meditation is whatever he happens
> to be doing. [2]

Now, there are times when, as a soul, you will
feel the desire for God, as a lover for her beloved.
The love in your heart will bubble up to express itself
as devotion to the Lord of the universe. This is the
noblest and best path for the soul, to focus on God
within itself with true humility and love, in simple
prayer and worship. Even after the supreme realization that your true Self is the universal Self, still
you will joy in the singing of His name, and in serving
Him in all His creatures and in remembering His
presence at every moment in every place.

And there will also be times when you will become
intensely focused and quiet, and your breathing will
become shallow and soft, and you will taste something
of the certainty of your eternal and limitless Selfhood.
And you will rest in that quietude, that solitary
joyfulness -- without thought, without movement,
aware only of your own infinite presence.

Because the one Reality is both subject and object,
both the personal and the Impersonal, both the manifest
and the Unmanifest, and because both of these aspects
are contained within man, both of these paths, or
methods, of Self-awareness are perfectly valid and
equally true. Just as a ray of sunlight is both distinguishable from and also identical with the Sun; as a
thought-image is both distinguishable from and yet
identical with the mind; as a wave is at once distinguishable from and identical with the ocean; we too
are both distinguishable from and identical to that

one Self.   Whether we turn to It as particularized
souls, or as Consciousness to Itself, we are looking
toward the one Light.

We should come to understand ourselves so well
that we can worship God with heartfelt love at one
moment, and know Him as non-different from our
Self at another moment, and not feel the slightest
contradiction in so doing. This whole world of creation
is God's, and it is also Himself. If God in the form
of His creature lovingly worships God, the Creator,
the inner Controller, the Self -- who is going to
object? Once again, listen to Jnaneshvar:

> Everything is contained in the being of God.
> If a desire for the Master-servant relationship
> arises, it is God alone who must supply both
> out of Himself. Even the devotional practices,
> such as repetition of God's name, faith and
> meditation, are not different from God. There-
> fore, God must worship God with God, in one
> way or another. [3]
>
> ... God Himself is the devotee; the Goal has
> become the path [in order to enjoy the journey].
> the whole universe is one solitary Being. It is
> He who becomes a God, and He who becomes a
> devotee. Yet, in Himself, He enjoys the kingdom
> of utter Stillness. [4]

I'd like to say a few words about the benefits of
meditation: Everyone knows that it is through meditation that we are able to know the Self; but there are
also many side benefits. Peace of mind lends itself
very beneficially to health of body. When the mind
becomes focused on God, and all your energies are
focused upward, the brain becomes infused with energy
and the light of Consciousness. Whatever you focus
on in your daily endeavors will be illumined by the
much increased clarity and intensity of your intellect,
and you will easily find solutions to all your problems.

You won't need to jog ten miles to feel healthy.
Just by raising that conscious Light within your body,
you will feel like a god. And you will radiate that
light of health to all around you. According to the
Svetasvatara Upanishad, the first fruits of meditation
are: "health, little waste matter, and a clear complex-

ion; lightness of body, a pleasant scent, and a sweet voice; also an absence of greedy desires." [5]   But, above all, of course, meditation enables one to become centered in the eternal Self; to rise above all the vicissitudes of life, and to remain established in peace and goodwill, attuned to the inner joy of the Eternal, while seeing the one God in all creation.

Here are a few suggestions to those who may be new to meditation: First, find a convenient time for your regular practice.   In the Vedantic tradition, the times for meditation are spoken of as the *brahmamuhurta*, the times just after the Sun goes down and just before the Sun comes up.   Most people find it difficult to meditate during the brightest of the daylight hours, as at those times the mind and body are most inclined to activity.

Second, have a regular place in which to meditate where it's quiet and you will be undisturbed.   Sit in a comfortable position.   Yogic texts recommend various postures, but always insist on a straight spine, so that the subtle energy (*prana*) may flow freely to the head.   As you breathe, draw the prana upwards with the inbreath and downward with the outbreath.

Third, the length of time for sitting will vary with the depth of your practice.   Beginners and even long-time practitioners find it difficult to concentrate for longer than one hour.

Fourth, don't let the mind just wander; you will only get into bad habits that will be difficult to break. Use one of the two methods or paths which I talked about.   If you're able to sit peacefully, absorbed in the Self, by all means do so.   But when, because of the forces of nature, which are always in flux, your mind becomes very active or agitated, then put it to work singing God's name.   Be very strict with your mind.   Tell it, "Please sing God's name with love, O my mind!   Please chant His name with a voice that is sweet with love!"   If you try to quiet your mind by force of will, it will only become more agitated and antagonistic.   But, if you lead it gently toward God with love, it will rush to bathe in the sweetness of devotion.   It will quickly soar with emotion to the heights of Divinity, and become absorbed in God.

Fifth, whatever you do, never become disgusted

with yourself -- not even in a dream!   Always respect your Self.   Love your Self.   Contemplate your Self. Your Lord lives within you as you.   Never forget that you are the Divine Self of all, ever-free, ever-blissful, the One in all.

Reflection

O my Lord, Father of the universe!   Let me put aside all thoughts and concerns, all activities of the body or mind, and let me sit silently in Thy presence. Let my mind be stilled in adoration, and let all voices within me be stilled.   Thy language of intimacy is silence, for my soul most nearly approaches Thy state when it is silent.   O Father, conform my mind to Thy peace.   Still me in Thy calming glance. Rest me in Thy cradling wings.   Dissolve me in Thyself.

How wonderful, Lord, is Thy stillness!   In quietude, I know fulfillment.   In nothingness, I know release. How good Thou art, O God of gods, to rest me in Thy peace, to grant me from within this taste of Thee, of Thy bliss.   What a great wonder it is that I can find Thee and touch Thee and enjoy Thee when I am empty and still!   How happy this, Thy silent, laughing Self!

*   *   *

THE MEETING OF HEART AND MIND

There is a saying that the man of devotion (the *bhakta*) and the man of knowledge (the *jnani*) are like a blind man and a lame man, respectively.   Neither can get about on his own; the *bhakta* without discrim- ination isn't able to   see where he's going, and the *jnani* without heart is lame and unable to go forward. A happy solution is found to both their problems, however, the the lame *jnani* is hoisted upon the should- ers of the blind *bhakta*.   For then, the *jnani* provides the *bhakta* with vision, and the *bhakta* provides the *jnani* with the means of forward motion.   The point of this saying, of course, is that this is what we must do with the two sides of our own nature: we must unite the two, so we have the benefit of both knowledge and devotion.

In the spiritual life, the intellect and the heart play equally important parts.   Like the blind man and the lame man, each is helpless without the other. Just think: how many times do we meet up with a simple, good-hearted person, full of sincere love for God, and yet who, because of a lack of discrimination, becomes lost on a path which leads only to a gushy sentimentality and misplaced affections.   And how often also do we see the overly intellectual, the stiff, proud person unwilling to let go of concepts long enough to feel the joy of love, or to simply pray with a humble, contrite, and loving heart.

Clearly, both are equally handicapped.   The heart without discrimination leads one only into darkness and confusion.   And the intellect without the sweetness of the heart makes of life a dry and trackless desert, without any flavor or joy.   It is my considered opinion that if a person is to reach the highest perfection possible to man, there must be a balance of heart and mind.   There must be both the knowledge of the Self, and at the same time, the love of God.

One of the great devotional works of the Vedantic tradition, the *Srimad Bhagavatam*, states: "The   essence of all yoga consists in withdrawing the mind from the objects of sense, and fixing it on God alone."   Contin- uing, it says, "The mind must be engaged in one thing or another: if it meditates on sense-objects, it becomes worldly; if it meditates on God, it becomes Divine." All the great scriptures of Vedanta similarly extol in one way or another the focusing of the mind on God. Some call it "devotion"; some call it "awareness of the Self". Narada, who was the epitome of the *bhakta*, states in his *Bhakti Sutras*, "The constant flow of love towards the Lord, without any selfish desire, is devotion." And Shankaracharya, who was the *jnani* of *jnanis*, says in his *Viveka-chudamani*, "Devotion is continuous meditation on one's true Self." Now, if we examine the matter closely, we can see that devotion to God is not in any way different from meditation on the Self; and that the experience of Divine Love is not different from the experience of the Bliss of the Self.

The mind experiences Unity as Consciousness and Bliss. The heart experiences God as the fullness of Love and Joy. Are these two different in any way? If the heart sings of God, does that take anything away from His Unity? If the mind speaks of Unity, does that add anything to His merciful goodness? The Truth remains, whether we make a noise or keep silent; whether we give Him this name or that, He remains the same. Whether we regard ourselves as the worshipper or the worshipped, there is nothing here but the One. Whether we call our intrinsic happiness by the name of Bliss or Love, its taste remains the same. We may call Him whatever name we like; we may sing it out to our heart's content. Whether we are gamboling in the streets or sitting quietly at home, we are always God playing within God. To remember Him is our only happiness; to forget Him our only sorrow.

When we speak of Self-knowledge, we must differentiate between such Knowledge as is identical with the Bliss of the Self and that knowledge which is simply the knowledge of such Knowledge. Intellectual knowledge of Vedanta is a wonderful thing, but it is only preparatory to true Knowledge, that Knowledge which is synonymous with Enlightenment. Conceptual knowledge we must certainly go beyond. To do so, it is necessary to utilize the heart. Devotion leads the mind beyond mere intellectual knowledge to the experience of the Blissful Self -- which is true Knowledge.

The 19th century saint, Sri Ramakrishna, was fond of bringing out this truth in his conversations and his songs. Here is one such song:

How are you trying, O my mind, to know the nature of God?
You are groping like a madman locked in a dark room.
He is grasped through ecstatic love; how can you fathom Him without it?
And, for that love, the mighty yogis practice yoga from age to age.
Then, when love awakes, the Lord, like a magnet, draws to Him the soul.
It is in love's elixir only that He delights, O mind!
He dwells in the body's inmost depths, in everlasting Joy.

Sri Ramakrishna himself became so full of desire for God, whom he regarded as his "Mother", that people began to fear for his sanity when they would see him rubbing his face on the ground and weeping for his 'Mother' to come. At times, he would sing this song:

O Mother, make me mad with Thy love!
What need have I of knowledge or reason?
Make me drunk with Thy love's wine!
O Thou, who stealest Thy bhakta's hearts,
Drown me deep in the sea of Thy love!
Here in this world, this madhouse of Thine,
Some laugh, some weep, some dance for joy:
Jesus, Buddha, Moses, Gauranga --
All are drunk with the wine of Thy love.
O Mother, when shall I be blessed
By joining their blissful company?

Such total abandon, such complete disregard for one's own reputation, status, future welfare, is typical of those who, in the end, attain to God. The great poet-saint, Kabir, spoke often of the need to renounce all other desires in order to attain God. "Love based on desire for gain," he said, "is valueless!

God is desireless. How then, could one with desire attain the Desireless?" Kabir then went on to say, "When I was conscious of individual existence, the love of God was absent in me. When the love of God filled by heart, my lesser self was displaced. O Kabir, this path is too narrow for two to travel."

You see, there's no room for two; one of the two must go. Whether your focus is on God or on the Self, you must transcend the individual self, or ego. The path of love, says Kabir, is too narrow for two to travel; the ego must get out of the way. "Very subtle," he says, "is the path of love! There, one loses one's self at His feet. There, one is immersed in the joy of the seeking, plunged in the depths of love as the fish in the depths of the water. The lover is never slow in offering his head for his Lord's service. This, Kabir is declaring, is the secret of love."

'How odd!' you may think; 'Must I really offer my life, be willing to give up my head in order to attain God?' Let me tell you a story: it is a story from the *Masnavi*, the Persian masterpiece of the great Sufi poet, Jalaluddin Rumi. In it, he tells the story of the Vakil of Bukhara. The Vakil is the prince; he represents the Lord, the ruler of all. One of the subjects of this prince is told that the Vakil is seeking him for the purpose of chopping off his head. The poor man, hearing this, flees the city into the desert, and wanders from small village to village, in his attempt to stay out of the hands of the Vakil.

For ten years the man runs and runs. Then, finally exhausted and humiliated, he returns in surrender to Bukhara. The people there who knew him previously shout to him from their homes to escape while he still can: "Run! Run for your life!" they cry; "The Vakil is searching everywhere for you; he has vowed to cut off your head with his own sword!" And, while everyone was shouting their warnings to this man, he just kept walking toward the palace of the Vakil, the prince. The people were calling to him from right and left; "Are you mad?" they shouted; "You are walking into certain death! Run! Run, while you have the chance!" But the man kept on walking, right into the palace of the Vakil.

When he reached the Vakil's antechamber, he entered it and walked right up to the throne, then he threw himself on the floor at the prince's feet. "I tried to escape you," the man said, "but it is useless. My heart knows that my greatest destiny is to be slain by you. Therefore, here I am; do with me what you will." But, of course, the prince had no desire to slay the man; he was very pleased, though, to see that the man had surrendered to him even when he thought he would lose his head. And so he raised the man up and made him his representative throughout the realm. And Rumi, the author of this story, says at the end, "O lover, cold-hearted and unfaithful, who out of fear for your life shun the Beloved! O base one, behold a hundred thousand souls dancing toward the deadly sword of his love!"

This is a recurrent theme among the devotional poets of the Sufi tradition. Kabir, whom I quoted a moment ago, asks of the devotee: "Are you ready to cut off your head and place your foot on it? If so, come; love awaits you! Love is not grown in a garden, nor sold in the marketplace. Whether you are a king or a servant, the price is your head and nothing else. The payment for the cup of love is your head! O miser, do you flinch? It is *cheap* at that price! Give up all expectation of gain. Be like one who has died, alive only to the service of God. Then God will run after you, crying, 'Wait, wait! I'm coming.'"

It is clear, of course, that what is necessary is not one's physical death, but the death of the ego-self. The little identity of 'me' and 'mine' is to be sublimated into the greater Identity of the one all-pervading Self through a continuous offering of the separative will into the universal will, an offering of the separative mind into the universal Mind, and the offering of the individual self in service of the universal Self.

Sri Ramakrishna knew very well how persistent is this false sense of ego, of selfhood. For this reason, he taught, not the suppression of this ego, such as the *jnani* practices, but rather the utilization of the ego in devotion and service to God. "The devotee", says Sri Ramakrishna, "feels, 'O God, Thou art the Lord and I am Thy servant.' This is the 'ego of devotion'. Why does such a lover of God retain the 'ego of devotion'? There is a reason. The ego cannot be gotten rid of; so let the rascal remain as the servant of God, the devotee of God."

You see, Sri Ramakrishna understood that, so long as this universe exists, the apparent duality of soul and God exists. Until such time as God merges the soul into Himself, both of these exist. We are the absolute Consciousness, to be sure; but we are also His manifested images. We are Brahman, but we are also Maya; we are Shiva, but we are also Shakti; we are the universal Self, but we are also the individualized self. It is foolish not to acknowledge both sides of our nature. Failing to do so only leads us into great conflicts and difficulties. If we deny and neglect the existence of the soul, asserting only, 'I am the one pure Consciousness', the active soul will rise up and make us acknowledge its presence. The only way to lead the soul to the experience of its all-pervasiveness is to teach it love, to transform it into Divine Love. The soul that goes on expanding its power to love eventually merges into absolute Love, and awakes to the truth that it *is* Love.

Remember, whatever you continually think of for a long time, that you become. So, if the mind continually thinks of God, it will attain the state of Love. No amount of knowledge will awaken the mind to love. Nor will the mind become quietened by force or the power of will. It will only become more frustrated, agitated and antagonistic. Instead of trying to do violence to the mind, lead it into meditation by the path of love. Soak it in the vat of love, and dye it in the crimson color of love; then it will merge into the sweetness of God.

I'd like to share with you a few words of inspiration from a modern saint who extolled this very truth of devotion to God for many years. In my search for someone who best represented the synthesis of the heart and mind, I considered many different saints, both ancient and modern. But, it seemed to me that one of the very best examples that could possibly be held up is that of a woman who was called "the Bliss-permeated Mother", Anandamayee Ma. Anandamayee Ma is mentioned in Yogananda's

Autobiography Of A Yogi, as a saint whom he met in 1935. Even then, she was a remarkable woman, inspiring everyone with whom she came in contact by her simple purity, and the depth of her God-realization.

She was born in 1896 in what is now Bangladesh. Since the mid-1920's she has been one of the most revered saints in all of India. She stayed in one place for only brief periods, preferring to travel about India, visiting her many devotees here and there, for the past sixty years. She recently passed from life, leaving this world a poorer place. For she was the epitome of a *jnani*, with the heart of a *bhakta*. Her exposition of the Self, from the standpoint of Non-Dualistic Vedanta, was flawless. She possessed the shining intellect of a god. She was always poised in the highest state. And yet, she was also a humble servant of God, exhorting others to give all their devotion to God alone. Listen to what she had to say:

Anandamayee Ma

It is by crying and pining for Him that the One is found. In times of adversity and distress as well as in times of well-being and good fortune, try to seek refuge in the One alone. Keep in mind that whatever He, the All-Benefic-ent, the Fountain of Goodness, does, is wholly for the best.

He alone knows to whom He will reveal Himself and under which form. By what path and in what manner He atracts any particular person to Himself is incomprehensible to the human intelligence. The path differs for different pilgrims.

The love of God is the only thing desirable for a human being. He who has brought you forth, He who is your father, mother, friend, beloved and Lord, who has given you everything, has nourished you with the ambrosia streaming from His own being -- by whatever name you invoke Him, that name you should bear in mind at all times.

Apart from seeking refuge in the contemplation of God, there is no way of becoming liberated from worldly anxiety and annoyance. Engage in whatever practice that helps to keep the mind centered in Him.   To regret one's bad luck only troubles the mind and ruins the body; it has no other effect -- keep this in mind!   He by whose law everything has been wrought, He alone should be remembered.

Live for the revelation of the Self hidden within you.   He who does not live thus is committing suicide.   Try to remove the veil of ignorance by the contemplation of God.   Endeavor to tread the path of immortality; become a follower of the Immortal.   ... Meditate on Him alone, on the Fountain of Goodness.   Pray to Him; depend on Him.   Try to give more time to *japa* (repeating His name) and meditation.   Surrender your mind at His feet.   Endeavor to sustain your *japa* and meditation without a break.

It is necessary to dedicate to the Supreme every single action of one's daily life.   From the moment one awakes in the morning until one falls asleep at night, one should endeavor to sustain this attitude of mind.   ... Then, when one has sacrificed at His feet whatever small power one possesses, so that there is nothing left that one may call one's own, do you know what He does at that fortunate moment?   Out of your littleness He makes you perfect, whole, and then nothing remains to be desired or achieved.   The moment your self-dedication becomes complete, at that very instant occurs the revelation of the indivisible, unbroken Perfection which is ever revealed as the Self.

These words of Anandamayee Ma constitute the ancient, yet ever-new, message of all the saints. Knowledge is essential to clear away our doubts, to understand where our greatest good lies.   But it is devotion that takes us to our Destination.   The determined dedication of the heart, mind, and will to God is the means to fulfillment, and the means to the perfect Knowledge which is the Self.

Reflection

What does it mean to remember God?   It means to awaken in yourself the awareness of His presence within you and all around you.   It is to transform the sense of selfhood into the sense of Spirit, and to transform the vision of 'others' into the vision of God's multiformed beauty.

He is the Source of all that exists, and He is our inner Guide and Teacher.   He is the majesty and greatness of our own soul.   Remember Him with every breath, and thus keep alive the flame of His unconditional Love in your heart.

Say to Him: "Father, do Thou guide my life and my every thought, for I have no other joy but Thee. Thou art the strength of my soul; my only confidant and source of guidance.   When I have forgotten Thee, I have fogotten my very heart's blood, and I have left aside the very fibre and backbone of my life.

"What I live for, Thou art.   My only desire, Thou art.   The sole fulfillment of all my dreams, the treasure for which my soul yearns, Thou art.   O God of my soul, blood of my heart, let me not forget Thee for a single moment!   O God of gods, grant me this boon that I may ever remember Thee who art my soul's support and strength, and let me love Thee and praise Thee ever in my heart."

*   *   *

THE WISDOM OF THE KATHA UPANISHAD

Today, I'd like to take up the *Katha Upanishad* for study. As you know, the Upanishads are independently written treatises or parables which were penned by various unnamed sages, widely scattered in time. The *Katha Upanishad*, like all the others, is undated; however, scholars guess its date of origin to be somewhere around the first few centuries before the Christian era, though we don't have any idea who might have written it. Nonetheless, it has stood the test of time due to the fact that its author was clearly a knower of the Self, a seer of extraordinary depth and clarity.

The Upanishad begins as a tale about a young boy named Nachiketas. It seems that Nachiketas' father, in his desire to atain heaven, performed a large-scale ritual sacrifice (*yajna*) in which he ostensibly offered the most highly-valued of his possessions, including a few head of cattle. Nachiketas, observing that the cattle offered were actually quite old and thin, wondered if his father might attain to a nether world of sorrow, rather than heaven, with such a poor sacrifice; and so he said to his father, "Why don't you offer me as well!" His father ignored this suggestion, and so Nachiketas repeated it three times during the course of the ritual offering. His father, finally angered by what he took to be his son's sarcasm, retorted, "Alright, I'll offer you to Yama, the king of death!"

And so, as the story goes, the guileless Nachiketas, in obedience to his father's word, willingly descended into the realm of Yama, the god of death. However, when Nachiketas arrived, Yama was not at home, but was apparently out on some sort of errand. And so Nachiketas had to remain there, awaiting Yama's return, for three nights, without food or water. When, at last, Yama did return to receive Nachiketas, he said to the boy, apologetically, "You came as my guest, and you were given no hospitality for three nights; and so, in order to make amends, I will grant you three boons."

Nachiketas accepted this offer, and said, "O Yama,

for my first boon, let my father's anger be appeased; and may he happily welcome me back when I return to him." This, of course, was a very clever first request, as it contained within it the assurance that he would return home from this place. And when Yama granted him this boon, Nachiketas said, "For my second boon, please explain to me the meaning of the *yajna*, the ritual of offering to the flames of the sacrificial fire, by which one is said to attain heaven." And so, Yama explained to him how to prepare the fire, what mantras to recite over it, and so forth. And then he said, "Now choose your third boon."

Nachiketas said, "When a man dies, some say he continues to exist; others say he ceases to exist. Please teach me the truth of this matter." And Yama immediately protested, saying, "Even the gods of old had questions about this. Ask me for another boon." But Nachiketas stood his ground; "There is no other boon I wish but to understand this," he said. And again Yama shook his head, saying, "I'll give you sons and grandsons who shall live for a hundred years! I can give you huge expanses of land, and you may live for as long as you like! Choose whatever you wish. I'll provide you with beautiful dancing girls with musical instruments to entertain you; but please don't ask me for the secrets of death!"

But Nachiketas was persistent; "All those pleasures," he said, "will only pass away; and while they exist, they only weaken a man's character and strength. Indeed, life is a very fleeting thing! Keep your horses and dancing girls. Can a man enjoy wealth when he has you in sight? How can we enjoy life while you stand in the background, waiting for the end to come? I repeat my request for the knowledge of life and death. This is the only boon I wish of you."

So, Yama had no choice but to honor his word. He sat down with Nachiketas, and began explaining to him: "There is the path of joy, and there is the path of pleasure," he said. "Both attract the soul. One who follows the path of joy comes to good; the follower of pleasure does not reach the ultimate destination. These two paths lie before everyone. The wise choose the path of joy; the fools choose the path of pleasure.

"You, O Nachiketas," Yama continued, "have pondered on pleasures, and you have rejected them. You have not accepted that chain of possessions wherewith men bind themselves and beneath which they sink and fall. There is the path of wisdom, and the path of ignorance. They are far apart, and lead to different ends. You, O Nachiketas, are a follower of the path of wisdom; many pleasures tempt you not."

Comment: This is the truth; the great majority of humans on this planet are as yet unevolved, and still addicted to pleasures of the senses. They strive, from the time of their adolescence, to acquire material goods, and throughout their lives they give no thought to penetrating beneath the appearances to discern the reality of this life. The 'good life', they feel, has been acquired only if it is filled with wealth and power. And then they grow old, fall into senility, and die, miserable and confused.

"Abiding in the midst of ignorance," Yama continued, "and thinking themselves wise and learned, fools go aimlessly hither and thither, like the blind led by the blind. What lies beyond life shines not to those who are childish, or careless, or deluded by wealth. 'This is the only world; there is no other', they say. Thus they go from death to death."

Comment: "From death to death" is Yama's way of saying that they transmigrate as souls, taking on new bodies to enjoy the pleasures of life; then, again, they die, and continue thusly, learning slowly through experience that pleasure only alternates with pain on this wheel of birth and death. Eventually, they learn to seek, through learning and introspection, the knowledge of the eternal Self which is the salvation from birth and death.

"Not many hear of Him (who is beyond life and death); and, of those who do hear, not many reach Him. He cannot be reached by much thinking. The way to Him is through a teacher who has seen Him."

Comment: There are many teachers of 'the spiritual life'; but, unless they have, themselves, become enlightened; that is, *seen* the Truth in themselves, they are more apt to mislead their students than lead them to experience the eternal Self. Those who

teach, without having attained that 'vision' for themselves, are often preferred by superficial students;
for they are apt to reduce 'the spiritual life' to a
more accessible level, offering, not the 'vision' of
God, but merely a healthy lifestyle, and membership
in a 'spiritual community'. This is not enlightenment,
but ignorance. It is the blind led by the blind.

"This sacred knowledge," said Yama, "is not attained
by reasoning; but it can be given by a true teacher.
As your purpose is steady, you have found your teacher.
May I find another pupil like you!

"Before your eyes has been spread, Nachiketas,
the fulfillment of all desire, the dominion of the
world, the reward of all ritual, the shore where
there is no fear, the greatness of fame and boundless
lands. With strength and wisdom you have renounced
them all.

"When the wise [person] rests his mind in contemplation on our God beyond time, who invisibly dwells
in the mystery of things and in the heart of man,
then he rises above pleasures and sorrows.

"When a man has heard and has understood, and,
finding the Essence, reaches the Inmost, then he
finds joy in the Source of joy. Nachiketas, you are
a vessel open to the experience of your Self, of
God."

Then, Nachiketas questioned Yama, his teacher:
"Tell me, please, O Yama, what is seen beyond the
opposites of good and evil, action and inaction, beyond
past and future."

And Yama, instructing his new pupil, said, "The
Self is never born and never dies. Nothing existed
before Him, and He remains One forever. He was
never born; He is eternal. He is beyond all times
gone by, and all times to come; He does not die
when the body dies. If the slayer thinks that he
kills, and if the slain thinks that he dies, neither
knows the Truth. The Eternal in man cannot kill;
the Eternal in man cannot die."

Comment: The author of the *Bhagavad Gita* was
apparently an admirer of the Katha Upanishad, for
he used several of the passages from this Upanishad,
almost verbatim, to place in the mouth of Krishna,
such as this one, above. Or, it may be that the

author of this Upanishad was quoting the *Bhagavad Gita*. In either case, however, it is important to note that there is no intention of implying, as some foolish people suggest, that the taking of life is justified or condoned by these sacred passages.

Yama continues: "Concealed in the heart of all beings is the Self -- smaller than the smallest atom, greater than all the vast spaces. The man who surrenders his human will leaves sorrows behind, and beholds the glory of the Self, by the grace of God."

Comment: The Self exists everywhere: in the sub-microscopic world of the atom and beyond the far-flung galaxies. He is realized as the sole reality of one's being. When the puny individual ego is surrendered to that higher Self, it is the merciful grace of God which leads one to know the Truth.

"At peace, He moves everywhere; unseeing, He sees everything. Who else but my Self can know that God of joy and sorrow? When the wise realize the omnipresent Spirit, who rests invisible in the visible, and is permanent within the impermanent, then they go beyond sorrow."

Comment: The paradox of an unmoving God who is manifest in all that moves is one which can never really be unravelled until the Truth is revealed within. He, in His transcendence, experiences nothing of the world; yet, He is the enjoyer and experiencer of all the senses of all creatures. Only the Self can experience the Self; and when It is revealed, the illusion of an individual ego is dispelled. Then, only the One is.

"Not through much learning is the Self reached, and not through the intellect and the study of the sacred literature. It is reached by the chosen of Him -- because they choose Him. To His chosen, the Self reveals His glory."

Comment: "Many are called," said Jesus, "but few are chosen." Here again it is emphasized that no amount of learning or intellectual acumen can open to man the 'vision of God'. It is He who grants this vision. It is a paradox: God inspires the longing; God fulfills the longing; God is the giver of the vision, the receiver of the vision, and the vision as well.

"Not even through deep knowledge can the Self

be reached, unless evil ways are abandoned, and
there is rest in the senses, concentration in the
mind, and peace in one's heart."

Comment: These, while they seem to be conditions
required for the attaining of grace, are, in fact, the
results of grace. All is His doing.

"Who knows, truly, where He is? The majesty of
His power carries everyone away at the time of
death: priests and warriors, the holy and the unholy.
Death, itself, is carried away ultimately."

Comment: When, at the end of the cosmic cycle,
the manifested universe is withdrawn into the eternal
Mind of God, life -- and therefore, death -- is no
more.

Yama continues to instruct Nachiketas, saying:
"In the secret place of the heart, there are two
beings who drink the wine of life: those who know
Brahman ... call them 'light' and 'darkness'."

Comment: This is similar to the parable of the
two birds in the Mundaka and Svetasvara Upanishads,
one of whom represents the individualized soul who
eats the fruits of life, while the other, the Self,
looks on in silence, as the eternal Witness.   These
two aspects of Reality, the transcendent Mind, and
Its power of creative manifestation, are named in
nearly every mystical treatise.   They have been called
"Shiva" and "Shakti", "Brahman" and "Maya", "Theos"
and "Logos", "Purusha" and Prakrti", and so on.   In
the New Testament book of John, they are referred
to as the "Light" and the "darkness"; this is a universal appelation for these two, found in nearly every
mystical tradition.   The Light, of course, is the
eternal Godhead; the darkness is the universal appearance of phenomena, the 'world' of form, which,
through transient and changing, is so often mistakenly
thought to be permanent and reliable.

"Know the Self," says Yama, "to be the Lord of
the chariot; and the body to be the chariot itself.
Understand the faculty of reason to be the charioteer;
and the mind to be the reins.

"The horses, they say, are the senses; and the
path ahead of them contains many objects of the
senses.   When the soul identifies with the mind and
the senses, he is called, 'one who has joys and sorrows'."

Comment: The transmigrating soul identifies with the body, mind, and senses, and is thus carried away by the impulse toward enjoyment of the sense-objects. At the heart of every soul is the Self, the one eternal Existence-Consciousness-Bliss. But, through ignorance of its real nature, it races about, identifying with the active mind and senses.

"He who has no correct understanding, and whose mind is never steady, is not the ruler of his life; he is like a bad driver with wild horses. But he who has right understanding, and whose mind is ever-steady, is the ruler of his life, like a good driver with well-trained horses.

"He who has no correct understanding, who is careless and never pure, does not reach the end of the journey [of life]; but wanders on from death to death. But he who has right understanding, is careful and ever-pure, reaches the end of the journey [of life], from which he never returns.

"The man whose chariot is driven by reason, who watches and holds the reins of his mind firmly, reaches the ultimate end of the journey, the supreme and everlasting Spirit."

Reflection

What, Lord, is the most I can hope for in this life? Is it not Thee, Lord, who art my greatest hope? To find Thy love and Thy serenity within me when trouble comes to me -- is this not my greatest hope and treasure? To feel Thy presence when all others abandon me, to receive Thy consolation when nothing on earth consoles me, to breathe freely in eternal Joy when this earthly breath fails me -- is this not my greatest hope, my highest good?

To be so firmly wed to Thee that I am never without the happy thought of Thee; to be so established in awareness of Thee that I see nothing before me that is not resplendent with Thy glory; to be so surrendered to Thy Will that I do not speak or act, but rather Thou dost speak and act through me -- is this not the most I can wish for in this life, O Lord?

Bring me, Lord, to this, my desire: that I may remember Thee with my every thought, see Thee in every form, and serve Thee with every word and deed that comes from me. For Thou art my Truth, my Joy, my very Self; and I have no other goal, and no other hope, but Thee and Thee alone.

*   *   *

THE WISDOM OF THE KATHA UPANISHAD
PART II

When we left off with the *Katha Upanishad*, Yama, the god of death, was explaining to Nachiketas, his pupil, that like the master of a chariot, the Self is the Master of the body. The mind he likened to the reins, held in the hands of the intellect, who is the charioteer. The horses, which are steered by means of the reins, are the senses; and their objects are the pathway before them. As we left off, Yama was saying to Nachiketas that, "The man whose chariot is driven by reason, who watches and holds the reins of his mind firmly, reaches the ultimate end of the journey, the supreme and everlasting Spirit."

Once again, Yama attempts to explain to Nachiketas the relationship of the Self to Nature, to the soul and to the intellect and the wayward mind:

"Beyond the objects [of sense] are the senses which perceive them; and beyond the senses is the mind. Beyond the mind is the faculty of intellect, and beyond the intellect is the soul (*jiva*) of man. Beyond the soul is the manifestory power of God (Nature, or *Prakrti*); and beyond Nature is the supreme Being (*Purusha*). Nothing is beyond Purusha. He is the final end."

Comment: It may be possible to understand this better by reversing the order and seeing how each manifests from the other: The Self, or Purusha, is synonymous with Brahman, the absolute Godhead. Emanating from It, as a Thought, is the manifestory power of God. This 'power' is the creative Energy which manifests as the phenomenal universe of form -- on both the subtle and the gross levels. From God's manifestory power, souls are formed, each one being God in essence, but unaware of it, due to the veiling power inherent in manifestation, which gives to each one a unique perspective. The pure Consciousness, which is the Self, is reflected in the soul as intellect, the reasoning power, and subservient to this reasoning power is the active effusion of thought and image which is the mind. The mind, in turn, is the 'ruler', so to speak, of the senses; their input is

filtered through the mind and there analyzed.   And,
of course, the senses could not function if there
were no objects of perception in the phenomenal
world to reflect.

Yama goes on to say: "The light of the Self is
invisible, concealed in all beings.   It is seen by the
seers of the subtle, when their vision is keen and
clear."

Comment: The Self is the original Light by which
all subtle and gross forms which emanate from It are
illumined.   As the senses and their objects are subsequent to the Self, that original Light cannot be perceived by the senses.   However, when the separative
identity, the false ego, is made subservient to the
Self, the Light of Consciousness rises to the surface,
as it were, and shines through as Divine Love, or Joy.
In a moment of absolute clarity, the Self becomes
aware of Itself, and all ignorance regarding Its true
Identity is dispelled.

"Awake, arise!" says Yama; "Strive for the Highest
and be in the light!   Sages say the path is narrow
and difficult to tread; narrow as a razor's edge."

Comment: This was the admonition of Jesus also:
"Strait is the way and narrow the path that leads
unto the Light."   What both of these Self-realized
sages meant to impart with this caveat was the understanding that what was required to attain 'the Highest',
'the kingdom of God', was a single-minded dedication
to the goal, comparable to that of a tight-rope walker
whose concentration is fixed on the rope before him.
Those who follow the soft-pedaled approach of those
teachers who have never made their way to the Highest will not find such methodology to their taste;
however, those who have reached that goal are unanimous in the prescription of dilligent one-pointedness
of mind.

"The Self," says Yama, "is beyond sound and
form, beyond touch, taste, or smell.   It is eternal,
unchangeable, and without beginning or end; indeed,
It is beyond reasoning.   When consciousness of the
Self manifests within, a man becomes free from the
jaws of death."

Comment: The realization of the Self, which Yama
is teaching to Nachiketas, is the means to be free of

the power of Yama himself. Little wonder that Yama was reluctant to teach this secret to Nachiketas.

Again, Yama speaks to his charge of the difference between the outer focus of attention, which is intent on the objects of sense, and the inner focus of attention, which is intent on God within:

"The Creator made the senses outward-going; they go to the world of matter outside, not to the Spirit within. But, it happened that a sage who sought the eternal Truth looked within himself and found his own eternal Soul.

"The foolish people of the world run after outward pleasures, and fall into the snares of all-embracing death. But the wise, who seek the Eternal, do not search for It in things that pass away.

"This, by which we perceive colors and sounds, perfumes and kisses of love, by which alone we attain knowledge, by which we can be conscious of anything: this, truly, is that Self."

Comment: Yama wishes to make clear that the substratum of consciousness which is our very Self, that same consciousness by which we think and know and experience the pleasures of the senses, is the one Consciousness of the universe. There is no other. Though that consciousness is limited at present by our false identification with such modifications as the intellect, the mind, the body, etc., still, the Self is always the Self; and that is our true Identity.

"When the wise man knows that it is through the great and omnipresent Spirit in us that we are conscious, both in waking and in dreaming, then he goes beyond sorrow.

"When he knows the Self, the inner Life, who enjoys like a bee the sweetness of the flowers of the senses, the Lord of what was and of what will be, then he goes beyond fear. This, truly, is that Self."

Comment: "This" means this very self which is seated behind the eyes that are reading these words; this Self, which is the witness of the activity of the mind and the senses, is the one and only Self. It does not come and go; It is always the Self of you and of everyone.

"There is a Spirit who is awake in our sleep, and creates the wonder of dreams. He is Brahman, the

Spirit of Light, who is rightly called 'The Immortal'.
All the worlds rest on that Spirit, and beyond Him
no one can go. This, truly, is that Self.

"As fire, though one, takes new forms in all
things that burn, the Spirit, though one, takes new
forms in all things that live. He is within all and is
also outside."

Comment: If just for a moment one could become
aware, while looking at other people, that here,
before one's eyes, is the Divine Spirit, manifesting in
all these various forms -- then, in that moment,
one's view of life and the world would be changed
forever. And because, ultimately, the Divine Spirit is
one's own Self, all this world of diversity and multiplicity is nothing else but one's Self.

"As the wind, though one, takes new forms in
whatever it enters, the Spirit, though one, takes new
forms in all things that live. He is within all and is
also outside.

"As the Sun, that beholds all the world, is untouched
by earthly impurities, so the Spirit, that is in all
things, is untouched by external sufferings."

Comment: The remark that God does not suffer
seems an obvious and unnecessary statement. But it
is not obvious to everyone that their real Self never
suffers. If we can realize that there is no Self but
God, the eternal Self, then we can see also that it
is only Nature, it is only the constituted appearances
which suffer disintegration and death. The Self is
ever-free of Nature, while projecting it on Its own
screen.

"There is one Ruler, the Spirit that is in all
things, who transforms His Unity into [the appearance
of] multiplicity. Only the wise who see Him in their
souls attain the Joy eternal.

"He is the Eternal among things that pass away,
the pure Consciousness of all conscious beings, the
One who fulfills the prayers of many. Only the wise
who see Him in their souls attain the Peace eternal."

Now, Yama draws all his thoughts together and
reiterates, by way of summary, all that he had said
before, in order to inspire Nachiketas to aspire toward
the realization of the Self:

"The whole universe," says Yama, "comes from

the Lord, and His Life burns [like a conflagration of Energy] throughout the whole universe. In the power of thunder one senses His majesty; but those who have known Him have found immortality.

"If one sees Him in this life before the body passes away, one is free from bondage; but if not, one is born and dies again in new worlds and new creations.

"When the wise man knows that the senses do not belong to the Spirit, but that their waking and sleeping belongs to Nature, then he grieves no more."

Comment: In other words, it is not the Self who acts, or enjoys, or senses; but, rather, it is the manifestory power of God, or Nature, who is acting, enjoying and sensing within this phenomenal world. The Self is always detached. It is the eternal Witness, the conscious Screen upon which all is projected. And when this is realized, one knows the Self to be ever-free, ever-blissful, without grief.

"Beyond the senses is the mind and beyond the mind is the intellect; beyond the intellect is the soul of man, and beyond this is the creative Energy of the universe, the Evolver of all. Beyond even this, is the Purusha (the Self), all-pervading, beyond definitions. When a mortal knows Him, he attains liberation and reaches immortality."

Comment: This is the course of the evolution of awareness: first, we identify with the senses as children; then we discover the mind, then the intellect; and, if we study and analyze Nature, we come to realize that all forms are nothing but manifestations of the one creative Energy. We sense our oneness with this creative Energy, this one effusive Life, and we feel that we are an integral part of one vast Nature. Only the contemplative soul passes beyond even Nature and knows the eternal Mind from which that creative Energy is projected, as a vast dream-image is projected from the mind of man. This eternal Mind, the Absolute, the Godhead, is realized within the mind of man as the substratum of Consciousness that manifests as all conscious beings. It is known, not as "He", but as "I".

"His form is not in the field of vision; no one sees Him with mortal eyes. He is seen by a pure heart, and by a mind and thoughts that are pure. Those who know Him attain life immortal.

When the five senses and the mind are still, and the intellect itself rests in silence, then begins the path supreme. This calm steadiness of the senses is called 'Yoga'. Then, one should become watchful, because Yoga comes and goes.

"... When all desires that cling to the heart are surrendered, then a mortal becomes immortal, and even in this world he is one with Brahman."

Comment: Even while living in this world of manifold appearance, one who has seen the Truth of existence will be free, will know that he is the Immortal. And, even should he forget, he remains ever-free, ever one with Brahman.

"When all the ties that bind the heart are untied, then a mortal becomes immortal. This is the sacred teaching."

Comment: When all personal, separative desires are dispelled in the satisfaction of the Self, then the heart is surrendered to God's will, and that heart becomes an instrument of God's Love, of God's Joy. The separative soul no longer has any substance or reality; and only the immortal Self lives and acts on earth so long as the body lives. This is the end of Yama's sacred teachings; and with this, the *Katha Upanishad* also ends:

"Nachiketas assimilated this supreme wisdom taught by Yama, the god of the after-life, and he learned the art of inner union, or Yoga. Then he reached Brahman, the supreme Self, and became immortal and pure. And so, truly, will anyone else who knows the *Atman*, the true, supreme Self."

Reflection

What may I give Thee, O my Lord, who hast given to me so greatly of Thyself? What, indeed, do I have to give that is not already Thine? And who is this upstart "I" who speaks of serving "Thee", whom everyone knows art both the server and the served?

It is this very sense of "I", this false ego, that I offer, Father, as my gift to Thee. For there is nothing that is not Thine own: this body, mind, and

intellect, all belong to Thee and serve Thy purposes
in reflecting Thy wisdom and Thy truth.   It is only
this mistaken sense of "I", this 'me and mine', that
stands before the clarity of Thy inherent Light and
the sweetness of Thy perfect Peace.

Then let this "I" be always prostrate at Thy feet
in adoration, silenced in surrender, awed and voiceless
in anticipation of Thy touch.   And let these eyes
turn ever upward unto Thee, though blinded by Thy
brilliant Light, until, transparent as a polished pane
of glass, this soul becomes the pure conduit of Thy
Truth, Thy Will, Thy Love, who art the only "I" that
truly lives.

*   *   *

THE SPIRITUAL LIFE

All of us are interested in learning more about the "spiritual" side of ourselves; but it's important for us to ask ourselves, "Why?" Is it to obtain some visual experiences? To acquire more personal power? To become a "spiritual" person in the eyes of others? Do you secretly wish to impress others with your supernormal abilities and your knowledge of subtle and esoteric matters? All these, of course, are the wrong reasons for pursuing spiritual knowledge. But if you are truly eager for self-knowledge out of an inherent love for truth, then there is a possibility that you will gain something of value in the study of Vedanta. If your life, from the time of your child-hood, has been concerned with understanding and living the truth, then you will rejoice at hearing the teachings of those who have seen the Truth, who have known God, the ultimate Reality.

But to those who are only seeking some unique experience to call their own, or some evidence that they possess some superior power, I must say that you will find nothing in the teachings of Vedanta that will please you; you will be very disappointed. Thomas à Kempis, writing for his novices in the 15th century, said it well: "He who seeks any other thing in religion than God and the health of his soul, shall find nothing there but trouble and sorrow; and he may not stand long there in peace and quietness who does not labor to be least and subject to all." [1]

Too often, we find among so-called "spiritual" people an overwhelming interest in psychic phenomena or occult sciences. Such people take all sorts of classes to learn techniques for developing their sensi-tivity -- both sensual and psychic. They evidence an interest in ghosts, ancestors, and other manifestations from the dead. They practice various methods of exercise, diet, and therapies for the health of the body. They ardently seek extreme mental states, whether induced by suggestion or by exotic drugs; and are facinated with all kinds of assorted phenomena associated with "spiritualism".

No doubt, some of these things can be of great

interest to the mind of the neophyte, which is recently opened to new vistas for exploration. For example,
today there is a great facination with UFO's and the
possibility of alien visitors from space. But think:
even should you be wisked away on a tour of all the
stars in the galaxy, would that provide you with the
knowledge you seek for perfect peace of mind, for
the realization of the ultimate Truth? That knowledge
you must find in you!

All these phenomena which can be approached
either on the physical or on the subtle, "astral",
level, are matters which we would classify, not as
"spiritual", but as occult or psychic. "Occult" means
hidden, obscured. But that does not make something
"spiritual". The occult sciences can be extraordinar-
ily facinating and useful to the understanding of both
physical and subtle-level phenomena; but insofar as
Self-realization is concerned, they lead only to a
dead-end.

Consider the occult science of Astrology, for
example. It is a subtle science of the relationship
between the motions of the planets and one's own
destiny on earth. It is a facinating field of study,
especially to those who have a proclivity for it. It
can be of great use in the purification of the soul
to one who has a clear grasp of its principles. It
certainly should not be disparaged. But it goes only
so far as the soul -- that is to say, the subtle, or
astral, level. It can give very useful information
about the subtle forces affecting the soul at any
given moment; but such information is irrelevant to
the Self. The Self transcends the subtle body called
the "soul". It is universal, unlimited by the motions
and irregular activities of the soul. The soul is
temporary; it is a transient dream. But the Self is
eternal. It is the realization of the Self that releases
us from all our dreams; it is our universal Self that
we must come to know and to identify with if we
are to be free; for that is our true, our eternal,
Identity.

And so, if we are to know the Self and live in
complete freedom from the suffering that inevitably
accompanies delusion, such knowledge as Astrology
can provide is only a prefatory knowledge at best; in

itself, it is absolutely useless as a means toward the knowledge of the Self. This is so for all such subtle-level pursuits. Just as we must pass beyond our facination with the gross manifestations on this physical plane, so must we pass beyond our facination with the subtle manifestations, if we sincerely wish to know God.

There is also the facination with psychic phenomena to deal with. Many regard visual experiences on the subtle plane as, not only essential to the spiritual life, but as the veritable *sine qua non* of spirituality, or "mystical" experience. However, these experiences are common only to a specific type of seeker and not necessarily to all spiritual aspirants. Those visionary experiences, which many men and women have told of, such as the visualization of prophets, saviors, angels, and heavenly landscapes, or of lights of various colors, are no doubt significant experiences of the mind or psyche, but they are, by the same token, significantly less than "the vision of God" and must be categorized as psychic experiences rather than "mystical" ones.

Throughout history, those who have experienced their ultimate Identity have attempted to explain this inexplicable experience to others and, in so doing, have repeatedly cautioned against the ever-recurring belief that "the vision of God" is the perception of some image or humanized form. On this, the 13th century German mystic, Meister Eckhart, had this to say:

> If the soul sees form, whether she see the form of an angel or her own form, it is an imperfection in her. But when all forms are detached from the soul, and she sees nothing but the One alone, then the naked essence of the soul finds the naked formless essence of the Divine Unity.
>
> ... Some simple people think that they will see God as if He were standing there and they here. It is not so. God and I, we are One. The eye by which I see God is the same as the eye by which God sees me. My eye and God's eye are one and the same -- one in seeing, one in knowing, and one in

loving. [2]

Others, of differing religious traditions, have made the same point. The 9th century Chinese Buddhist mystic, I-Hsuan, for example, in his endeavor to point Truth-seekers beyond all perceivable forms, cautioned his followers to reject even the Buddha, should he appear in their meditations. "If you see the Buddha, destroy him," he said. By way of explanation, he added:

> Those who truly seek after Truth will have no use for the Buddha. ... The Buddhas of the ten cardinal directions may appear before me and I shall not feel happy for a single moment. Why? Because I know that all manifestations are devoid of Reality. They exist only due to the transformations of Energy within the One. The three worlds are but one Mind, and all manifestations are Consciousness only. They are all dreams, illusions and flowers in the air. What is the use of grasping and seizing onto them? O seekers of the Way, if you want to achieve knowledge of the Truth, don't dwell either on internal or external objects.

And yet, what amazing and captivating things are all these subtle-body experiences! How facinating they are! But they are much like dreams. They are facinating, even useful; but they are not to be pursued or clung to; for, ultimately, they are obstacles to the clear realization of the Self. It is not necessary to see lights, to hear sounds or to envision chakras; such phenomena are symptoms and sign-posts along the way, but not at all a necessary ingredient in the spiritual growth of a soul. If you are not experiencing any visions, any movements, any obvious indications of the activity of Energy within you, don't imagine that this is a sign that you are not growing spiritually.

There are many who have made Energy and the manifestations of Energy their God and turned away from the Truth which is the source of all Energy. Shiva, the Lord of all Energy, and not Shakti -- the Energy itself -- is our true aim. Shakti promises power, glamor, wealth, fame; these are its highest manifestations. And they can be had -- at the right price. But in the end Shakti is realized to be nothing but the power of illusion -- God's power of illusion. And when the bubble bursts, there is nothing at all left to which one may cling.

God may be had by refusing the illusions. It may seem boring in contrast: God offers only Love, Peace, Joy, Consciousness. 'How dull!' some may think; 'I'll take the power, the wealth, the glory', they say. And, of course, they have their reward. Manifestations of Energy without the awareness of the transcendent Self and devotion to that inner Lord will have no positive results. Therefore, practice your devotion, your meditations; keep your mind free of attachments; do not identify with your limitations; see God, identify with God, take the time to be with God and melt into His love. This is the spiritual life. All else is superfluous and non-essential. Be at peace and go on loving God in yourself and in all.

In His time, He will lift you into His embrace and make you one with Him. Until then, let us sing His name and praise Him in our hearts.

Reflection

What is a "spiritual life"? How does one live who chooses such a life? It is a life devoted to the awareness and realization of the Self. And one who undertakes to live such a life fashions his or her worldly existence in such a way as to allow the greatest opportunity for the awareness and realization of the Self.

An early rising is absolutely necessary, in order to take advantage of the stillness of the outer and inner landscape. This is the time to sit for meditation. Meditation is the life-blood of the spiritual life. But it does not end with sitting. The spiritual life requires a continual meditation throughout one's working day, remembering only God, seeing only God, serving only God.

The spiritual life does not aim at casual amusement; it is founded on the self-discipline necessary for the one-pointed focus of the mind. And the aim of that one-pointed focus is God, the Divine Self.

The mind may be easily distracted from this focus simply by the relaxation of one's purpose. But one who sincerely wishes to live the spiritual life will arrange his life with disciplined boundaries, so the mind is helped and not hindered in its endeavor.

To live so as to enable the mind to be pure, and free to gaze intently into the heart of Truth, into the very clear sky of Eternity, into the Divinity who lives as the Self of all selves -- that is the spiritual life.

*   *   *

BURNING UP KARMA

First of all, what is karma? *Karma* is the Sanskrit
word for "action".   The word is also used sometimes
to represent the "fruits", or results, of actions.   The
so-called 'law of karma' is the law of action and
reaction.   It is the same as the law governing physical
phenomena, as defined by Newton: "For every action,
there is an equal and opposite reaction."   This is the
law by which our actions rebound upon ourselves,
either for good or for ill.   Now, karma, or actions,
are not merely physical phenomena; actions are performed at the subtle, mental, level as well; and it is
there, at the root of all physical actions, that all
good and all evil, all pleasure and all pain, has its
origin.   And it is there, also, that we are able to
initiate, control, and negate our actions, our karmas.
Once karma has reached the physical level as bodily
activity, it is too late for negation; such karma must
bear its fruit.

We can understand the different kinds of karma
by the use of a picture-analogy frequently used in
the Vedantic tradition: it is of an archer who has
just shot an arrow from his bow. He is just placing
another arrow in his bow, and he carries a quiver full
of arrows on his back.   Now, the arrow already shot
is karma which cannot be called back; it must bear
its fruit.   This is one's past (*prarabdha*) karma.   Even
the realized saints must accept the fruits of their
past karma -- those actions which have already been
performed.   The arrow that was just placed in the
bow, but which has not yet been shot, represents the
present potential (*kriyaman*) karma.   And the quiver
full of arrows represents the future potential (*sanchita*)
karma.   These last two, the present and the future
karmas, can be cancelled out, burned up by the knowledge of the Self.

Now, before we get into the subject of how karmas
are burned up, let's understand what it is that is
affected by karmas, by actions, on the subtle and the
gross levels.   It is the *jiva*, the individualized soul,
that receives the fruits of actions.   The Self is not
affected at all by actions; only the *jiva*.   In fact, it

is by our actions that the *jiva*, the soul, continues to
exist. The effects of actions accrue to the *jiva* and
are the cause of rebirth. The *jiva* is nothing else
but the package of impressions, memories, and karmas
which we ourselves create. This is what was meant
by Heraclitus when he said, "Character is destiny."
From our deeply ingrained impressions (*samskaras*),
come desires, which draw us to be reborn in this
world. It is this ephemeral bundle of impressions and
desires which reincarnates as a "soul".

This should not be seen as a fatalistic view, however. Some hold the mistaken view that if we are
merely products of our past actions, we are fated to
repeat endlessly the mistakes of the past. This is
not true. We are all born with a certain blueprint
of our life, which consists of impressions born of the
actions of our previous life. This can be seen reflected in the unique pattern created by one's natal horo-
scope. But, our present acts and thoughts, modified
by our learning-experiences, in the same way, creates
our future. Man, therefore, is the architect of his
own fate and the builder of his own future. Though
past impressions, habits, memories, are deeply rooted
in our soul-fabric, they *can* be modified and even
rooted out by new habits. The burning up of all
karma is achieved by the realization of the Self,
which is the substratum of all souls and all actions.

To understand this clearly, we must first understand
the nature of the Reality in which we live, and move,
and have our being. This is where the knowledge of
those who have realized the Truth of reality can be
of benefit to us. They tell us that the Source and
Origin of all phenomena is pure, unqualified, Consciousness; and that this Consciousness, by Its very nature,
projects upon Itself a living universe of forms by Its
power of projection. The projected universe is not
that Consciousness, but is Its projection. Vedantists
call it "Maya"; Muslims call it "Khalq"; and Christians
call it "the Logos" or "the Word". This "Maya" is
produced in a way very much like what we do when
we project a thought, an image, or a dream upon our
own consciousness. The consciousness and the thought
are not separate and yet we would not say that the
thought *is* the consciousness. The consciousness is

manifest as the thought, and is nothing but consciousness; and yet the consciousness remains distinct from and independent of the thought -- as the ocean is distinct from its waves.

In exactly the same way, the one pure Consciousness, called variously by the name of "Brahman", "Haqq", or "God", remains independent of the projected universe, and is unaffected by the universe, even though the universe is nothing but Its own manifestation. In some ways, the analogy of the ocean and its waves is a good one. The waves are produced by the ocean and are nothing else but ocean. Yet the ocean is the reality, independent of whether the waves exist or not. Without the ocean, where are the waves? They cannot exist, for they are nothing but ocean. Likewise, the One Reality, the continuously existent Consciousness, is unaffected by the appearance of souls and actions.

This brings us to the understanding we were seeking regarding actions, and how we can transcend their effects. We receive the effects of actions only because we imagine that we are the actor; that is to say, the agent of our actions. Again, using the wave comparison, think of a wave experiencing the horror of being dashed on the rocky shore. But, if that wave realizes that he is not merely the wave-form, but is, in fact, the ocean, he experiences no horror. He sees that he remains unchanged regardless of what happens to his wave-form. It is simply a matter of identification. The world and all perceivable objects within it, including our bodies, thoughts, emotions, is the projected manifestation of the One Reality, the one pure Consciousness, Brahman; and are comparable to the waves of the ocean. We, like the hypothetical wave, identify with the form, and fail to recognize that we are the substance, the Essence. We are Brahman, and not Maya or its forms. We are free, never bound. Bondage is nothing but the lack of true identification; it is delusion. And "liberation" is nothing but the awakening from this delusion about who you are.

When you realize that you are the ocean, the dissolution of each momentary wave is of little consequence to you. When you are Brahman, the occurrances within Maya do not disturb you or affect you in any way. When there is no "selfish" activity, there can be no karma. For there is no "self" to receive the fruits, either good or bad, from one's actions when those actions are without selfish motive. Liberation is not the result of Self-knowledge; it *is* that knowledge. Bondage to cause-effect, action-reaction, giving-getting, is the result of wrong identification. He who knows who he is, that he is the Eternal, the unchanging One, cannot be attached to actions or the result of actions. One who knows he's everything, and beyond everything, cannot seriously desire anything. He is therefore free. "Knowledge of the Self" and "Liberation" are synonymous terms.

This knowledge of the Self is also spoken of as "liberation from the wheel of rebirth" because rebirth of the soul (*jiva*) occurs only when there is an uncontrollable desire to enjoy worldly life. When the Self no longer identifies with objective phenomena or the enjoyment of objective phenomena, there is no more pull toward rebirth. Such a person is said to be liberated. He continues to live and enjoy due to his *prarabdha* karma, but he is a soul no longer; he is nothing else but the one Self. Such a being knows himself as the all-pervading *akasha*, the sky of Consciousness, when he leaves the body. He is also aware that he is That even while living and acting in the body. He is known as a *jivanmukta*, a soul freed while living.

It is the attainment of the direct knowledge of the Self which alone is capable of burning up all karma and all ignorance. However, until we are graced with that direct knowledge, we can only fortify our faith in the Self through indirect knowledge. In such a case, how does one go about modifying one's karmas? How does one go about changing the way one acts on the subtle level, so as to be not only more cognizant of the Self, but also faithful to the truth of the Self, and therefore less susceptible to error and the pain accompanying it? Only by great effort. That is the truth. The spiritual life is a life of inner warfare. It is a life of great challenge, with obstacles around every corner. It requires a constant vigilance over the mind, and a determination toward the Truth in the face of all the wiles of the enemy, ignorance. This is known as discrimination.

The first step in the spiritual life, it seems to me, is the recognition of the fact that there is a fundamental, undifferentiated Reality which is the Divine basis of our own being. This is the grace of awakening. The second step is to acknowledge, with regret and remorse, our past error in identifying with the separative ego -- regret for our stupidity, and remorse for all the pain we caused others in our ignorance. Repentance is not something that can be demanded of others, as some Christian sects seem to think; rather, it is the spontaneously-occurring wrenching of the heart of one newly awakened to the Truth, when he or she reflects on the errors of their past ways. From this, there comes a re-setting of priorities; a choosing of a new path ahead, a rethinking and rededication of one's life toward the realization and manifestation of Truth. This is what it means to be reborn in the Spirit.

But that is just the beginning. The life of awareness, the life of Truth, is never accomplished; it is a never-ending pursuit. It is a daily battle of the Spirit against old, deeply-entrenched habits of Nature. The Spirit must have the victory, for It is the Truth. But we have for so long habituated our minds to act in ways that are based in untruth, in ignorance; that we feel outnumbered, overwhelmed, and, at times, defeated. We stumble, we fall, we wonder if we shall rise again. And then, somehow, the inner Light uplifts us, and we climb to our feet to try again to walk in the Light of Truth. It's an old story; but it is replayed anew in earnest in each and every one of us, as we grow and learn, and relearn the art of love and the joy of life.

When we make terrible mistakes, hurtful mistakes, it is necessary, first of all, to surrender to what is; to resolve to make amends and then to go on with one's best efforts. The burden of failure does not seem so terrible, so unredeemable, if we can say to ourselves, "So, I made a blunder! I'll probably make many more. The instrument through which I operate, the manifested body, brain, etc., is imperfect. It is subject to failure, to error. Let it. I am not merely this instrument, this entity. I am pure, eternal Consciousness. I am the unblemished Lord of the universe. It is only this instrument that requires purification; I am ever pure." This is the truth: "I am not in the leastwise affected by the happenings in this world; I am the ever-free, ever-unchanging, universal Self!" This is the truth that will make you free.

The true knowledge of the Self is, of course, a direct knowledge. It is not merely an understanding, nor a conviction. However, the thought, "I am the Self. I am Brahman", is necessary as a counter-active to the thought, "I am in pain. I am resentful. I am needy; etc." It is a corrective to the wrong thinking, wrong identification, with which all of us are afflicted. It is a counter-offensive to the whining of the ego-mind, and the discomfort which accompanies error. But its purpose is to alleviate the need for thought at all. Once it has destroyed that wrong thought, the true assertion also ceases; it is no longer necessary, and it dissolves on its own -- like the dying of a flame when its fuel is exhausted. Then, one can enjoy the silent awareness of God's all-pervading presence.

In that awareness, love begins to flow toward the one Existence of its own accord. One feels a delicious thrill moving upward through one's body; this manifests in feeling as loving devotion, and the yearning for contact with the Highest, with God, our supreme Self. That devotion, that thrill of love, will lead you to God. It is the thread by which you may draw yourself nearer and nearer to the Truth; until, finally, your mind becomes solely fixed on Him, your breathing becomes suspended, and you merge in Him and know Him as your true Self.

This is the ultimate liberation from karma, from actions -- because then, you will know that your true Identity transcends the world and all actions. You will know without any doubt that you are the eternally unchanging Consciousness from which is projected all worlds, all beings, and all actions. They are all your play, your drama, your enjoyment, while you remain forever one and whole, unsullied by the creation, the ongoing drama, or the final dissolution of the universe. To what action, then, should

you become attached and call "mine"?   No action is
"yours", and all actions are Yours.   There is no one
here at all but the One.   The entire play of universal
creation and destruction is His dream-like fantasy.   In
truth, only He exists.   And that is who You are.

Reflection

What do I really want in life?   Some say this
world is a wish-fulfilling tree and that we choose
what we shall have in this life according to our desires.
If this is true, what then, shall I wish for?   What, of
all the things that bring delight, shall I choose to
have in this life?

What about a large family and many loving friends?
Lots of children would be nice; and so would loving
and supportive friends.   Much happiness would be
found in that.   But, ... children grow up and change.
Friends come and go.   These do not last and therefore
cannot bring me any permanent or satisfactory joy.

What about wealth, then?   Wealth is very handy; it
provides many enjoyments of the senses, and a certain
freedom of action.   But wait, ... will wealth give me
a permanent happiness, the unchanging satisfaction my
soul desires?   No, I think not.   In fact, the accumulation and guarding of wealth seems to bring with it
many difficulties and much mental unrest.

What about fame?   I shall attain great heights of
achievement!   I shall be famous for my contribution
to the world!   But that, too, is ephemeral and illusory;
and besides, I know it would not provide any deep and
lasting satisfaction.

Where, then, can I find a joy that never diminishes
or changes?   Is it not in God, the eternal Spirit within
my own heart?   Is not my very nature Joy?   Am I
not, in fact, eternally perfect and eternally fulfilled
within?   Let me make this eternal Joy within my Self
the sole focus of my life; for it is this I most desire.
Let me leave all other thought -- of family, friends,
wealth and fame -- to those who wish for them; but
let my heart be with That which I most treasure: my
God-Self, my eternal Freedom, my own clear light of
Consciousness and Joy.   For there is all I love and all
that I desire.

*   *   *

SHANKARACHARYA:
THE MAN AND HIS MESSAGE

One of the greatest names in the annals of Vedanta is that of Shankara, usually referred to as Shankara- charya, "Shankara, the teacher". Shankara was born in Kaladi, a remote village in Kerala state in South India, in the 7th or 8th century. His father was Shivaguru and his mother's name was Aryamba. According to legend, the childless couple had gone on pilgrimage to the Shiva temple in a nearby town to ask the Lord for a child, and stayed to worship and pray at the temple the whole day. That night, the Lord appeared to Aryamba in a dream and asked her if she would like to have a brilliant son who would live only a short time or a dullard who would live a long time. She chose the former. Within a year, Aryamba gave birth to a son, whom they called Shank- ara, in remembrance of Shiva, who is also known by that name.

At the age of eight, Shankara related to his mother his desire to renounce worldly aims, to become a *sannyasin* (monk), and devote his life to the realization of God. His mother refused permission, saying he was too young. Then one day, while Shankara was walking with his mother to the river bank, a crocodile got hold of his foot and began dragging him into the water. He cried out to his mother, "Mother, I'm being dragged to my death! At least now, grant my final request and consent to my taking the vows of renunciation!" And his mother, without hesitating, said, "Yes, of course!" At that moment, Shankara cried out, *"Sannyasthoham* ("I am a renunciant!")" loudly three times, and the crocodile let him go. In this way he succeeded in getting his mother's permission to take the vows of monkhood.

Now the eight-year old boy began his search for his guru. He had heard of the legendary Gaudapada, a famous sage; but Gaudapada was now old and had vowed to remain in solitude, so Shankara sought out the sage's disciple, Govindapada. He travelled on foot northward to Omkarnath to find him. And when he found him, he remained with Govindapada as his student-disciple for a few years, attaining the realization of the Self under his tutelege. When Govinda-pada took *mahasamadhi*, Shankara journeyed to the holy city of Kashi (Benares), as his guru had instructed him, and there he gathered and taught a few loyal disciples. He was only twelve years old at this time.

One day, returning from his morning bath, he found his pathway blocked by a Chandala, a low-caste, black-skinned man. Shankara asked him to move aside, as he didn't want to touch such a person. And the Chandala retorted, "You teach that all is God, all is the Self, do you not? Who, then, do you wish to avoid? Am I not the Self as well?" And Shankara, feeling that he had received a great lesson, bowed down humbly before the Chandala and begged his forgiveness. On that day, he would later say, the Chandala had been his guru.

After this, Shankara felt Divinely inspired to write some modern commentaries on the various Vedantic scriptures of old, so as to bring out the ancient truths in a way that would be fresh and comprehensible to the men of his own day. So, with his few disciples, he travelled to Badrikashram, where he stayed for four years writing his commentaries on the *Brahma Sutras*, the twelve *Upanishads*, and the *Bhagavad Gita*.

Then, after this period of seclusion and creative activity, Shankara resumed his travels on foot, traversing the length and breadth of the Indian sub-continent. For a while, he stayed at Sringeri, where a large temple and ashram was built. It was there that he wrote some of his greatest Vedantic treatises, such as *Viveka-chudamani* ("The Crest-Jewel of Discrimination"), *Atma-bodha* ("Self-knowledge"), *Upadeshasahasri* ("The One-Thousand Teachings") and others. During the approximately sixteen years of his mission on earth, he founded many monasteries, organized ten Orders of monks and wrote numerous treatises and songs to teach and celebrate the knowledge of the Self. He was a reformer and a restorer of the Non-Dualist philosophy of Vedanta; and he did more than any other man, of his time or any other, to lift the Indian religious tradition out of the mire of ritualism and priestlyism into which it had fallen.

The quintessence of Shankara's philosophy was stated by himself in a half-verse:

Brahma satyam
Jagan mithya
Jivo Brahmaiva naparah

("Brahman is the Reality;
  The phenomenal universe is merely an appearance;
  The soul is, in fact, nothing but Brahman.")

Let's examine this formula line by line: "Brahman is the Reality." The meaning of this is that God alone exists. This is the basis of all true religion and all true knowledge. The mystical vision reveals this truth clearly; all that exists is nothing but God. For He is Existence itself. The mystic, who experiences identification with God, sees all creation as the effusive production of his own Consciousness. He realizes the fundamental truth expressed by Shankara, that God alone is the Reality, and that He alone is.

"The phenomenal universe is merely an appearance." This is a truth that is impossible to deny when we consider the findings of modern physics. Scientists have convincingly demonstrated that all the forms in this world are composed of tiny cellular structures, which are composed of smaller building-blocks called molecules, which in turn are made of atoms, which in turn are comprised of electrons, neutrons, and other sub-atomic particles, which in turn are ultimately seen to be mere charges of energy that are governed in their behavior by an undetected intelligence. All matter, in other words, turns out to be an illusion, a mirage, created by the ordered movement of energy charges that have no "material" substance at all. The world-appearance, therefore, is much like the appearance of a circle of light created by the whirling of a torch in a circular motion. The world is appearance only, an appearance that is incessantly changing, yet whose *real* substance is eternally unchanged. The Reality, the substance, is the One who is Existence, Consciousness, and Bliss. It is He who appears in the form of the world.

Shankara's third proposition is that "The soul is, in fact, nothing but Brahman." 'If the world is an illusion', cry those who object to this line of reasoning, 'who then am I? Am I an illusion also?' And the answer, of course, is "No. You are truly the Reality. You are truly Brahman." Your belief that you are merely this phenomenal appearance with which you identify is the misperception which prevents you from seeing who you really are. It is, in fact, this deep-seated ignorance which constitutes your individuality, your soul-identity. When, at last, you know the truth of your Identity, you will transcend the limited identity which is the soul, and you will know that, truly, you are and have always been, the one Self of the universe.

In this three-lined formula of Shankara's, the ultimate knowledge, the essence of Vedanta, is expressed. The Western "materialist" view is, of course, just the opposite of this. God and the soul are dismissed as unreal, and the world is affirmed as the only reality. However, physicists from the materialist's own ranks have shown the world to be only an appearance created by the vibrations of energy; and so, the materialist view is utterly shattered by the very evidence gathered to support it. The scientists, who've place so much emphasis on the causal relationships taking place in the phenomenal world, are unable to find any 'real' substance to this world. Furthermore, these scientists can find no firm basis for a belief in independent causes or effects, but rather a body of evidence is growing to show that all things move together of one accord in a vast web of interrelationships within one contiguous whole.

However, Shankara's position is not at all based on empirical evidence; it is based on the experience which he and countless souls have had of the Reality through direct, not indirect, knowledge. For those who have experienced It, the one infinite and eternal Consciousness is a certainty, and not a theory. It is the unquestionably ultimate and indubitable Truth of all existence. The idea, therefore, that the knowledge of the Self is the sole means to be free of ignorance forever, is not, for Shankara, an article of faith, but a matter of absolute certainty. And, says Shankara, in order to attain that knowledge, one's method or means, should be the same as the end. If the final

" The Truth shall set you free, "

truth, known by the enlightened, is that the Self and
Brahman are one, says Shankara, then take that truth
as your practice as well. The truth is "I am Brahman"; therefore, let your practice be the continual
recollection: "I am Brahman."

'In the experience of Unity, you will see, in place
of the world,' says Shankara, 'only God, pure Consciousness, everywhere. So, take that as your method
as well. Learn to see only God in everything before
you. Haven't all the scriptures said, "In Him we live
and move and have our being"? Then reform your
vision and see only God. All around you is but one
continuous ocean of Existence-Consciousness-Bliss.
Remind yourself every moment of this truth. Acclimate
your mind to the knowledge of Truth; then, it will
easily merge into the clear awareness of Truth.'

Shankara advised also such traditional methods of
sodhana, or spiritual practice, as *viveka* (discrimination
between the Real and the unreal), and *vairagya* (detachment from the attractions of sense-objects); and
all the normal principles of conduct traditionally
associated with sadhana -- like truthfulness, non-stealing, non-harming, etc. But we should remember that
the ethical principles in Vedanta are not presented
as principles of conduct for the sake of social harmony
or some such end, but are geared rather toward the
attainment of Self-knowledge.   When Self-knowledge
is attained, ethical principles of moral conduct are
no longer necessary, as a person illumined acts out
of a true sense of unity with all being, and his conduct
is in perfect accordance with the Truth, without any
such constraints as moral principles.

Here, in the West, where materialistic ideals are
so prominent, religion is almost totally ethical in
nature.   That is, its ultimate goal is seen to be
ethically moral behavior. Not many years ago, heaven
was seen to be the ultimate reward by Western religious teachers; but that is now regarded as "pie-in-the-
sky" morality. The goal of Western religion today is
"heaven on earth". Religious teachers of today offer
us the hope and prospect of an infinite increase in
good and a complete eradication of evil, resulting in
a perfect world of the future. This is known as
"secular humanism": the idea that the perfection of

humanity is the only proper religion -- not for the sake of some "other-worldly" reward, but simply for the harmonious survival of the society. All ethical principles and moral imperitives, from the secular humanistic viewpoint, have as their impetus and goal, the survival of the individual and the harmonious functioning of the society. Now, survival is certainly essential; without it, nothing else matters. But is it the ultimately satisfying end and purpose toward which all men strive?

Vedanta -- Shankara's as well as the classical Vedanta of the Upanishads -- asserts that the ultimate satisfaction toward which all men strive is the freedom from ignorance which comes from knowing one's true nature. And that, therefore, all ethical or moral principles must be founded on, and have as their objective, the attainment of Self-knowledge. Such virtues as detachment, mental calm, compassion, humility, etc., are not, in Vedanta, mere means to promote social harmony; but rather are behavioral characteristics in conformance with man's true nature which conduce to the experience of Self-knowledge and hence perfect fulfillment.

When a person knows the Self, he no longer has any need of rules of behavior; he transcends all moral imperitives, as he has transcended both good and evil in that perfect state which is beyond all such dualities. The One is neither good nor evil; it is the Whole which contains both and yet partakes of neither. It is the undivided Unity. And he who has known the Self is not swayed by considerations of whether an act is regarded as good or evil, but rather, he acts spontaneously from the awareness that all is nothing but his own Self. He is not "compassionate"; he is simply naturally loving. Love is his nature. He is not motivated by fear of punishment or promise of reward; he lives and acts in the best interest of all, having no special interest of his own. He works to bring about the enlightenment of all beings, and to spread the joy of Truth wherever and whenever he can.

To attain this perfect state, Shankara extolled most emphatically the practice of *jnan-abhyasa*, the practice of remembering the truth: "I am Brahman, I am the one Self." However, he did not exclude the practice of *bhakti*, or devotion, as some think.   In fact, the practice of remembering the Self *is* devotion. As Shankara put it, "the endeavor to know one's true nature is devotion."   Whether we regard our goal as God or the Self, the direction in which we must turn is the same -- within.   It is there one finds both God and the Self; for they turn out to be one and the same.

Devotion to God is both a means and an end in itself.   Devotion is itself the transcendence of the world of duality.   Both the joys and the sorrows of earthly life are cast aside when the heart turns toward God in devotion.   Devotion is an act of the soul and takes place entirely at the subtlest level of consciousness, at that place where the apparent duality is resolvable into unity.   There, the world and its pleasures, the world and its evils, is completely vanquished, for the soul is elsewhere -- at the feet of God, immersed in the Self.

As the light of consciousness becomes pure and clear, the soul, that is, the limited "I", awakes to the awareness that it is much greater than it had previously thought, that it is, in fact, the entirety of Existence.   As the awareness of a limited "I" fades away, so does the "Thou" to which it directed its entreaties.   The soul is no longer a soul, but the one pure Consciousness within whom the dialogue between "I" and "Thou" had been taking place.   From the viewpoint of enlightenment, the illusory duality of "I" and "Thou" was "superimposed" upon the one undivided Existence-Consciousness-Bliss.

According to Shankara, "superimposition" (*adhyasa*) is a process that begins at the subtlest level of mind. In the unitive consciousness of man, prior to the manifestation of thought, there arises the sense of "I", the experiencer; and at the very same time arises the perception of the "other", that which is experienced.   This is the subtle-level bifurcation of the one Self into subject and object, "I" and "Thou". It is a superimposition of duality upon what is truly One.   All duality, and hence all conflict and confusion, results from this original, subtle-level superimposition.

If we would realize and know the unity of the

Self, we must return to that subtle-level of mind where this original bifurcation or superimposition occurs. We must recognize and clearly witness this process of Self-division at the subtle level in order to fully realize the truth that the Self is the one Reality, and contains in Itself the impulse which gives rise to duality. Eventually, we must come to recognize that there is only the one consciousness (misperceived as a limited subject), and that all objective phenomena -- from the original "other" to the multiplicity of forms experienced as the objective world -- is a superimposition on the one pure Consciousness. Both subject and object, both "I" and "Thou" come into existence simultaneously from this initial impulse in Consciousness.

That impulse is called "Shakti" or "Maya", the principle of manifestation. It is the duality-producing tendency inherent in the one Consciousness. From it, the entire world of so-called "objective" phenomena is created. In man, the one Consciousness becomes convinced of the existence of the "other", and is limited by that very perception. He takes on an identity as the limited "I". This is the individual soul, or *jiva*, whose characteristics are determined by the thought-tendencies it has accumulated.

The light of intelligence, the clear awareness in man, is the Divine Consciousness. Yet, the duality-producing tendency inherent in that one Consciousness keeps us bound in delusion and ignorance of our true nature. However, we have within us also the ability to realize our true Self, and become freed of that binding delusion. How does this realization come about? Is it accomplished by our own self-efforts or through the unassisted grace of that one Intelligence? As there is only one -- the one Intelligence *appearing* as the soul -- the question of which one is responsible is invalidated as making no sense. He, the One, is doing everything.

Here are a few selections from Shankara's *Viveka-chudamani* on the nature of the Self:

Now I shall tell you the nature of the Self. If you realize It you will be freed from the bonds of ignorance and attain liberation.
... The Self is distinct from Maya, the primal cause, and from her effect, the universe. The

nature of the Self is pure Consciousness. The
Self reveals this entire universe of mind and
matter. It cannot be defined. In and through
the various states of consciousness -- the
waking, the dreaming, and the deep sleep --
it maintains our unbroken awareness of identity.
It manifests itself as the witness of the intelligence. [1]

... The fool thinks, 'I am the body'. The
intelligent man thinks, 'I am an individual soul
united with the body'. But the wise man, in
the greatness of his knowledge and spiritual
discrimination, sees the Self as the sole reality
and thinks, 'I am Brahman'. [2]

The Self is the witness -- beyond all attributes, beyond action. It can be directly realized
as pure Consciousness and infinite Bliss. Its
appearance as an individual soul is caused by
the delusion of our understanding, and has no
reality. By its very nature, this appearance is
unreal. So long as our delusion continues, the
rope appears to be a snake. When the delusion
ends, the snake ceases to exist. [3]

... Know the Self, transcend all sorrows
and reach the fountain of Joy. Be illumined
by this knowledge, and you have nothing to
fear. If you wish to find liberation, there is
no other way of breaking the bonds of rebirth. [4]

I spoke earlier of *jnan-abhyasa*, the practice of knowledge: this is the method of sadhana recommended
by Shankara. "The means to dispel ignorance," he
says, "is the uninterrupted practice of the awareness
of the Self." This is how he describes the practice:

...Know your true Self as the witness of
the mind and intellect, and of the thought-waves
that arise in them. Raise one single wave of
thought constantly: 'I am Brahman'. Thus you
will free yourself from identification with
non-Self. [5]

... You are pure Consciousness, the witness
of all experiences. Your real nature is joy.
Cease this very moment to identify yourself
with the ego, which is created by ignorance.

Its intelligence is only apparent, a reflection of the Self, which is pure Consciousness. It robs you of peace and joy in the Self. By identifying yourself with it, you have fallen into the snare of the world, [to experience] the miseries of birth, decay, and death.

You are the Self, the infinite being, the pure, unchanging Consciousness, which pervades everything. Your nature is bliss and your glory is without stain. Because you identify yourself with the ego, you are tied to birth and death. Your bondage has no other cause.[6]

This idea of 'me' and 'mine' relating to the body, organs, etc., which are non-Self, must be terminated by identifying with the Self. Know your Self to be the witness of the intellect and its modifications, and, constantly revolving the positive thought, 'I am That', conquer this identification with the non-Self.

One should know 'I am Brahman. I am without attributes and actions, eternal, without doubts, unsullied, changeless, formless, ever free and pure. Like space, I pervade everything inside and outside. Never fallen, I am eternal, unattached, pure and motionless; the same in all.' Thus constantly practiced, this innate impression, 'I am truly Brahman,' destroys agitations caused by ignorance just as medicine destroys disease. [7]

Reflection

Do you say I am only a ray of His Light? Ah, but while this ray must vanish when night-time comes, that Eternal Sun will always shine. I am not the ray, but I am Light itself. Glory be to me!

Do you say I am but a thought, an imagination, in the universal Mind? Wait -- this thought will cease when the time comes for sleep! And yet the Mind from which it sprang, that infinite Consciousness which thinks forth this world, can never cease. It is pure and clear forever, like the infinite reaches of space. That Mind am I. Glory be to me!

Do you say I am but a wave on the ocean of

Existence?   Ah, but this wave will break upon some shore, and be dispersed.   Yet, I shall rise up again in calmer or in rougher weather; for I am the very Ocean whose surface tosses in this multitude of wave-like forms.   In my depths, I am ever still; yet I am the Origin of all life.   None can sound my depths or chart my ways.   I am boisterous and uproarious; I am silent, I am still.   I am full, yet I am empty; abundant, yet a void.   I am the One who, while changing, is ever-unchanged.   I am the Light, the Mind, the Ocean!   Glory be to me!

*   *   *

SELF-KNOWLEDGE

Today I'm going to talk a little about knowing your Self. 'But,' you may say, 'I already know who I am. I'm Mr. or Mrs. so-and-so. I'm a doctor, lawyer, teacher, wife, mother, father, student, etc., and I see myself every morning in the mirror.' It is these things with which most of us identify. We regard as our self not only our physical bodies, but our constructed identities; that is to say, our professions, our opinions, our memories, our social status, our education, our familial relations, etc. And most of us would strongly protest against any assertion that we do not know who we are.

Well, Vedanta philosophy asks you to examine just what it is you are identifying with. Are you the body? When you think about it, you must answer, 'No, I can't be just the body.' Well, what, then? A soul that retains its unique proclivities and memories and personality? 'Well, I just don't know!' you might say; 'I've never really thought about it.' The philosophy of Vedanta represents the voice of those who do know, those who have thought about it; and it says you are none of these things -- certainly not the body, but also not the soul, for that too must come to an end. The individualized 'soul' is merely a temporary formation of tendencies which arise from the veiling power of that one transcendent Mind which creates all souls from Itself.

Vedanta speaks of the "veiling power" of God as *Maya*, or sometimes simply as *avidya*, or ignorance. Now, this is not simply the ignorance of not-knowing this or that bit of factual information; it is a primal ignorance which is produced by God in His creatures in the very act of creating. Manifestation itself is the act of the diversification of the One into many. The one "I" has now numerous reference points to regard as Its subjective vantagepoint, and It identifies with the entity through which It experiences conscious awareness. Over eons of transmigration, this point of awareness becomes firmly established in ignorance of its Origin, its real nature, and continues so, until sufficiently evolved and experienced to recognize the truth when it is presented.

This ignorance, or Maya, is said to be beginning-less; i.e., it is 'built-into' the process of manifesta-tion, which itself brings time into being.   However, this ignorance, while beginningless, is capable of being dispelled, and thus ended.   Because, just as the Self has the power of presenting to Itself this vast illusion of multiplicity, It also has the power to reveal Itself to Itself, to awake from Its self-induced ignorance.   This is known as "Self-realization," or "Knowledge of the Self."   This brings immediate liberation from all the fears and anxieties attendant upon the isolation of individual existence, just as the turning-on of a light in a room that has been dark for centuries immediately dispels centuries of darkness. Once the Self is revealed, the ignorance of many lifetimes is vanished forever.

In order to examine this topic at length, I'm going to utilize one of the great scriptures of Vedanta philosophy which deals with it: namely, the famous work by Shankaracharya called, *Atma-bodha* ("Self-knowledge").   Shankaracharya, who lived in the 7th or 8th century in India, had experienced the Self, and realized That which the Upanishadic seers had known.   Following his own Self-realization, he wrote many commentaries on the Upanishads and other Vedantic scriptures of his time in order to explain and make clear to others their message; and he wrote some independent works as well.   This, the *Atma-bodha*, is one of his most clear and unequivocal statements on the nature of the Self, and the means to realize It.   This is how he begins:

1.   This *Atma-bodha* is being composed to serve the needs of those whose sins have been removed by austerities, who are calm, free from desires, and yearning for liberation.

Comment: You see, this information about the Self is completely useless to someone who is still greedily gobbling up the fruits of his desires, who is utterly unaware of the worth of others, but sees only his own wishes to be fulfilled.   Such an agitated per-son, who has not even entertained the thought of leaving this phenomenal world of delights, is not only unable to appreciate this information which follows, but is capable of angrily persecuting those who speak of such matters. He believes only in his own ego, and greatly resents those teachings which suggest the restraint of his egoistic desires, and the need for self-examination. Furthermore, he has not the subtlety of mind to comprehend the notion of his own Divinity, and sees this information as a blasphemous and corrupting ideal. Thus, Shankaracharya states in the beginning that this work is solely for those who have reached the stage of evolution in which they are capable of comprehending his message.

2.   Of all spiritual disciplines, knowledge of the Self is truly the real means for Liberation, just as fire [is required] for cooking. Liberation [from the suffering of ignorance] cannot be attained without knowledge of the Self.

Comment: Shankaracharya is stating what appears to be an obvious tenet only in order to make clear to those who believe that they can reach the ultimate salvation through the performance of rituals, the following of religious injunctions, the worship of deities, the giving of charity, or the performance of other humanitarian duties, that they are sadly mistaken; that there is no way to be free of illusion, of misery, of crippling ignorance, except by the realization of the Truth, the gracious revelation of the universal Self. In the following verses, he explains why this is so.

3.   Actions (*karmas*) cannot destroy ignorance (*avidya*), as the performance of actions is not opposed to the ignorance of the Self. Knowledge alone destroys ignorance, just as light destroys the densest darkness.

Comment: This utterance is solidly backed by this statement from the *Mundaka Upanishad:* "Ignorant fools regarding ritual offerings and humanitarian works as the highest, do not know any higher good. After enjoying their rewards in heaven [which were] acquired by good works, they enter into this world again. But those wise men of tranquil minds, ... contemplating that God who is the Source of the universe, depart, freed from impurities, to the place where that immortal

Self dwells whose nature is imperishable."

4.   The Self appears to be finite because of ignorance.   When that is destroyed, truly the Self alone shines by itself, as does the Sun when a cloud passes away.

Comment: Here, Shankaracharya compares ignorance to a cloud which prevents the true light of the Sun from shining through.   The Self is always there, just as the Sun is always there; but our lack of awareness of It is like a nebulous cloud, or a dark glass, through which we cannot see.   Ignorance, we must remember, is not a 'thing'; it has no positive reality.   Rather, ignorance is a negative; it means "not-knowing".   It is an absence of clarity, of conscious Light, just as darkness is an absence of earthly light.   Therefore, we must be careful not to invest 'ignorance' with some kind of essence, as though it were an actual entity of sorts.   It is much like a cloud that conceals from us the full extent of our infinite Being.   For when the Self is revealed, that ignorance is nowhere to be found -- just like a cloud that has been dispelled by the light of the Sun, and is no more.

5.   The practice of knowledge thoroughly puri-fies the ignorance-stained Self, and the knowledge itself disappears, as salt [disappears] in water.

Comment: Shankara introduces the phrase, "the practice of knowledge" (*jnan-abhyasa*), as a method of establishing the continual awareness of the Self. According to him, vestiges of wrong-identification remain even after the realization of the Self.   Old habits of identifying with the separative ego die hard, and must be eliminated by a constant vigilance of consciousness.   This vigilance may take the form of a repetitive verbal reminder to oneself whenever ignorance raises its ugly head; a reminder such as "I am not the body; I am not this wayward mind; I am the unchanging Absolute!"   This has the effect of clarifying the awareness, and dispelling any wrong notions that may have crept in.

Shankaracharya anticipates the objection that this is mere words, and not true "Self-knowledge", by explaining that, while this verbalized conceptual knowledge is not the true, direct Knowledge, this ideational knowledge has the effect of bringing about true Self-awareness into which the idea dissolves away, just as salt dissolves in water. It is like using a fuel to ignite a fire; then, when the fuel is consumed, the fire also dies, and nothing is left. Just as the fuel is sacrificed to the fire, and disappears, so does ideational knowledge fuel pure awareness, and is sacrificed, disappearing in the process.

6.   The world, full of attachments, aversions, etc., is truly like a dream. While it exists, it appears to be real, but when one awakes [to the Self], it is realized to be unreal.

Comment: God is not dreaming this world, of course; He is ever-awake. But, as Shankara says, this world is *like* a dream insofar as both seem to be very real at the time one is experiencing them; and yet, once one "awakes" from either condition, then, and only then, does one become aware that he had been under an illusion-producing influence. If we consider the persuasiveness of dreams, and recall the many personalities that people our dreams on occasion, we may get some insight into the illusory nature of this world and our own souls. What becomes of the soul when one awakes to the eternal Self is very similar to what becomes of the personalities that people our dreams when we awake from them. They were mere figments of our imagination, and therefore they dissolve away into the nothingness from which they came. This is also what becomes of the individualized 'soul' when one awakes to the Self. And so, while this world may not truly be regarded as a dream, the comparison is quite valid.

7.   The world appears to be real as long as the non-dual Self, the Substratum of all, is not realized; just as silver may appear only until one realizes the object perceived to be mother-of-pearl.

Comment: Shankara continues his comparison of the world to a dream which appears to be real so long as the dreaming-self is not realized. By "real", Shankara means the permanent, eternal, Reality. But "real" has several various gradations of meaning ordinarily. For example, a dream is not a permanent reality, but it does have a phenomenal reality insofar as it does have a kind of existence. This world, too, though it is not the ultimate Reality, does have a temporal existence, and therefore must be regarded as "real" to some degree. It should be clear, however, that Shankaracharya is extending his analogy with a dream in order to show the similarities between the two kinds of "reality", and to show that, just as there is a more permanent reality behind the dream: i.e., the dreamer; likewise, there is a permanent Reality behind the phenomenal universe: i.e., the one universal Self. And that, when one awakes to the Eternal, the one Self, the world is realized to have been a mere appearance, much in the manner that a dreamer awakening from a dream realizes the dream to have been a mere appearance.

8. As bubbles [arise from, exist in, and dissolve into] the water, the [many] worlds arise from, exist in, and dissolve into, the supreme Lord, who is [not only the "efficient" cause, but] the material cause and support of everything.

Comment: In other words, the Lord, the Self, is not only the Cause of the universe, in the sense of His being the Author and initiating Cause of the effect, but He is the Cause also in the sense of being the very "material" of which the universe is made. All this exists in Him; is, in fact, His very substance, just as a dream which exists in the mind of a dreamer is inseparable from the dreamer, and is made from the very consciousness of the dreamer. The Self is the Support of all in the same way that a dreamer is the support of the dream-world which he creates within himself.

9. The manifested world of plurality is superimposed, by [a process which can be likened to] imagination, upon the eternal, all-pervading Lord whose nature is Existence and Consciousness, just as various objects of jewelry are superimposed upon [the substance] gold.

Comment: Just as a dream, which is produced

from the consciousness of man, is superimposed upon
that consciousness, and is witnessed by that consciousness, so is the world produced from the eternal Consciousness, superimposed upon that eternal Consciousness,
and is witnessed by that eternal Consciousness.   And
just as golden ornaments of jewelry, while assuming
various forms, are essentially gold, and nothing but
gold, so this world, while appearing in innumerable
forms, is really the Self, and nothing but the Self.   It
is we individualized subjects who superimpose upon the
one Reality multiple names for the various forms we
perceive; but truly, there is nothing here but the Self.

Reflection

Who am I?   Am I my name?   No, of course not!   I
could have any number of names, and yet I -- my
Self -- would not be changed on that account.   Am I
this hulk of a body that sits here?   No.   I am an
awareness -- not merely an inert mass of bones and
flesh.   Over the years, this body has changed, and
become different in appearance from what it once
was, but *I* -- that which I am -- has never changed.
And when, one day, this body falls away, and decays
in the earth, I shall not be in the least bit affected
by these events.   It would be foolish to think so.
      Am I, then, this mind -- this bundle of thoughts,
desires, past memories, and peculiarities that makes
up my individuality, my personal soul?   No.   I cannot
be this fluctuating mind, this kaleidoscope of thoughts,
impressions, and images.   For I am the one who watches this display, this subtle show, from within.   I am
the Witness, the Judge, and the Critic, on whose screen
these thoughts and images are projected for my viewing.
They arise from me, like bubbles rising out of the
ocean, or like clouds forming in the sky.   They are
evanescent; they quickly change and pass away, but I,
like the deep ocean or the clear sky, remain pure and
unchanged by their passing.
      Everything arises from Me, and passes in time, but
I am beyond time, and beyond the forms that arise.
I am the eternal Quietude, beyond even the cold reaches
of space.   Within Me, the whole universe rises and
sets -- while I remain, My Peace forever undiminished,
my Joy forever unstained.

*   *   *

SELF-KNOWLEDGE

PART II

As was stated in the beginning of our study of Shankara's *Atma-bodha*, his philosophy is an expression of his own "visionary" experience. In that experience, one knows the Unity beyond all apparent duality. One realizes the nature of the Self to be absolute, transcending all phenomenal appearance. The phenomenal world is seen to be a projection, or emanated thought, of the transcendent Self. Thus, while it is only the One who is both transcendent God *and* projected universe, there is an *apparent* duality, since the transcendent aspect of the Reality is ever-whole, ever-unchanging, ever-pure and unblemished; while the universe of form, which is Its complementary aspect, is ever-changing, divisible, and transient.

Our very existence illustrates this duality-in-unity, and reveals the contradictory nature of these two aspects of being: our bodies and psyches constitute the transient, phenomenal aspect of our lives; while our consciousness constitutes our eternal Divinity, transcendent and free. These two aspects of our being, indeed, of all being, are so intertwined, one superimposed upon the other, that they are inseparable. We struggle with the conflict between body and "spirit"; and yet, ironically, they are ultimately One. In order, however, to discriminate between these two, the Eternal and the temporal, we separate them out conceptually.

The eternal Self, our permanent reality, is experienced as pure Consciousness, the witness of the activity of the mind and the body. The phenomenal existence, which we perceive as form -- on both the subtle and the gross levels -- is the manifestation of Nature, the Self's projected Energy. This Energy (*Shakti, Maya, Prakrti*) is God's power of creation; all form is constituted of it. It is the subtle, psychically-perceived, forms; and it is all the various forms perceived in the physical world. It is not the Self; it is the "projection" of the Self. The Self is Eternal, but Its projected appearances are transient, illusory.

This is a subtle theological distinction, made in every religious tradition based on true mystical experience. These two, the Eternal and Its projected Energy (which appears as form), have been called by many different names: "Brahman-Maya", "Purusha-Prakrti", "Shiva-Shakti", "Theos-Logos", etc. Here, in the following verses, Shankara distinguishes between the Self and the products of Its projected Energy:

18.　　　One should understand the Self to be distinct from the body, sense-organs, mind, intellect and its tendencies (*vasanas* or *samskaras*), and always a witness of their functions, as a king [is a witness of the various activities going on in his kingdom].

Comment: Here is the classical discrimination between the Real and the unreal, the Truth and the appearance. When we discriminate in this way, we learn that our eternal Consciousness is separable from the manifold activities of the mind and body. Meditation is just this very discrimination; it is a centering upon the pure Awareness that is the Witness of all subtle phenomena. In this way, one is enabled to identify with the eternal Self, and regard the mind's activity from a detached distance.

19.　　　To the non-discriminating, the Self appears to be active when the sense organs are functioning, just as the moon appears to be moving when the clouds are moving.

Comment: Most of us, until we learn the difference, identify almost completely with the body as receptor of sensory experience. When the body is moving, we say, "I am moving"; when the eyes are seeing, we say, "I see"; and so on. But the discriminating person realizes that it is only the body and the senses which are operating, and that "I" (i.e., the Self) am never affected by any motion or activity whatever, but remain always the transcendent Witness to the activities of Nature. It is worth noting also that, in the analogy provided, just as the motion of the clouds is noticeable by virtue of the moon's remaining relatively motionless, and the clouds are only visible because of the moon's light -- so, likewise, it is only because the Witness is unchanging that all change can be observed by It, and it is that Self also which is illumining all objects of perception.

20.   The body, sense-organs, mind and intellect perform their respective activities due to the Light and Energy (shakti) of the Self -- just as all beings are dependent upon the light and energy of the Sun.

21.   But, owing to non-discrimination, the qualities and activities of the body and the sense-organs are superimposed on the stainless Self, which is absolute Existence, Consciousness, and Bliss. [We attribute qualities and activities to the Self] just as we attribute the blue color to the sky.

Comment: The Self is always pure Consciousness, eternal and infinite; It is always transcendent to, and unaffected by, the phenomena of Nature, just as the infinite sky is colorless and unaffected by the impurities such as clouds which occupy it.   But because Nature, with all its forms and activities, is superimposed upon the Self, we identify our Self with the forms and the activities, and remain unaware of our true nature -- just as one who regards the sky as blue is unaware of its true nature.

22.   The agency of action, which belongs to the modification of Nature which we call the mind, is attributed, through ignorance, to the Self -- just as ripples on the water are attributed to the moon reflected in the water.

Comment: It is the water that is rippled; not the moon.   It is the mind which is actively producing thoughts and imges; not the Self.   the Self never performs any actions; therefore, the results of actions never accrue to the Self, and the Self remains ever-free.

23.   Attachment, desire, pleasure, pain, etc., arise when the intellect is present.   They do not exist in deep sleep when the intellect is absent.   Therefore, they are of the intellect but not of the Self.

24.   The nature of the Sun is luminosity, the nature of water is wetness, the nature of fire is heat; likewise, the nature of the Self is absolute Existence, Consciousness, Bliss, Eternity and Purity.

25.   By the indiscriminate superimposition of these two -- the Self which is the true Consciousness, and the intellect, there arises the notion, "I am knowing."

26.   The Self never undergoes modification; the intellect is never endowed with Consciousness. Yet, an individual, experiencing the act of knowing, becomes extremely deluded with the notions of "I am the seer, I am the knower."

Comment: This is how false identification occurs. For many deluded people, it is possible to realize that they are not the body only when the death of the body occurs. But it is even more difficult for them to realize that they are not the psyche, i.e., the mind, intellect, memory, etc. The intellect is active, cunning, and capable of producing confusion, fear, etc. The Self is none of these. Yet, when the intellect functions in any of these modes, one identifies with the state of the intellect, and says, "I am thinking, I am deciding, I am afraid, I am confused," etc. By this wrong identification, one suffers mistakenly.

27.   Mistaking oneself for the individualized intellect, just as by mistaking a rope for a snake, one is overcome with fear. [However,] if one is known, not as the individualized intellect, but as the supreme Self, one becomes free from fear.

Comment: How should one fear, knowing he is the eternal and all-pervading Self? When all is one's Self, what is there to fear? This was pointed out very ably in the *Taittirya Upanishad,* which states, "When a man finds fearless support in That which is invisible, incorporeal, indefinable, and supportless, he has then attained fearlessness. If he makes even the slightest differentiation in It, then he is once again susceptible to fear." [1]

28.   The Self alone illumines the intellect,
mind, sense-organs, etc., as a light illumines
clay pots or other objects.   One's Self is not
illumined by inert objects [such as the intellect,
etc.].

Comment: In other words, we see the mind's
activity by the light of the Self. It is the one Consciousness which empowers all and gives the light of
perception to all.   Neither the mind nor the intellect
have the ability to shed light on the Self.   The Self
cannot be known by the power of the intellect; the
intellect is itself empowered by the Self.   Many make
this mistake of attempting to know the Self by the
light of the intellect; but it cannot be done, for reasons
made obvious.   The Self alone has the power to reveal
the Self; and the Self alone has the power to perceive
Itself.

29.   Just as a light does not need another
light to illumine it, so too, the Self needs no
other knowledge to make Itself known, as Its
nature is Knowledge itself.

Comment: Clearly, one must go beyond the mind
and the intellect in order to realize the Self.   Meditation on the Self is the practice of abandoning the
thought-producing mind and the activity of the intellect,
so as to clear the pure sky of Consciousness of all
objects and obscuring clouds.   The pure Awareness
which is the witnessing Self can then be experienced
by Itself.

30.   Having negated all limiting modifications
of Nature with the declaration, "Not this, not
this (*neti, neti*)," one should realize the oneness
of the individual self and the supreme Self.

Comment: This is what is called, in the Christian
tradition, the *via negativa*, or "the negative path".   It
entails the elimination of all those phenomena which
belong to Nature, such as the body, the senses, the
mind, etc., by realizing that, one by one, "I am not
this, not this!"   By this process of elimination, one
comes at last to what one truly is: the pure and
eternal Consciousness which is the Self of the universe.

31.   Visible objects, like the body, mind, etc., are born of the primal Energy (*shakti*) and the ignorance (*avidya*) attending it, and are evanescent like bubbles.   One should realize the pure, eternal Self, which is other than these, and know, "I am Brahman (*aham brahmasmi*)."

32.   "Being distinct from the body, I have no birth, old age, senility, or death.   Since I am not the sense-organs, I am not attached to sense objects like sound, color, form, etc.

33.   "Since I am not the mind, I have no grief, desire, hatred, fear, etc., and indeed the scriptures declare that the Self is not the mind nor the prana; it is pure and eternal.

34.   "I am without attributes and actions, eternal, without doubts, unsullied, changeless, formless, ever-free and pure.

35.   "Like space, I pervade everything inside and outside.   Never fallen, the same in all, I am eternal, unattached, pure and motionless.

36.   "I am nothing else but that supreme Self which is eternal, pure, liberated, one, unbroken Bliss, undivided Existence, and unlimited Knowledge."

Comment: Shankara asserts that, by discriminating in this way, and continually reasserting one's true Identity, the old habits of wrong identification will be dispelled, and the true identification will take its place.   This will result in an alleviation of all the fears and anxieties attending the false sense of separation and isolation resulting from the identification with the individual mind-body complex.   The mind will become stilled from its normal agitations, and peace will infuse both the body and the mind.

37.   Thus constantly practiced, the innate impression, "I am truly the Self," destroys agitations caused by ignorance, just as medicine destroys diseases.

Comment: We find this same practice of knowledge (*jnan-abhyasa*) recommended in the *Yoga Sutras* of Patanjali: "The incessant practice of discrimination is the means [to establishment in the awareness of the Self]." [2]

In the following verses, Shankara describes the details of this practice:

38.   Seated in a solitary place, free from desires and with senses controlled, one should meditate on that one infinite Self without any other thought.

39.   Having dissolved the entire objective world in the Self alone by the process of discrimination, the wise person should constantly meditate upon the one Self as the stainless sky of Consciousness (*nirmalakasha*).

Comment: When meditating on the Self, the intellect with all its questioning and reasoning is not at all required. In fact, such activity of the intellect is an obstacle to the pure sky of the Self, just as clouds overhead obscure the vista of a clear, blue sky. The Self is the eternal Ground upon which all thoughts appear; and it is of that Ground that one must become aware. This is the declaration of all authentic scriptures, such as the *Vijnana Bhairava* of the Kashmir Shaivites: "Meditate on yourself as a vast, cloudless sky, and realize the true nature of your Self."

Reflection

What is Truth?   Truth is who you are!   Yes, Truth is your real Identity! It is the ocean of Existence on which all these variously-formed waves arise and fall.   Truth is not a set of principles; there are no words in It at all.   The taste of sugar cannot be captured in words; nor can the taste of Truth.   It seems to be concealed from Itself, as a forest seems concealed by the trees.   Yet, It is closer than our breath, closer than a laugh.   It is the wellspring from which each breath is drawn.   It is the river of Joy from which each laugh is born.   It is the Light that glistens in our eyes; It is the bright sky of Awareness that looks upon each thought that dances 'cross It's face.

What is Truth? Oh, It is the silent, joy-filled, sky of Light from which our very soul, cloud-like, forms, and on which it drifts, and eventually disperses piecemeal, disappearing; till only That -- our sky of Truth, our cloudless Reality, our infinite Self -- shines radiant, deep, and still, through all eternity. And we know sweetly, clearly, lovingly: "The Truth is all there is, and -- Truth be known -- That is who I am!"

*   *   *

SELF-KNOWLEDGE

PART III

Continuing with Shankara's *Atma-bodha*, we come to the final portion, in which he describes the state of awareness possessed by one who has realized the Self:

> 40.   He who has realized the supreme Self discards all forms, castes, etc., and rests in his own intrinsic form which is infinite Consciousness and Bliss.

Comment: On realizing one's identity to be the one all-pervading Reality, all previous identifications, limited to one's body or one's social position, etc., are naturally discarded. While there may be some residue of habit which causes one to inadvertently slip into identifying with temporal conditions, one eventually becomes established, through the disciplined practice of discrimination, in one's eternal Identity and sheds all identification with such limiting conditions.

> 41.   Since It is, Itself, pure Knowledge and Bliss, there are no distinctions of knower, knowing, and known in the supreme Self; It shines by Itself alone.

Comment: The apparent duality between the experiencer and the experienced causes one to imagine he is an individual soul, separate and isolated from the Eternal. But the truth experienced in the awareness of Unity reveals that the duality of experiencer and experienced is a mirage, a mere illusion. In that illuminating "vision", the duality of subject and object vanishes; the wave that searched for the ocean realizes suddenly that it *is* the ocean. It is the only one who was. It is eternally alone.

> 42.   Thus, by the constant churning of contemplation on the wood of the Self, the flame of Knowledge is born, which burns up the entire store of ignorance-fuel.

Comment: Utilizing, as an analogous image, the

operation of the small bow and pestle with which brahmin priests start the *homa* fire used in the *yajna* ritual, Shankara reminds us that, in a similar way, we must make an effort to lift the mind to a continual contemplation of the Self; in this way, the Knowledge will become clearly established, and the tendency toward wrong indentification will be eradicated.

43.   Just as the Sun rises of its own accord, and dispels the darkness of night by the light of day, so does the dawning of Self-awareness dispel ignorance by the light of Knowledge.

Comment: The darkness of ignorance in which we live, in a way similar to physical darkness, prevents us from seeing the real nature of existence; and when that unitive Knowledge dawns, It reveals the previously unseen Truth, just as the light of the Sun, dawning, reveals the world previously hidden to the sight.

44.   The Self is indeed an ever-present Reality; yet, because of ignorance, It is not realized. When ignorance is vanquished, the Self seems to be gained, just like the proverbial necklace around one 's neck.

Comment: There is an illustrative story which tells of a woman who looked in a mirror and happened to notice that her expensive necklace was missing. After raising a great fuss about it for quite a long time, she was immediately silenced by someone nearby who pointed out to her that the necklace had simply slipped beneath the neckline of her gown, and that, in fact, the necklace had never been lost.   The Self, likewise, has never been lost; it is always present as "I".   It is only due to our misperception that we imagine It to be absent.

45.   An individuality (ego) is superimposed on the Self through delusion, just as the form of a man is superimposed on a post. But that individuality disappears when the real nature of the Self is realized.

Comment: Just as a person walking on a dark road at night might take a wooden post to be a man lurking in the shadows, and become fearful that he was about to be robbed or harmed, so do we, in our delusion, imagine an individual ego-identity where there is only the one pure Consciousness. The individual ego-identity is superimposed upon the one Consciousness, just as the imaginary 'man' was superimposed upon the post. When the one Self is known, the imaginary ego-identity vanishes, just as the 'man' vanishes when it is realized to be a wooden post.

46.   The knowledge born out of the realization of the supreme Self instantly removes ignorance and the notions of 'I' and 'mine', in the same way as the knowledge of direction removes confusion regarding direction.

Comment: As soon as the Self is known, all notions about one's identity as a separate and limited being are instantly dispelled, however long one may have held such notions. It is similar to the vanishing of one's confusion regarding one's whereabouts in that moment at which a familiar landmark is recognized. Where, then, does the confusion go? It just vanishes. So does ignorance of one's Divinity vanish the moment one realizes the supreme Self.

47.   A yogi of complete enlightenment sees with his eye of wisdom the entire universe in his own Self, and the one Self pervading all.

Comment: The realization of the Self is enlightenment. In that clear awareness, all is known to be one's own manifested form. The entire universe is realized to be the embodiment of one's Self.

48.   The entire universe is truly the Self. There exists nothing at all other than the Self. The enlightened one sees everything as his own Self -- just as one sees pots and other earthen vessels as nothing but clay.

Comment: Objects made of clay are nothing but clay; likewise, all the universe and all objects in it are nothing but God. One who has realized the nature of his Self knows he is God and that all that exists is God.

49.   A liberated being endowed with Self-knowledge gives up identification with the

traits of his previous conditions (*upadhis*); and he becomes the Self, knowing his true nature to be Existence-Consciousness-Bliss, just as a larva becomes a wasp.

Comment: The *upadhis* are the limiting conditions, such as the bodily characteristics, the family environment, the social status, etc. Until a man realizes the Self, he identifies with such temporal conditions, and regards himself as a certain kind of person from a certain family, with a professional status, etc. But, just as the larva of a wasp, or a butterfly, once its transformation is completed, spreads its wings and leaves its larva-life behind, the Self-realized sage leaves behind all past identifications, and lives as the all-pervasive Self -- the one Existence-Consciousness-Bliss.

52.   Though associated with the limiting conditions, the all-knowing sage is untainted by their traits, as the sky is untainted by the clouds floating about within it. He lives [to all appearances] like a fool, and moves about unattached, just like the wind.

Comment: Though the Self-realized sage knows he is the unlimited Consciousness, still, while he lives in the body, he is associated with the various conditions of the body, mind, etc. Nevertheless, though associated with it, he does not identify with the body and its conditions. As the sky is unaffected by the appearance or non-appearance of clouds, so is he unaffected by the conditions with which he is associated. In his awareness, he is unattached to any object, thought, or condition. He views them as mere clouds passing by.

53.   At the destruction of the limiting conditions (i.e., at the death of the body), the sage becomes one with the all-pervading Reality, just as water mixes with water, or light with light, or space with space.

Comment: Even while living in the body, the Self-realized sage rises above the limiting conditions of body, mind, intellect, etc. He retains the awareness that he is the unlimited Self, the witness of the various conditions with which he is associated. But when the limiting conditions no longer exist, when his association with them is severed by bodily death, he is freed of even the appearance of limiting conditions, and becomes what he has always been.

54.   Realize that to be the Self, beyond the attainment of which there is no greater attainment, beyond whose bliss there is no greater bliss, and beyond the knowledge of which there is no greater knowledge.

Comment: All worldly attainments, however great; all worldly satisfactions, however satisfying; all worldly knowledge, however vast; pales into insignificance when compared to the attainment, the satisfaction, the knowledge, of the eternal Self.

55.   Realize that to be the Self, having seen which there is nothing else to be seen; having known which there is nothing else to be known, and having become which there is nothing else to become.

Comment: The realization of the Self is the ultimate vision, the ultimate knowledge, the ultimate achievement. It is experienced as the final stop at the 'end of the line'; for it is the reduction of all that exists to a single 'I', beyond which there is no further reduction. That it is the ultimate Goal is therefore self-evident.

56.   Realize that to be the Self which is all-pervading across, above, and below; which is Existence-Consciousness-Bliss, and which is undivided, infinite, eternal and One.

Comment: There is nothing that is not the Self. He is the One, without a second. This has been experienced and declared by countless men and women throughout history. It is the indisputable truth. We are never justified, therefore, in attributing existence to anything other than the one Self.

63.   The Self is not other than the universe. There exists nothing that is not the Self. If anything other than the Self is seen, it is as unreal as a mirage.

Comment: Shankara holds that this universe is Brahman, the Self. When he says, in another place, that "the world is illusory", he does not deny that it is Brahman *appearing* as the world. The world-appearance, with all its manifold forms, leads one to believe in the independent existence of multiple entities; whereas, in fact, there is nothing but Brahman. The Unity is real; the multiplicity is illusory. The one absolute and transcendent Mind is the eternal Reality; the world-appearance is transient, and therefore unreal. This duality is apparent only; the ever-present God, the eternal Self, is always One and undivided, whether the world-appearance exists or not.

64.   Whatever is seen or heard cannot be anything other than the Self; and on the realization of Truth, one recognizes that Self as Existence-Consciousness-Bliss, the One without a second.

Comment: When experiencing the variety of phenomena through the senses, one can, by an effort of concentration, become aware that everything is a manifestation of the Self, and that, all around one, nothing is experienced but the Self. But, for the certain and indubitable proof of that fact, one must realize the truth of one's own Self in contemplation, at the height of devotion. Then the perfect knowledge shines forth, revealing the Self to be the source and manifestation, the root and flower, of all that is.

65.   One with the eye of wisdom sees the all-pervading Self, whose nature is Existence-Con-sciousness-Bliss; one whose vision is obscured by ignorance does not see it -- just as the blind do not see the resplendent Sun.

Comment: The Truth is realized by the wise, and laughed at by the foolish. Just as the blind are deprived of the joy of seeing the brilliant Sun and all it illumines, so are the pridefully ignorant deprived of knowing the Unity, and of tasting the joy of the all-pervasive Self.

66.   The individual soul (*jiva*), heated in the fire of knowledge, which has been kindled by listening to the truth, reflecting on its signif-

icance, and contemplating and meditating on it, is freed from all impurities, and its true nature shines forth, as gold [shines forth when all the dross is burned away].

Comment: Here, Shankara uses the process of smelting gold as a metaphor for spiritual purification. He describes the kindling of this process in the traditional Vedantic terms associated with the learning process: *sravana*, listening to the truth; *manana*, reflecting on its meaning and significance; and *nidhidhyasana*, making it one's own through meditation and contemplation.

67.   The Self, the Sun of knowledge, that rises in the firmament of the heart, destroys the darkness of ignorance, pervades and sustains all, and shines and causes everything to shine.

Comment: When the knowledge of the Self dawns, all darkness of ignorance is dispelled, and all existence, including one's own being, is seen to be the radiant light from the one Sun -- the Lord and Self of all that lives.

68.   He who, renouncing all other activities, worships at the holy shrine of his own Self -- which is independent of time, space, and direction, which is present everywhere, which is the destroyer of duality, which is eternal Bliss and stainless -- becomes all-knowing, all-pervading, and immortal.

Comment: If you wish to know the Self, says Shankaracharya, have no other occupation than the worship of the Self. Let this be your only activity, regardless of place, time, or circumstance. Whether you are doing bodily labor or sitting quietly, whether you are giving or getting, whether you are speaking or listening, let your mind and heart be lifted up in worship of the Highest. Be aware every moment that you are present at the feet of your God. Only in this way, by the reforming of your mind and heart, will your soul become transformed, enabling you to become aware of the Self at every moment. When your soul is established in Unity-awareness, when you experience the bliss that emanates from your own eternal Self, and when you experience the truth that all before your eyes is the glorious play of the One, then your soul will merge in Him, and know its own immortality.

Thus, Shankaracharya ends his lucid and concise directions for the acquisition of Self-Knowledge, known as *Atma-bodha*.

Reflection

Teach me, Lord, to look with love upon Thee and all Thy doings; for Thy love is my only delight and my only good.

Teach me, Lord, to correct my wayward mind whenever it falls from remembrance of Thy goodness and the presence of Thy omnipotent hand in all that occurs here on earth.

Lift me into Thy light, O Lord, for without Thy grace, I am but a burden on the earth.   Teach me to become perfect in wisdom, perfect in knowledge, perfect in contentment, perfect in love.

Let me be Thy instrument, Lord, in spreading Thy perfect joy to Thy children in whatever measure is ordained by Thee.

Father, remove from me all darkness of ignorance, and all self-serving motivations, that I may truly serve as an instrument of Thy truth and Thy grace on earth; and I shall give adoration to Thee in my heart, and sing Thy praise throughout all the days of my life.

*   *   *

THE PHILOSOPHY OF RECOGNITION

The great medieval revitalizer of Vedanta philosophy, Shankaracharya, set forth in very explicit terms
the philosophy of Non-Dualism.   In explaining the
apparent duality between God and the world, he
referred to the world as a product of the creative
Power of God -- His *shakti* or *maya*; and asserted that
the phenomenal world produced by *maya* was "illusory",
or "unreal".   The phenomenal universe, said Shankaracharya, is a "superimposition"(*adhyasa*) upon Brahman.
Let me try to explain what he meant by this:
For the mystic who has experienced in himself
the clear revelation of the nature of Reality, the
world is truly a "superimposition" upon the absolute
Consciousness, very much the way a thought or mental
image is superimposed upon our conscious awareness
when it is produced in our mind.   Consider: a thought
is projected from the conscious mind, is made of
nothing but mind, and at the same time is superimposed upon that conscious mind.   The thought is not
the same thing as the mind; and yet, who would say
they are different?   They are like the ocean and its
waves.   They are different, and yet they are the
same.   It is the same with God and the world; they
are different, and yet they are the same.   One is
the (eternal) substratum, and the other is a transient
manifestation, superimposed upon that substratum.
The expression of this relationship between God and
the world often presents a quandary for those who
have clearly experienced it in "the mystical vision".
From the standpoint of the absolute Unity, there
is, of course, no differentiation; there is only one
undivided Consciousness.   It is only from the standpoint
of the individual soul at the phenomenal level that
'the world' exists at all.   What is seen as 'the world'
is the same Reality that is Brahman; it is just that
it is seen from a limited and isolated perspective.
Shankara called this apparent duality a "superimposition" -- not an unreasonable manner of expressing in
language this paradoxical duality-in-Unity.   However,
his terminology was regarded as unfortunate by many,
as it seemed to imply a *real* duality between God and

the world.   If there is something superimposed, some
reasoned, it is not exactly the same as Brahman.

Shankara, in his many writings, frequently differ-
entiated between God, the eternal Self, and Maya's
product, the world, simply in order to guide the
earnest seeker away from attention to the transient
appearance (the phenomenal world), and toward the
eternal Reality (the Self).   He never intended to
imply, however, that the transient appearance was
anything but Brahman.   Here, let him explain in his
own words:

> Brahman is the Reality, the one Existence.
> Because of the ignorance of our human minds,
> the universe seems to be composed of diverse
> forms; but it is Brahman alone.   ... Apart from
> Brahman, the universe does not exist.   There is
> nothing beside Him.   The universe is superimposed
> upon Him.   It has no separate existence/ apart
> from its Ground.

And again:

> The universe is truly Brahman, for that
> which is superimposed has no separate existence
> from its substratum.   Whatever a deluded person
> perceives through mistake is Brahman and Brahm-
> an alone.   The silver imagined in mother-of-pearl
> is really mother-of-pearl.   The name, "universe",
> is superimposed on Brahman, but what we call
> "the universe" is [really] nothing but Brahman. [1]

Shankara never intended to imply by the use of his
word, "superimposition", that there was something
other than Brahman superimposed on Brahman.   But,
unfortunately, that is what arises in the minds of
some when they hear this word, "superimposition".

Jnaneshvar, the 13th century Maharashtran saint,
objected to the notion of superimposition as an implication of duality, and attempted to clarify the doctrine
of Non-Duality in the following passage from his
Amritanubhav:

> When it is always only the one pure Conscious-
> ness seeing Itself, why postulate the necessity of
> a superimposition?   Does one superimpose the
> sparkle on a gem?   Does gold need to superim-

pose shininess on itself? [2]   A lamp that is lit does not need the superimposition of light; it is resplendent with light.   Likewise, the one pure Consciousness is resplendent with radiance. Therefore, without obligation to anything else, He easily perceives Himself. [3]

... Whatever form appears, appears because of Him.   There is nothing here but the Self. It is the gold itself which shines in the form of a necklace or a coin; they, themselves, are nothing but gold.   In the current of the river or the waves of the sea, there is nothing but water.   Similarly,   in   the   universe,   nothing exists   or   is   brought   into   existence   that   is other than the Self.   Whether appearing as the seen,   or   perceiving   as   the   seer,   nothing   else exists besides the Self. [4]

Perhaps it is impossible to adequately express in words the differentiation between the eternal Consciousness and Its creative Energy without making it appear that they are two separate things.   This would seem to be the case, since every time one mystic gives expression to his vision, another mystic takes exception to the way it is described, and tries his own hand at it, only to have another mystic come along somewhere down the line who takes issue with *his* terminology. In any case, Shankara's writings gave rise to many misunderstandings, and to clear up some of these misunderstanding of terminology, the philosophy of Kashmir Shaivism arose.   Now, as we already know, the word, *Shiva*, had been used since the very earliest recorded history in India to represent God, the absolute Being.   And so, "Shaivism" was no new thing.   But the movement called "Kashmir Shaivism" arose in the northern kingdom of Kashmir in the 9th century with the writings of the sage, Vasugupta, and his disciples.

Legend tells that Vasugupta had a dream in which Lord Shiva told him the whereabouts of a large rock on which Shiva himself had inscribed some teachings in the form of brief aphorisms regarding the nature of God, the soul, and the universe.   These inscriptions were copied from the rock by Vasugupta and later became known as the *Shiva Sutras*. Thus, like many other religious traditions, Kashmir Shaivism claims Divine revelation as its source.   Such revealed scriptures are called *agamas* by those who embrace this tradition. Other *agamas*, besides the *Shiva Sutras*, are the *Malini-vijaya*, the *Vijnana-bhairava*, and the *Rudra-yamala*.

There are also some subsidiary scriptures which explain the *agamas*; these are called *spandas*, or *spanda-karikas*, which formulate doctrine.   Then there are the philosophical works which attempt to present the teachings in a logical and ordered form; these are called the *Pratyabijna shastras*. Some of these are *Shiva-drshti* by Somananda (ca. 875-925 C.E.), *Ishwara-pratyabijna* and *Shivastotravali* by Utpaladeva (ca. 900-950 C.E.), and *Pratyabijnahridayam* by Kshemaraj. This philosophy expressed by Kashmir Shaivism also came to be known as *Pratyabijna Darshana*, "The Philosophy Of Recognition"; and also as *Purna Advaita*, or "Perfect Non-Dualism".

The ultimate Reality, according to Kashmir Shaiv-ism, is *Paramashiva*, "The Supreme Shiva".   This is, of course, synonymous with *Parabrahman*, "The Supreme Brahman", of Vedanta.   Indeed, in all cases, there is no difference whatever between the vision of Vedanta and that of Kashmir Shaivism, except for the differences in terminology.   For example, Vedanta holds that Brahman "projects" the world by His creative Power (*Maya*), and Kashmir Shaivism says that Parama-shiva "appears" as the world through His creative Power (*Shakti*).   Vedanta says the universe is a "super-imposition" upon Brahman; Kashmir Shaivism says the universe is simply Paramashiva appearing as form. There is not the slightest difference between them except for their terminology.   It is commonly found in this world that isolated groups of people tend to regard their way of saying things to be "righter" than the way some other people say it.   The truth is, it is the sage who knows the Truth by experiencing It directly who really knows the truth.

The Kashmiri sages say that Paramashiva is the one Reality; all is taking place within Him.   But He remains unchanged and unmoved by all this multiplicity and apparent change.   He is the (transcendent) Total-ity, and so He remains the same, no matter what. To Him, there is only the pure sky of Consciousness-

Bliss.   He remains awake to His oneness always, while the "creation" comes and goes.   It is breathed out by Him and breathed in again, in an ever-recurring cycle.   It is manifested, and then re-absorbed back into Him.   This emanation is called *abhasa*, a "shining forth".   Then, when it is withdrawn again, that is called *pralaya*.   The complete cycle is a *kalpa* -- which amounts to 4 billion, 320 million years of earth-time.

According to the sages of Kashmir Shaivism, a *kalpa* begins with a *spanda*.   *Spanda* is the first movement of will, the initial flutter or throb of movement in the Divine Will, or *shakti*.   And, as for the question, "Why does He create at all?", the answer given by the Kashmiri Shaivites is the same as that given by the Vedantists: "It is simply His nature to do so." It is His innate nature to breathe forth the universe of multiplicity; and yet, at the same time, it is asserted, He manifests the universe of His own free will, as a play or sport.   In fact, the very first sutra of the *Pratyabijnahridayam* is, "The absolute Consciousness, of Its own free will, is the cause of the manifestation of the universe."

The Pratyabijna philosophers say that, from *spanda*, then comes the bifurcation into *aham* and *idam*, subject and object.   These two aspects of the One are also spoken of as *prakasha* and *vimarsha*.   *Prakasha* is the conscious light, the witness, the "subject" aspect of Paramashiva.   *Vimarsha* is Its power of self-manifestation; i.e., the "object" aspect of Paramashiva. Thus, inherent in the process of manifestation, is this Self-division of Paramashiva into subject and object; from this initial polarity, all other dualities come into being.   And, according to the Kashmir Shaivite philosophy, while there is never anything but Paramashiva, the souls thus created by this Self-division experience a limitation of their originally unlimited powers.   As stated in the *Pratyabijnahridayam* of Kshemaraj, "Consciousness Itself, descending from Its universal state, becomes the limited consciousness of man, through the process of contraction.   Then, because of this contraction, the universal Consciousness becomes an ordinary human being, subject to limitations."

The truth is, of course, the Lord, the one supreme

Consciousness, is never subject to limitations. He lives in absolute freedom. He is all-pervading and all-knowing. By His Power, He can do whatever He likes. And so, in order to become many and play within the multiplicity which is the universe, He sheds His undifferentiated state of Unity and accepts differences. Then, His various powers of will, knowledge and action appear to have shrunk, though this is not really so. This limited state is the state of ordinary people, subject to limitations.

When Shakti manifests as individual conscious entities, the one Consciousness becomes bound by Its own Self-imposed limitations; Its primal powers of omniscience, perfection, everlastingness and all-pervasiveness are then experienced in a reduced condition. Although omniscient, He knows only a few things; though omnipotent, He feels helpless and acts effectively only in a small sphere. The master of perfect Bliss, He is ensnared in pleasure and pain, attachment and aversion. The eternal Being cries aloud from fear of death, regarding Himself as mortal. Pervading all space and form, He grieves because He is tied to a particular place and a particular form. This is the condition of all creatures whose Shakti is reduced, and who are caught in the transmigratory cycle. Again, quoting from the *Pratyabijnahridayam*: "To be a transmigratory being, one needs only to be deluded by one's own Shakti."

It is because Shiva, the Self, has become involved in His own Shakti -- that is, manifested in form, that He finds Himself in the state of "an ordinary being, subject to limitations." But, we must see, it is His sport to do so. Without such an "involution", there could be no evolution. The evolution, or unwinding, of a watch-spring could not occur without there first being an involution of the watch-spring created by the winding of the watch. A log burns, i.e., evolves into energy, only because energy, in the form of sunlight, water, and soil, has become involuted as the log of wood. Evolution is the reverse transmutation of an effect into its cause. Paramashiva, or Chit-Shakti, has "involved" Himself in the form of gross matter, and through the human form, must "evolve" back to Himself.

It is only in the human form that one is able to choose to take the evolutionary path back to the Source, because of the development of mind.   It is the mind that is capable of development toward intelligence, concentration, meditation, and, finally, absorption in pure Consciousness.   This is evolution. It is also known as "Liberation", as it is the freeing of one's Self from identification with the body and the activity of the mind, and thus from rebirth.

Liberation, or *moksha*, is freedom from the vicious circle of births and deaths which from eternity are whirling a soul around.   In fact, life is not worthy of the name, "life", as it is really no more than a series of limitations, the very nature of which pinches the soul and makes it hanker after something real, something permanent, beyond the pale of sensual pleasures and pains, something not clouded with the gloomy, lusty, desires, which are never quenched and are never satiable.   Real "life" is that for which the soul yearns with an incessant longing, though not knowing where and how it is to be had.   Still, it feels its existence with some inborn conviction as a tangible reality.   Everyone yearns for it, because life, eternal life, is the soul's very nature.

The astute student will recognize the afore-mentioned doctrines of Kashmir Shaivism as quite consistent with the precepts of Vedanta.   The ultimate goal of the "bound" soul is the knowledge of the Self, which constitutes "liberation" from the wheel of transmigration.   This is the teaching of both Vedanta and Kashmir Shaivism, revealing once again their undeviatingly common perspective.   But, of course, it is only natural that all philosophies stemming from real "mystical" experience will find agreement in nearly all their conceptual elements.   Listen, for example, to what is said in the *Ishvara Pratyabijna-vimarshini* of   Abhinavagupta (ca. 950-1000 C.E.):

> The knowledge of the identity of the soul (*jiva*) and God (*Shiva*), which has been proclaimed in the scriptures, constitutes liberation; lack of this knowledge constitutes bondage.

In other words, it is ignorance of our true nature that binds us, and nothing else.   In fact, it is clear that we have never been really bound.   This is brought out in the *Tripura rahasya*, attributed   to   Dattatreya, which states:

> Though, in reality, there is no bondage, the individual is in bondage as long as there exists the feeling of limitation in him.   ... In fact, there has never been any veiling or covering anywhere in Reality.   No one has ever been in bondage.   Please show me where such a bondage could be.   Besides these two false beliefs -- that there is such a thing as bondage, and that there is such as thing as mind -- there is no bondage for anyone anywhere.

Both Vedanta and Kashmir Shaivism recognize the possibility of *jivanmukta*, liberation from the wheel of transmigration while still living in the body.   However, it is not merely the mystical experience of Unity which constitutes this self-liberation; one must also assimilate the knowledge thus acquired into one's everyday consciousness, and make the knowledge of the Self an ever-present awareness.   Here is the statement of this ultimate liberation from the *Pratya-bijnahridayam*:

> Final realization is possible only when the complete nature of the Self is realized.   Though there might be release after death, there can be no release in life unless the universal Self is grasped through the intellect.   Indeed, the equanimity in the experience of worldly enjoyment and in the experience of Unity is what truly constitutes the liberation of the soul, while living.   ... The individual who identifies with the Self, and regards the universe to be a sport and is always united with it, is undoubtedly liberated in life.

And this is reiterated in the *Spanda-karika*:

> This entire universe is a sport of universal Consciousness.   He who is constantly aware of this truth is liberated in this life, without doubt.

Reflection

Liberty is loved by everyone. It is our natural birthright, our very nature. Liberty is freedom -- not only the freedom from coercion which we call political or social freedom, but a deeper, more fundamental kind of freedom, which we call spiritual liberty. It is a freedom from the tyranny of ignorance, from the tyranny of the restless mind, from the false ego. It is this ego, this false sense of who we are, which fuels the restless mind, and tyrannically oppresses us with ignorance and untruth. It is the source of all worry, all unrest, all bondage.

Let us then cast off this ego, this self-pitying, self-asserting, bundle of erroneous assumptions which burden and bind us like a heavy weight. Let us be free -- with a mind clear and pure, like the morning air. Freedom is quietude, a mind free of burdens, free of thoughts. Freedom is peace, the calm and quiet rest of the heart and mind in the silent perfect light of pure Being.

Let us, then, be free in God, free in Spirit; and all our lives will be as a carefree song of joy on the lips of God.

*   *   *

THE PHILOSOPHY OF RECOGNITION
PART II

Sadhana is the period of one's spiritual journey, in search of the Self. And the *sadhana* of Kashmir Shaivism is the same as the *sadhana* of Vedanta: it consists of self-effort and grace. Self-effort is in the form of learning about the Self, contemplating the knowledge gained and meditating on the Self. It is a self-effort toward Consciousness; but Self-realization comes of grace. There is nothing to be done to receive it, but to be true to the Self, to give our hearts to the communion with God within. In this way, we prepare ourselves for grace.

Every great spiritual teacher, including Jesus, taught that one realizes God through His grace alone. This may be verified in the Christian scriptures; for example, when Jesus was asked by some of his disciples, "Who, then, can enter the kingdom of God? (in other words, 'Who can realize the Self?')", Jesus replied, "For man it is impossible; but for God all things are possible." [1] He was saying, in other words, 'Don't ask me how to know God. It can't be done by you or me or anyone! It is God Himself who makes Himself known. Only He has the power to reveal Himself. What we can do is to open our hearts and minds, our souls, to receive the light of His grace; and this alone is the skill, the art, if you will, that we must acquire. The giving of His gifts is entirely in His hands. If anyone can dispute this of his own experience, and has the power to experience the Self at his own whim and convenience, I have yet to hear of such a person.'

The philosophers and sages of Kashmir Shaivism hold exactly this same view; furthermore, they hold that this grace is absolutely undetermined and unconditioned. As it is stated in the *Tantraloka* of Abhinavagupta: "Divine Grace leads the individual to the path of spiritual realization. It is the only cause of Self-realization, and is independent of human effort." If it were dependent upon some conditions, it would not be absolute and independent grace.

Grace is the uncaused Cause of the soul's release. What appears at first glance to be a condition of grace, is, in reality, a consequence of it. For example, devotion, which may seem to bring grace, is, in fact, the result or gift of grace. In the Kashmir Shaivite tradition, the Absolute is said to carry on the sport of self-bondage and self-release of His own free will; and the postulation of conditions or qualifications would be against that doctrine of free-will. This position is made clear in the *Malini Vijaya-vartika:*

> The learned men of all times always hold that the descent of grace does not have any cause or condition, but depends entirely on the free will of the Lord.

And again in the *Paramartha Sara:*

> Throughout all these forms, it is the Lord who illumines His own nature. In reality, there is no other cause of these manifestations except His freedom, which alone gives rise to both worldly enjoyment and Self-realization.

Here, the question may arise that if Divine grace has no regard for the merit and demerit of the recipients, does it not amount to an act of partiality on the part of God? How is it that He favors some individuals by bestowing His grace and disfavors others by keeping it away from them? And the answer is that grace is operative all the time on all individuals. The difference in the descent of grace is really the differences in the receptivity of the individual souls, each of whom evolves at his own unique pace. Moreover, this problem does not have much significance in the Non-Dualistic philosophies of Vedanta and Kashmir Shaivism; because it is the Absolute Himself who appears first as bound, and then as liberated, owing to His own free will. He cannot be accused of partiality, since it is only Himself whom He favors or rejects.

As for self-effort, this is accomplished by our inherent power of will. Shakti, the Divine power of will, exists in us in a limited form. This will, which we possess, is the faculty by which a person decides upon and initiates action. Fickleness of mind flutters and weakens the will-power; and conversely, a strong

desire and one-pointed longing strengthens it.   But
too many desires and hankerings after many objects,
and aimless running about in pursuit of sense-pleasures
dissipates the creative energy, the will-power.   As
one clear-minded sage said, "A definite purpose of
action, backed by a strong will, is a sure way to
success in any endeavor.   Therefore, minimize your
desires, make a deliberate choice, and focus the whole
energy of your will-power in that particular direction,
and you will never miss your goal."

The will of a person may be made to flow in two
different, and opposite, directions: outwardly, toward
secular goals, or inwardly, toward spiritual goals.   If
one wishes to concentrate one's energy toward spiritual
goals, then the creative energy, the will, must be
diverted from its normal outward-flowing course; by
closing all such outlets in the form of objective desires,
one at last attains the state of desirelessness.   Then,
it is possible to turn the mind inwardly to the Self,
and attain spiritual knowledge.

It is desires for worldly objectives that distract
one from the attainment of spiritual objectives.   But,
for one who is established in the pursuit of spiritual
goals, worldly gains have little charm, and the necessary
duties one must perform in the world take on a spiritual significance.   To such a person, every act on the
worldly plane is a service to the Lord, in the fulfillment of His will, and a stepping-stone for the upward
progress toward spiritual enlightenment.

Therefore, when the objective, or outward, trend
of the will is checked, and is given a turn in the
opposite direction, the 'involved' Shakti begins its
evolutionary journey; and, instead of experiencing a
poverty of Shakti, a person begins to expand his or
her powers, and to feel greater abilities and an expanded sense of well-being and completeness.   Turning in
the direction of its source, the mind begins to sense
its identity with the Self, the pure and all-perfect
Consciousness of the universe.   This is the beginning
of the evolution from the human to the Divine.

Now, if it were an easy thing to revert the flow
of the will from worldly to spiritual objectives, everyone would be able to manage it.   But it is not easy.
The mind is totally deluded by the amazing and wonder-

ful appearance spread out before it; and, unaware that it is all its own projection, it reaches out eagerly for satisfaction and pleasure from the ephemeral and empty mirage.   Intellectually acquired knowledge helps us to recognize the mirage for what it is -- but still, old habits must be overcome.   And that is not an easy task.   To subdue the habits of nature, instilled by long practice and conviction, to subdue the old outgoing tendencies of the mind, requires great effort.   This is known as *tapasya*.

To understand what *tapasya* is, we must understand that it is *Shakti, the Divine Energy*, that manifests as our minds and bodies and their various activities. And, frequently, we expend that Energy in thoughtless and frivolous ways, and thus remain listless and groggy through much of our lives.   But, if we could learn to conserve our natural *Shakti*, then we could reap the benefits in the form of greater physical and mental energy, and a clearer awareness of the blissful Self, our eternal Identity.   *Tapasya*, which literally means "making heat", is the restraint of the outgoing tendency of the mind and senses, which conserves and heats the Shakti.   The Shakti, turned inward, then begins to nourish and invigorate the brain and the whole body, expanding one's natural powers as well as one's consciousness.

Here are some of the traditional methods of *tapasya* which conserves and evolves the Shakti toward its source, Shiva (the Self):

(1) *Mantra repetition:* This conserves the Shakti by subduing the wandering mind and the prana, and focusing the attention upon God within.

(2) *Devotional singing:* This heats the Shakti through emotion, and elevates the awareness to God.

(3) *Concentration of the mind:* By deep thought, attention, study, or meditation, the Shakti is concentrated and focused, and the mind becomes subtle and clear.

(4) *Surrender of the fruits of actions:* This relieves the mind of futile exertions, conserving the Shakti and retaining the steadiness of the mind.

(5) *Eating properly, moderately and regularly:* It is the Shakti which is the central regulator of the mind and body; it preserves the heat and cold of the body,

and distributes the effects of various foods and drinks to the different parts of the body through the nerve currents.   The Shakti absorbs within seconds the cold in cooling foods, and one becomes sleepy and lethargic; it absorbs the heat of heat-producing foods and drinks, and makes the body and mind restless.   The choice of a proper, moderate, and regular diet is therefore most important.

(6) *Continence:* When the Shakti has been given an evolutionary turn, and begins to flow inward and upward instead of outward through the senses, there is an accumulation of heat in the region near the base of the spine.   It is there the Shakti gathers and creates the heat which causes it to rise.   Much of that heat is transferred to the sexual glands, causing an increase in stimulation there.   If one allows that energy to be expended frivolously in sexual indulgence, one loses a great portion of one's Shakti.   But if it is conserved, it rises, and is absorbed into the body, resulting in greater bodily vigor and lustre, as well as greater mental power.   This is a practice recommended for *brahmacharis* or *sannyasins* (monks). Householders, of course, are exempt from this kind of *tapasya.* For married people, normal moderation is best.

(7) *Longing for liberation:* Most important, for conserving and increasing the Shakti, is a strong aspiration toward, and longing for, liberation from ignorance.   Such aspiration will draw the grace of God, and will focus the energy upward toward the seat of Consciousness, and will be a strong protector against inertia and dullness.

According to the philosophy of Kashmir Shaivism, there are three different levels of spiritual practice; these levels, or methods (*upayas*), are: *anava upaya*, which takes place on the physical and sensual level; *shakta upaya*, which is mental in nature; and *shambhava upaya,* which engages the will and the intuition.   As I have dealt with these *upayas*, or methods, in detail in the following chapter, "The Physical, The Mental, And The Spiritual", I will pass over the subject of the *upayas* for now.   But I would like to make mention of a meditative practice which is described in the *Pratyabijnahridayam* as a practice suitable for everyone:

It is called the meditation on the *pancha-krtya*, the "five acts", of Shiva -- the Self.   These five-fold acts are: manifesting, sustaining, destroying, concealing, and revealing.   These are the cosmic functions of Shiva; but, even after becoming limited as an individual soul, Shiva continues to perform these five acts, or functions, albeit on a lesser scale.

The nature of the Self, even in the state of bondage, is Consciousness; and so, through our limited consciousness, we, who are really the Self, continue to perform these five functions -- in our own limited way.   When, within our own limited consciousness, a thought is formed, that is the act of creative *manifestation*.   As we continue to dwell on that thought or fantasy, that is -- in a limited way -- God's power of *sustenance* at work.   *Destruction* is the vanishing of an object into the mind after having appeared there, as when one object is replaced in consciousness by another.   *Concealment* occurs as the Self is concealed in the process of manifesting the manifold thought-waves that arise in the conscious mind.   *Revelation* is the recognition that eventually dawns that the diverse thought-forms arise from the one undifferentiated Light of Consciousness, one's Self.   This is known as Self-realization.

So, it becomes clear that, just as Shiva, the supreme Consciousness, creates, sustains, and destroys the world by His power (*shakti*), the individual soul is also continually performing these same functions -- only in a limited way.   Creation, sustenance, destruction, concealment, and grace are constantly going on, both on the cosmic level and on the individual level.   As it is said in the *Pratyabijnahridayam*,

> When one acquires full knowledge of this five-fold process within oneself, he regains his status of pure Consciousness.   By reasserting one's inherent powers, one recognizes the universe as one's own.   When the bliss of Consciousness is attained, there is the lasting acquisition of that state in which Consciousness is our only Self, and in which things that appear are identical with Consciousness.   Even the body is experienced as identical with Consciousness.

According to the Kashmir Shaivite philosophy, a
true yogi will be conscious of these five processes
going on within.   He will see the creation of thoughts
as the playful sport of *Chit-Shakti*.   In this way, one
is able to become aware of his Divine Identity.   He
sees the entire universe as the expansion of the Self.
He contemplates the activity of these five processes
going on within himself, and becomes intoxicated,
identifying with Shiva.   He sits calmly and watches
the play of his creative effulgence -- but he does
not make the mistake of identifying with these productions; he is aware of himself as eternal Bliss,
unsullied Consciousness, infinite Being.   The creation
and dissolution of countless worlds is his marvellous
play.

'Therefore', say the seers of the Self, 'recognize
who you are!   Clear away the cobwebs of lethargy;
open your eyes to the Reality before you.   You are
the Self of the universe!   All this is but the infinite
variety of your own effulgence.   Let your mind become
still; become aware of your greatness.   Taste the
nectar of your perfect and unending Bliss.'

Reflection

Awake, O mind!   Do you not know who you are?
The time for dreaming is past.   The Sun of Knowledge
is rising, and the light of day is expanding through
the morning air.   See!   This light that fills the world
is you!   Awake, O mind, and know!

Awake!   Turn up the wick of your inner lamp;
clear away the webs of sleep, and see!   More light!
More light!   Nothing else but light.   The inner sky is
clear, an ocean of blue light.   The clouds are gone;
and you alone spread out your light of love to fill all
space.   Open your eyes and see, O mind!   This life
that sweetly sings, this glorious show of shows, this
silent Source and Center of light, is you.   Awake, O
mind, and see!

*   *   *

THE PHYSICAL, THE MENTAL,
AND THE SPIRITUAL

The 19th century God-realized saint, Sri Ramakrishna, frequently emphasized the fact that it was God's grace by which we are able to know God, but he also stressed that it is our responsibility to get His attention. A baby does not get picked up and nursed by its mother until the mother bestows her grace and actually picks up the child; but the child has to make a racket first. He cries, and wails, and screams, and sounds like he's dying -- then the mother says, "Poor baby, what's the matter?" And she picks up the child. So we, likewise, must get the attention of the Self, of God, if we are to receive His grace. Our efforts must pass from the gross level to the subtler levels; that is how we reach to God, for He is at the ultimate level of subtlety.

We exist on three levels: let's call them "the physical", "the mental", and "the spiritual". Our activities in pursuit of the Self take place on each of these progressively subtle levels, and become increasingly effective as we reach to increasingly subtle levels of activity. Recall, in this connection, how Rama in the *Ramayana*, asked his monkey-servant, Hanuman, "How do you regard me?" And Hanuman replied, "When I regard myself as the body, I'm your servant; when I regard myself as the mind, I'm a part of you; and when I regard myself as the spirit, the Self, you and I are one." Note how Hanuman's realization became more subtle and closer to the absolute Truth as he went from identification with the physical body to the mind, and from the mind to the spirit.

All our efforts to know God manifest on one or another of these levels of reality. At the grossest level, we perform physical acts: acts of service, ritual worship, Hatha yoga postures, the sounding of mantras, etc. These are necessary and beneficial practices, but they are at the gross physical level only; we must go deeper toward the subtle if we are to reach God. At this level, we identify with the body; we regard ourselves as the servant of God, as His instrument.

The next level of activity is the mental. Here, we perform many practices: we study the scriptures and other writings of the realized saints; we do mental worship, such as prayer, or the mental repetition of the name of God; we continually attempt to refine our understanding, and remind ourselves inwardly of the Truth. And here, at this stage where we identify with the mind, we come to regard ourselves as a spark or a ray from the one Sun which manifests and illumines the world. All is seen as God, and we are a part of Him.

Then, on the spiritual level, the activity is very subtle; we may also call it the level of consciousness. It is simply the constant alertness to reject any obscuration of conscious awareness. It is the jealous guarding of the pure Consciousness that is the witness, the Self. At that level, there is no duality of I and Thou, mine and Thine; there is only 'I AM'. Notice that each one of these levels of activity leads to the next, subtler, level. For example, when you do physical acts of service, or worship, this brings with it the mental level of service or worship, as our concentration deepens. Or, if we repeat the name of God on the physical level, such as when we chant aloud, that physical repetition brings with it, by sympathetic resonance, the mental awareness of the name, and we find that we're repeating the mantra on the mental level as well. The idea, of course, is for our worship, our prayer, our meditation, to reach to deeper and deeper levels of subtlety, becoming a transforming force to re-create us at the spiritual level.

Practice at the mental level is superior, of course, to mere physical action, because it is by the transformation of our minds that we truly become transformed into Divine beings. As Krishna said to Arjuna in the *Bhagavad Gita*, "The Self is realized by the purified mind!" This is also what Jesus taught when he asked his disciples to be transformed by the renewal of their minds. Also, we have seen what great emphasis is placed on the mental practice of Self-knowledge by the great Shankaracharya, who said, "The practice of knowledge thoroughly purifies the ignorance-stained mind, and then that [intellectual] knowledge itself disappears, just as a grain of salt disappears in water."

This analogy can be easily understood by one whose concentration on the knowledge, "I am pure Consciousness," leads the mind, through concentrated effort toward understanding, eventually to perfect mental quietude -- and thus to the experience of pure Consciousness. Through one-pointed concentration on this one thought, "I am not merely this body, this mind; I am the Absolute; I am pure Consciousness," one goes beyond thought and attains the thought-free state. It is in this way that the mental practice leads to the subtler level of spiritual practice. The story of king Janaka and Ashtavakra is a good illustration of this:

King Janaka was sitting one day on the river-bank, repeating his mantra aloud. In a loud, powerful voice, he repeated over and over, "I am That! I am That!" Then, along came his guru, Ashtavakra, who sat on the opposite bank. Observing that king Janaka was involved in the physical practice of mantra-repetition, with maybe a touch of mental practice thrown in, Ashtavakra decided to elevate king Janaka's practice. So he began to shout aloud, "This is my water bowl; this is my staff!" As he did so, he alternately lifted each of the items mentioned. Soon the king's mantra-repetition was disturbed and he quickly became annoyed. Finally, he could take it no more, and he shouted across to Ashtavakra, "Hey, why all this racket? Who says those things are *not* yours!" And Ashtavakra shot back, "And who says you are *not* That!" Immediately king Janaka's mind ceased its activity and became absorbed in the silent awareness that he *was* That, was the Self, and didn't need to go on engaging his mind or his lips in repeatedly asserting it. In other words, by the grace of his guru, his mental practice merged into spiritual practice.

This last, and subtlest practice, is that which Hanuman spoke of when he expressed the fact that he and God were one, without distinction or separation, when he was aware of his universal Self. Such a practice does not call into play either the body or the mind, but rather what we would call simply, 'the will'. It is the practice of keeping a willful check

on the impulses of the mind, and a willful retention
of pure awareness, with a sense of identification
with the one all-pervasive Consciousness. It is, in
other words, a direct awareness of the Self by an
effort of will. In its highest stage, this subtle practice, which we have called, "spiritual", becomes no
practice at all. It simply remains spontaneously,
habitually. It is the state of consciousness which the
Zen Buddhists call the state of "No-mind", and which
Vedantists refer to as *sahaj samadhi*, "the natural state
of unity".

To explain how one level of practice leads to a
subtler level, let's take, as an example, the practice
of mantra repetition. You may begin by just repeating
it on the physical level. And, even on this level, the
sound-vibrations have a certain effect on you, instilling
peace and a sense of well-being. Then, you begin to
reflect on its meaning. Now, it is no longer just a
sound; it's a meaningful thought: *So-ham*, "I am
That!" That's mental practice. You repeat the
mantra on the mental level with an awareness of its
meaning. Then, as you begin to sense the reality of
it, as you begin to experience it, you transcend the
mantra, and hold yourself poised in the thought-free
state. That's the spiritual level of practice. When,
eventually, this awareness becomes natural and spontaneous, one transcends all practice, and becomes
established in the awareness of the Self.

Now, to make all this really clear, I'm going to
give you some sample practices from each of these
three levels. And, to do that, I'm going to use an
ancient scripture from the tradition of Kashmir Shaivism, called the *Vijnana Bhairava*. "Bhairava" is another
name for Shiva, the Lord, the Self. And "Vijnana"
means supreme awareness, or knowledge. This book

is a manual of how to experience the Lord, to attain
to the highest awareness or knowledge. And it takes
the form of a dialogue between Shiva and his consort,
Shakti.

In this imaginary dialogue, Shakti asks Shiva to
explain His true nature and the practices by which
He can be known; and Shiva then details 112 different
practices, utilizing those from each of the three
levels we've discussed. First, we'll hear of some of

the physical practices, some of which have to do with the breath, the prana, or the visualizing of inner lights and sounds. Listen to some of the practices Shiva recommends to Shakti. You might like to try them out as I mention them to you:

> The breath is exhaled with the sound, *Ham*, and inhaled with the sound, *Sah*. Thus, the individual soul always recites the mantra, *Hamsah* (or *So-ham*, "I am That!").[1]

> *Prana* (inhalation) goes upward, and the *apana* (exhalation) goes downward. This is the expression of the creative Shakti. By becoming aware of the two places where each originates, experience absolute fulfillment.[2]

> There is a momentary pause, when the out-going breath has gone out, and there is a momentary pause when the ingoing breath has gone in. Fix your mind steadily on these places of pause, and experience Shiva.[3]

> Always fix your mind on those places where the breath pauses, and the mind will quickly cease its fluctuations, and you will acquire a wonderful state.[4]

(*Note*: In the *Bhagavad Gita* (4:29), Krishna says, "Some yogis, devoted to *pranayama*, offer as sacrifice the outgoing breath into the incoming breath, and the incoming into the outgoing, restraining the course of both." It is this very practice that is being spoken of here in the *Vijnana Bhairava*, which goes on to say:

> When the in-breath merges with the outgoing breath, they become perfectly balanced and cease to flow. Experience that state and realize equality.[5]

> Let the breath remain balanced, and let all thoughts cease; then experience the state of Shiva.[6]

That's enough practices on the physical level; let's move on to the mental practices. Here, we enter into the realm of ideas. These practices deal entirely

with formulated intellectual knowledge.   Shiva says
to Shakti:

> Concentrate your mind on whatever gives
> you satisfaction.   Then experience the true
> nature of supreme satisfaction.[7]

> Meditate on yourself as a vast, cloudless
> sky, and realize your true nature as Conscious-
> ness. [8]

> Becoming detached from the awareness of
> the body, meditate on the thought, "I am every-
> where!" and thus experience joy. [9]

> Hold this thought in your mind: "All the
> waves of the various forms in this universe have
> arisen from me -- just as waves arise from
> water, flames arise from fire, or rays from the
> Sun. [10]

> Contemplate with an unwavering mind that
> your own body and the whole universe are of
> the nature of Consciousness, and experience the
> great awakening.[11]

> Contemplate your body and the whole universe
> as permeated with Bliss.   Then experience
> yourself as that Bliss.[12]

Okay.   Now we come to the spiritual practices;
these are at a subtler level of consciousness.   Here,
you don't have to think at all.   You need only to
become aware, focusing on that clear, thought-free
awareness that is your Self.   Shiva says:

> Observe the arising of a desire.   Then immed-
> iately put an end to it by reabsorbing it into
> That from which it arose.[13]

> What are you when a thought or desire does
> *not* arise?   Truly, the one Reality!   Become
> absorbed in and identified with That.[14]

> When a thought or desire arises, detach
> yourself from the object of thought or desire,
> and witness the thought or desire as a manifest-
> ation of your Self, and thus realize the Truth.[15]

The same conscious Self is manifest in all forms; there is no differentiation in It. Realize everything as the same one, and rise triumphantly above the appearance of multiplicity.[16]

When under a strong impulse of desire, or anger, greed, infatuation, pride, or envy, make your mind steady and become aware of the Reality underlying the mental state.[17]

Perceive the entire universe as a magic-show, or as forms painted on a canvas, or as so many leaves on a single tree; and becoming absorbed in this, experience great happiness.[18]

Leaving aside your own body for the time being, contemplate your Self as the consciousness pervading other bodies, and thus become all-pervasive.[19]

Free the mind of all supports, without and within, and let no thought-vibration take form. Then the self becomes the supreme Self, Shiva.[20]

At the onset or culmination of a sneeze, or at the moment of fright, or deep sorrow, or at the moment of a sigh, or while running for your life, or during intense facination, or extreme hunger, become aware of Brahman.[21]

What cannot be objectively known, what cannot be held in the mind, that which is empty, and exists even in non-existence: contemplate That as your Self, and thus attain realization of Shiva.[22]

Meditate on yourself as eternal, all-pervasive, the independent Lord of all; and thus attain That.[23]

About the ultimate state, beyond all practice, there is really nothing one can say. It is the pathless path, beyond both the mental and verbal levels. This is what Jnaneshvar, the 13th century yogi, says in his *Amritanubhav* about such an advanced soul:

One who has attained this wisdom may say whatever he likes; the silence of his contempla-

tion remains undisturbed.   His state of action-
lessness remains unaffected, even though he
performs countless actions.   Whether he walks
in the streets or remains sitting quietly, he is
always in his own home.   His rule of conduct
is his own sweet will.   His meditation is whatever he happens to be doing.[24]

Such a knower of the Self lives in perfect freedom.

You too, by utilizing all these levels of practice --
the physical, the mental, and the spiritual -- can
attain to that state.   As you meditate, just sit quietly;
let the mind be still and become aware of the Self.
If you can't do that immediately, then take the help
of the mantra, the name of God, the name of the
Self.   Reflect on its meaning.   Identify with that
One.   And if you cannot do that, at least practice on
the physical level: repeat the mantra with the in-breath,
and again with the out-breath.   Let it carry you to
the awareness that you and your beloved God are one.

Reflection

Father, I turn to Thee, who art the Fountain from
which I sprang, the Ocean on which I, wave-like, rise.
Thou art the Source of all my thoughts; in Thee each
word or subtlest motion spreads its waves, as ripples
spread on the surface of a lake.   Thou art the lake
of Consciousness, the ripples, and the Source of all
motion.   Father, even the thought of Thee is Thyself!
The thinker, thought, and object of thought -- all are
Thee!   How may I imagine that I could ever be apart
from Thee and lost, who am Thy very Self -- as a
wave on the ocean is nothing but ocean!   Even such
an imagination is a ripple of Spirit upon Spirit; even
this 'I' that calls to 'Thee' is but an imaginary separation.

Whither shall I flee from Thy Spirit?   How shall
what is Thine be separate from Thyself?   There is no
place in all the vastness of the universe or beyond
where I might be apart from Thee; for Thou art the
One, the all-inclusive Reality, to which there is no
beyond, no 'other'.   O wondrous joy that I am Thee
and Thou art me, and we are one, inseparable, and

infinite Bliss forever and forever!   O may Thy grace and glory shine in this, Thy fragile, momentary form; and may Thy light illumine all the subtle ways of my mind, and make me to know the Truth!

VEDANTA AND BUDDHISM

One meets with a great objection from the so-called "learned" community when one tries to explain that there are not many religions, but that "religion" is one thing taught by many different teachers. The pretenders to learning say, "That's a very naive view of the world's religions; Presbyterians are not the same as Catholics, nor are Christian Scientists the same as Mormons or Jehovah's Witnesses -- not to mention the vast differences between Christians and Hindus, Moslems and Jews, Buddhists and Confucianists, for example. How can you possibly say that all religion is one?"

In order to answer this, we must first explain what is meant by the word, "religion". It is from the Latin root, *religare*, which means to re-tie or re-unite. We find the same meaning in the word, "yoga"; it is from the Sanskrit root, *yuj*, which gives us the English word, "yoke", as in "Yoke the oxen to the cart." It means to connect or unite. And both of these words, "religion" and "yoga" mean to re-unite our minds, our awareness, our souls, to our Source, to the universal Being who is our true and lasting Self.

Now, what Jesus of Nazareth taught was certainly "religion" in this true sense of the word. But, whether Presbyterians or Baptists, Mormons or Catholics teach "religion" in this same sense of the word, depends, I think, on the understanding of the individuals who practice these "religions". You see, we have come to use this word in such a way that it can be pluralized as "religions", just as the word, "yoga", is often used to speak of various paths, or "yogas", such as "karma yoga", "bhakti yoga", etc. We've corrupted the meaning to the extent that our Western culture finds it difficult to define "religion". The dictionary definition states that it is "a *belief* in" a Divine or superhuman being. This allows just about any kind of nonsense to be subsumed under the label, "religion".

Well, for our purposes, let us understand by the word, "religion", 'the attempt to reunite one's mind with the Source of all minds.' We have already

determined that Jesus taught "religion" in this sense.
What, then, of the teacher who became known as
'the Buddha'? Did he teach "religion" in this same
sense Yet, he did. Do not believe those sectarian
religionists and "learned" people who say that Buddhism
is simply an atheistic, intellectual philosophy, similar
to Existentialism. The Buddha did not invent a new
"religion"; he merely re-discovered the eternal religion
known in Sanskrit as the *sanatana dharma*, which had
been established on the earth long prior to his time.

Like Jesus, the Buddha came to fulfill the ancient
teachings, not to destroy them. The Upanishadic
tradition of re-uniting with the Divine Self had been
very much alive previous to the Buddha; he only
re-confirmed it in his own experience and re-affirmed
it in his teachings. His experience -- and this is
the crux of the matter -- his expeience of the eternal
Truth was not different from the experience of the
eternal Truth known by the Upanishadic rishis. Is
there more than one Unity to be experienced? Are
there many different eternal Truths out there?
What fools people are to think that the realization
of Jesus or of the Upanishadic sages was different
from that of the Buddha! But, of course, such people
do not even accept the fact that Truth can actually
be "seen", "experienced", for oneself; they believe
that each of the various religious teachers throughout
history only devised in his own mind a separate truth
in which he or she strongly believed. Or else they
imagine that their representative was designated by
God as the "authentic" representative of truth, and
all others are phonies -- but this is politics, not
religion.

Those who do not understand that the eternal
Truth is, and has always been, experiential, naturally
have no basis from which to recognize what true
"religion" is; they imagine either that it is a mere
intellectual formulation of theological and moral
principles, or they imagine that it is a racially inherited favorite-nation status, or that it is something
like a family business, in which God, the father, sent
his son as an emissary to set up a franchise on
earth. Those who believe such absurdities usually
claim exclusive rights to the truth; "Ours is the true

and only religion!" they cry. And with their claims, they set up fences, which, while intended to exclude all others, only serve to isolate themselves from the commonwealth of man.

Those who do not understand the nature of enlightenment are those most often heard to exclaim that the Buddha taught something quite different from what Jesus taught. Such people do not understand what either of these men taught. Can the enlightenment of the Buddha be different from the entrance into the kingdom of God of which Jesus spoke? They are not different. God's kingdom is the place where the flimsy ego is dissolved, and the soul awakes to its true nature as unending Bliss. It realizes, "I am none else but the one Divine Consciousness from which all this universe is projected; I and the Father are one." That is the kingdom of God. And that is also the experience of enlightenment. "Buddha" means "the awakened"; it is the eternal Truth, the unchanging Identity, to which he awakened; and it is that direct experience of Truth which constituted his awakeness, his "Buddhahood".

As illustration of this, listen to what the Buddha said regarding that eternal Identity beyond birth and death, beyond what is created or what exists as a compound of elements:

> There is, monks, an Unborn, an Unevolved, Uncreated, Uncompounded. If, monks, there were not this Unborn, Unevolved, Uncreated, Uncompounded, there would not be any escape here from the born, the evolved, the created, the compounded. But, because there is an Unborn, an Unevolved, Uncreated, Uncompounded, therefore, there is an escape from the born, the evolved, the created, the compounded.[1]

The "Unborn", etc., is that same eternal One whom the sages of the Upanishads called, "Brahman" or "Purusha" or "the supreme Self". It is this unnameable One which the Upanishadic sages experienced, and it is this same One which the Buddha experienced in his solitary contemplation. The *experience* of Unity, the *experience* of the eternal Consciousness of the universe, is the basis of all that the Buddha taught.

In the attempt to convey something of his own experience to his fellow monks, he said to them:

> There is, O monks, a condition where there is neither this world nor any other world, nor is there any Sun or moon. There is neither a coming nor going, nor remaining, nor passing away, nor arising. Without support, without movement, It is the Foundation of everything. It is hard to see That which is selfless; it is not easy to perceive the Truth. Only one who has put an end to craving, who no longer clings to anything [in this world], is able to see [the Truth]. [2]

The Buddha had "seen" It; and he knew that others before him had seen It. But the seers of Truth have always been few; and the ignorance of the many always holds sway as the popular view. Siddhartha, the Buddha, had been born into a time when the esoteric understanding of the mystics, the seers, had been almost entirely subverted by the priests of the brahmin caste, who promulgated an interpretation of the ancient Vedic teachings based on their own ignorance of enlightenment. They had corrupted true religion into a superstition of primitive ritual, in which they, themselves, took the position of intercessors between God and His devotees, pandering to the fears and worldly desires of the people.

We see the same thing throughout history and today as well. The vast majority of "religious" men and women know nothing of the true meaning of religion. Their highest aspiration is "faith", not knowledge; and their greatest hope is that they can enjoy prosperity and happiness with their children and grandchildren here in this earthly realm. This is certainly not an ignoble attitude; it is just that it doesn't go deeply enough toward our true potential. It is superficial and doesn't really advance us toward the realization of our true and lasting Bliss. Indeed, a strong attachment to such superficial and transcient aims can be a great obstacle to the attainment of Truth.

Because the corruption of religion was so prevalent in his time, the Buddha felt that perhaps it was necessary to explain his experience of the Truth in a way that would leave little opportunity for the corruption of his message.   He knew that others had spoken before him of the mystical experience of the eternal Truth; the Upanishads were replete with such descriptions and declarations.   And yet the people ignored such high things, and followed what they could understand: the propitiation of gods through ritualized worship and offerings of sacrifice.   The Buddha wished to turn men toward the Eternal within themselves; not to foster more idolatry and dependence upon some "god" without.   He knew that it was the revealed knowledge of the Eternal within that constituted man's ultimate good, his ultimate freedom.

And so, the Buddha didn't speak of "God"; he didn't speak of "Shiva", or of "Brahman", or even of the "Atman".   He spoke of the *experience* of the Eternal, which he called, *nirvana* -- the extinction of the false ego.   He didn't attempt to formulate a systematic metaphysics; he saw that such intellectual learning had failed in the past to lead the people out of superstition and self-delusion.   Rather, he taught what he called "the Four Noble Truths": (1) That everything that is born and dies must experience suffering; (2) That there is a cause for this suffering (i.e., *kama*, desire, which leads to rebirth); (3) That there is a release from suffering (i.e., the mystical experience called, *nirvana*); (4) That there is a means, or methodology, by which to attain release from suffering; and this means or method he subdivided into what he called, "the eight-fold path".   These are:

1. Right understanding
2. Right aims
3. Right speech
4. Right behavior
5. Right livelihood
6. Right efforts
7. Right thinking
8. Right concentration

After the Buddha attained enlightenment, he taught what he had come to know to his fellow *sadhus*, or truth-seekers, with whom he had wandered during his own search for Truth.   One of the earliest and best known Sermons which he gave was the Sermon at the Deer Park, from atop a hill, as Jesus

would do five-hundred years later. This is what he
said in that Sermon:

> Whatever is born must die; it is vain to
> worry about the self. The [sense of an individu-
> alized] self is like a mirage, and all the tribu-
> lations that touch it will pass away. They will
> vanish as a nightmare vanishes when a sleeper
> awakes.[3]

The Buddha distinguishes between the transient,
temporal existence and the eternal Truth, which constitutes one's permanent Identity. The false identification
with the transient mind and body is what we regard
as our self; but that, says the Buddha, is merely a
mirage. Such an independent self does not exist; it is
a mere convention which we have come to regard as
real. When one awakes to the Reality, the Truth, the
true Self, one realizes that the transient life and
personality which seemed so real is like a dream; and
that who one really is is that eternal One who exists
as each and every person and creature on earth.

> He who has awakened [from this dream] is
> freed from fear; he has become a Buddha. He
> knows the vanity of all his cares, his ambitions,
> and his sufferings as well.[4]

A "Buddha" is one who is awakened. He has
become freed from the fears accompanying identification with the dream-person and his many adventures.
All his posturing, all his proud blustering, all his loves
and fears, and long-sufferings are seen as having no
more significance than the events occurring in a dream.
The fear and anxiety one experiences throughout life
for one's own well-being is comparable to the fear
that arises when one sees a rope and thinks it is a
snake.

> It sometimes happens that a man, when
> bathing in a river, steps on a wet rope and
> imagines that it is a snake. Terror will over-
> come him, and he will shake with fear, antici-
> pating in his mind all the agonies caused by
> the serpent's venomous bite. What a relief
> does this man experience when he sees that the

rope is no snake. The cause of his fear lies in his error, his ignorance, his illusion. If the true nature of the rope is recognized, his tranquility of mind will come back to him; he will feel relieved; he will be joyful and happy. This is the state of mind of one who has recognized that there is no [independent] self, and that the cause of all his troubles, cares, and vanities is a mirage, a shadow, a dream. [5]

The Buddhist doctrine of the illusory nature of the individualized self (the ego) is a teaching fundamental to all religion; it is, indeed, the mark of true understanding, based on the realization of the Real. Some, however, who possess only word-learning, declare that this doctrine (of *anatta*) runs counter to the Vedantic doctrine of the reality of the Self (*Atman*). Not at all. Only a little discrimination will reveal that the Self of Vedanta is identical to what the Buddha refers to as "the Unborn", or "the Truth"; and that both the Buddha and the Upanishadic sages declared the illusory nature of the individualized self, or ego. There is truly only one Self; we, through our ignorance, imagine that we are many. We identify with a separate viewpoint, a separate set of physical characteristics; and thus we create a separate self where none exists in fact.

[An independent] self is a fever, says the Buddha; self is a transient illusion, a dream; but [the eternal] Truth is sublime. Truth is everlasting. There is no immortality except in Truth; for It is only the Truth that lives forever.

He who has overcome [the illusion of an individual] self is happy. He who has attained peace is happy. He who has found the Truth is happy. [6]

What else needs to be said? Whether we call It "the Atman", "Brahman", "Purusha", "God", or "Truth", it is the realization of *That* which constitutes man's release from suffering, from ignorance, from all illusion. This is the message of the Buddha, of the Upanishads, of Shankara, of Jesus, and of all those who have known the Truth. Let us put to rest all notions that the

Buddha taught something other than the *sanatana dharma* taught throughout history by the seers of Truth.

There are, of course, many different scriptural texts of the Buddhist tradition, all written long after the Buddha was gone; and each conveys its own perspective of the Buddha's teachings. One of the best, in my estimation, for getting a well-rounded and fairly accurate rendition of the teachings of the Buddha is the little book from the Pali canon, called *The Dhammapada*, or "The Path of Truth". Here, as a sampling, are a few passages from it:

The Twin Verses

1. Our life is shaped by our mind; we become what we think. Suffering follows an evil thought as the wheels of a cart follow the oxen that draw it.

2. Our life is shaped by our mind; we become what we think. Joy follows a pure thought like a shadow that never goes away.

3. He was angry with me, he attacked me, he defeated me, he robbed me! Those who dwell on such thoughts as these will never be free from hatred.

4. He was angry with me, he attacked me, he defeated me, he robbed me! Those who do not dwell on such thoughts will surely become free from hatred.

5. For hatred can never put an end to hatred; love alone can. This is an unalterable law.

6. People forget that their lives will end soon. For those who remember, quarrels come to an end.

7. As a strong wind blows down a weak tree, Mara, the tempter [comparable to Maya], overwhelms weak people who, eating too much and working too little, are caught in the frantic pursuit of pleasure.

8. As the strongest wind cannot shake a mountain, Mara cannot shake those who are self-disciplined and full of faith.

11. The deluded, imagining trivial things to be vital to life, follow their vain fancies and never

attain the highest knowledge.   But the wise,
knowing what is trivial and what is vital, set
their thoughts on the supreme Goal and attain
the highest knowledge.

15.   Those who are selfish suffer here and hereafter; they suffer in both worlds from the
results of their own actions. But those who are
selfless rejoice here and rejoice hereafter.
They rejoice in both worlds from the results of
their own actions.

17.   Those who are selfish suffer in this life and
the next.   They suffer seeing the results of the
evil they have done and more suffering awaits
them in the next life.   But those who are
selfless rejoice seeing the good that they have
done and more joy awaits them in the next
life.

19.   Those who recite many scriptures, but fail
to practice their teachings are like a cowherd
who counts another's cows.   They do not share
in the joys of the spiritual life.   But those who
know few scriptures yet practice their teachings,
overcoming all lust, hatred, and delusion, live
with a pure mind in the highest wisdom.   They
stand without external supports and share in
the joys of the spiritual life. [7]

The Path

1.   Of all paths, the eightfold is the best; of
truths, the noble four are best.   Of mental
states, detachment is the best; of human beings
the illumined one is best.

2.   This is the path: there is no other that
leads to the purification of the mind.   Follow
this path and conquer Mara [Maya].   This path
will lead to the end of suffering.   This is the
path I made known after the arrows of sorrow
fell away.

3.   All the effort must be made by you; Buddhas
only show the way.   Follow this path and practice meditation; thus you will go beyond the
power of Mara.

4.   All created things are transitory; those who
realize this are freed from suffering.   This is

the path that leads to pure Wisdom.

5.   All created beings are involved in sorrow; those who realize this are freed from suffering. This is the path that leads to pure Wisdom.

6.   All the various states of the mind occur without the existence of an individual self; those who realize this are freed from suffering. This is the path that leads to pure Wisdom.

7.   Now is the time to wake up, when you are young and strong. Those who wait and waver, with a weak will and a divided mind, will never find the way to pure Wisdom.

8.   Guard your thoughts, words, and deeds. The discipline of these three will speed you along the path to pure Wisdom.

9.   Meditation brings wisdom; lack of meditation leaves you in ignorance. Know well what leads you forward and what holds you back, and choose the path that leads to Wisdom.

10.   Cut down the whole forest of selfish desires, not just one tree only. Cut down the whole forest and you will be on your way to liberation.

11.   If there is any trace of lust in your mind, you are bound to life, like a suckling calf is bound to its mother. Pull out every selfish desire as you would pull out a weed with your hands. Follow the path to *nirvana* with a guide who knows the way.

12.   "I will make this my winter home, have another house for the monsoon season, and dwell in a third during the summer;" those who are lost in such fancies as this forget their final destination.

13.   Death comes and carries off a man absorbed in his family and possessions, just as the monsoon flood sweeps away a sleeping village.

14.   Neither children nor parents can rescue one whom death has seized. Remember this, and follow without delay the path that leads to *nirvana* [the extinguishing of the illusory ego in the experience of the unitive Truth]. [8]

Reflection

Is there but one path to God? Is there but one line that can be drawn from the circumference of a circle to its center? The answer, of course, is No. An endless number of lines may be drawn from various points on the circumference; they all meet at the center. Likewise, regardless of where they start, all paths that take the eternal Truth as their focus must lead to God.

Some look upward at the nightime stars, and pray to the Father who created all things.

Some sit in the silent darkness of their rooms, and quiet their wayward minds, to know the Self.

Some chant the peaceful sounds that drown all thought in waves of bliss.

Some worship before an image of their holy master in humble homage, or envision his form within their hearts.

Some sing with love to the Mother of us all, and beg Her for Her blessing.

Some raise affirmations of perfection in their thoughts, and expand their souls to include all souls.

Some call the name of God within, and fill their hearts with the sweetness of devotion.

All seek the same embrace; all look to the same unnameable Source who gives them life. The paths are many, the Truth is One. He guides the heart and soul of all, and leads them, one by one, by infinite paths, to Him alone.

*   *   *

THE MEANING OF RENUNCIATION

In the Buddhist literary tradition, there is a saying that, 'As a lotus-flower blooms upon the surface of a pond, but is untouched by the water, so does the sage, while living within the world, remain untouched by the world.' The lotus has been a symbol of the spiritual life in the East for no one knows how long. It is a large, beautiful and elegant blossom which rises up out of the muck of a lake or pond, and presents itself there above the water, as if to say, "See! This is how you too must rise above the muck and show your splendor even in the most inhospitable of circumstances." But, we must not imagine that this is the extent of its symbolism; it has a deep metaphysical significance as well. The lotus is the perfect symbol of the eternal Principle that lives within the world-illusion, and remains ever the same, ever-glorious, ever unstained, by the surrounding sea of illusion.

Corresponding to the lotus in the Christian tradition is the "Light" that lives within the "darkness" and which the darkness does not perceive. It is the "Father" opposed to the "world" in Jesus' saying, "I am not of the world, but I am of the Father." The lotus and the pond together symbolize the universal One that appears as two. These two have been called by many names, such as "Brahman and Maya", "Shiva and Shakti", "Theos and Logos", "the Transcendent and the immanent", etc.; they appear under one appellation or another in every metaphysical tradition. To discover their significance, one must turn to the mystical experience of unity wherein they are revealed.

In the mystic's experience of unity, the experiencer knows he is the eternal Consciousness which is forever unchanging, unmoving, beyond all manifestation. In that experience, he is one with It; It is his very Self. And yet, he is not *just* this emptiness, this pure Consciousness which has been termed by some as a "Void." He "sees" also that this infinite Consciousness which he is, is also replete with dynamism. It emanates, projects, thinks, a vast cosmogeny of worlds upon worlds spread out through darkest space and fills them with Its own life.   And so, It has a paradoxical reality: It is pure, formless, Consciousness; and It also teems with activity and form.   Only those who have become one with It in their deep contemplation know with certainty the truth of It.   But It can be understood at a level somewhat removed from actual "vision" by the analogy with our own normal (limited) state of consciousness and its own power of thought-projection.

Your own mind is the best possible analogue, because your own mind is nothing else but a contracted replica of the one Divine Mind.   Consider: Your consciousness is the background awareness out of which all thoughts, images and mental constructs are created.   That consciousness itself is the featureless ground; and yet it is also the source of all the dynamic activity that is projected from it in the form of thoughts, etc.   Consciousness is the witness, the seer, of those thoughts and images, and is at the same time the thoughts and images themselves.   It is one mind; but it creates, by its power of effusion, a duality of seer and seen, of subject and object, where there is really only one.

Now, this is precisely the way the universal Mind creates out of Itself this myriad universe.   It is one; yet It produces an *apparent* duality between Itself (as transcendent Godhead) and Itself (as immanent Creation).   We, as sentient beings within this Creation, partake of His reality -- insofar as we are nothing but projections of the one Mind.   And so we, who are but images, have as our animating power and our very consciousness, the one Mind, the one Self of all -- even while existing in the projected world of thought-creation, this phenomenal universe.   We are "in" it, but not "of" it.   We are the Unlimited, while appearing as limited; we are the Divine Self, the ultimate Reality, while living in this dream-like phantasmagoria as human forms.

And so, we begin to see the relevance, the significance, of this symbol of the lotus: It is to know and retain awareness of our true Divine Identity, while living in the very convincing appearance of divisible forms.   So long as we are embodied, we must live and act within this apparent duality.   But, if we retain the awareness of who we really are, there is nothing in this dark pond that can touch or affect us. This is freedom. This is liberty.

The truth is that even this ocean of darkness, this multiformed illusion, is our own production, our own play; and when the truth is known, and when patience and other virtues are developed, one learns how to live as a pure and beautiful lotus -- even while living in this murky pond. For all is then seen as God's design, the merry play of Consciousness. And the apparent duality dissolves away into unity -- even in this life. Then one knows, "I am above *and* I am below; I am the transcendent Void, *and* I am the phenomenal universe; I am the lotus *and* I am the pond; I am both the subject *and* the object!" This is the attainment of Truth. In this Truth is nothing but Unity. In this Unity is nothing but Truth.

Why then, do we hear so often of the need for renunciation of the world if we are to know the Self? Because, in order to know the Self, it is necessary to focus one's attention, *not* on the world-appearance, *not* on the effusive Energy's manifold productions, but on the Source, the transcendent Self.

In Sanskrit, the word, "renunciation" is *sannyas*. A *sannyasin* is a renunciant, a monk; he is addressed as "Swami". You can learn about the meaning of this renunciation in the *Bhagavad Gita*. It does not mean someone who renounces activity, or society, or articles of his clothing. It refers only to the renunciation of suffering, or rather the cause of suffering: the ego. Ego is the false identification with the transient personality; because it is false, it's fruit is suffering. It is this ego which is to be renounced. There is a story which illustrates this truth:

Long ago in India lived a king who, despite all his attempts at understanding, despite all his devotional practices, still had found no peace. He complained to his wife that all his efforts had brought him no Self-realization, no peace. But his wife, unbeknownst to the king, was a great Yogi possessing many wonderful powers. By her miraculous power, she took the form of a wandering Guru and appeared before the king. The king, eager for Self-knowledge, asked the Guru for instruction, and the Guru simply said, "Renounce!"

The king pondered on this instruction and then he renounced his kingdom and went off into the forest to find peace. After some time, the Guru, who was really the kings's wife in disguise, appeared before the king in the forest and found him living in a very abject manner, cooking his own food over a fire. When he saw the Guru, he complained that he had not yet attained peace; and the Guru simply said, "Renounce!"

So the king got rid of his cooking pot and his fire, and from then on ate only raw fruits and nuts. He even got rid of his water jar and drank directly from the streams. And when the Guru appeared again, he still had not found peace. The Guru simply said, "Renounce!"

After this, the king cast off his clothes, renouncing even his modesty, and from that time on went about the forest naked. Still, when the Guru found him again, he had found no peace. And the Guru simply said, "Renounce!"

The king burst into tears; "My dear teacher," he cried, "I have given up my entire kingdom, the warmth of my fire, my very sustenance, the barest necessities, and even my clothing! What more could I possibly renounce? Shall I renounce even this body?"

And the Guru, taking pity on the king, said, "My dearest, renunciation does not mean the discarding of all these things needed for daily sustenance; there is only one thing which it is necessary to renounce; and that is the ego -- the false identification with the individual body and mind. Vow to renounce this false ego and never take it up again. Live in the awareness of your true and eternal Self, which is all-pervading, unlimited, untarnished, and unaffected by the existence of anything; for everything belongs to the Self, and is nothing else but a manifestation of the Self. It is only the forgetfulness of the true Self, and the identification with the illusory ego, which is the cause of all suffering. And it is that which is to be renounced."

After saying this, the Guru left the king alone to contemplate these words, and the king entered into a deep meditation, during which his mind became still and fixed on the eternal Self. At last he merged into the bliss of Unity and remained in that state for some time.

When the king returned to awareness of the world, he opened his eyes and saw his Guru sitting nearby. Eager to re-enter that state of Unity-awareness, he closed his eyes once more. But the Guru immediately took his hand and pressed him to explain what was to be gained *there* that was not *here*. The king said, "O Gurudev, I've found pure unalloyed bliss! I cannot find any pleasure in the activities of the world. Please let me be in peace so I can become immersed once more in that perfect state!"

The Guru smiled and said to the king, "O king, you do not yet know the highest state, reaching which the wise transcend duality and are never perplexed. How can that state be a perfect one if mental or physical activity can influence it, or if the displacement of the eyelid by the width of a grain of rice makes all the difference to it? It cannot be a perfect state if it can be attained or lost. What you consider to be the state of bliss with your eyes closed cannot be the perfect state, as it is intermittent and not unconditional. Therefore, learn to see wherever you turn the one undivided, eternally blissful Self. Watch the whole universe reflected as it arises and subsides in the Self. See the Self both within you and without. Do not separate the witnessing Self within and the seer of the universal Self without, for they are one and the same. Remain in the continual peace of your true Self in all conditions."

After this speech, the king understood, and became established in the perfectly free state. He had at last found peace. And he went back to his palace and once again assumed rulership of the kingdom. But, this time, he ruled in perfect equanimity and justice, seeing all his subjects as manifestations of his own Self. And he was not hindered in the least by the articles of wealth and beauty which surrounded him; for he was established in the knowledge and awareness of his

true Self, in whom everything exists as one and equal.
And so he never fell prey to desire or attachment.
He kept the teaching of his Guru in his heart and
kept his vow of renunciation, while living as a king in
the midst of plenty, and while carrying on all the
varied duties as ruler of a large kingdom. He lived,
in fact, like the lotus on the pond -- in the midst of
the world, but untouched by the world. His wife, by
the way, lived by his side, as his beloved Self; and
each saw in the other only the one Divinity.

So, you see, renunciation does not mean denying
the world. The world goes on, whether you deny it
or not! We must live in the world and yet remain
above it. That is the challenge. We have to work in
the world; and this can be very challenging, to be
sure. But, while you work at your task in life, reflect
often on the truth that you are the one, undivided,
Self. Turn your mind to continual meditation on the
Self. Identify with that Self.

Naturally, this is not simple matter. To be the
Self, to be God, all sense of limitation must be renounced. The limited existence must become all
Existence. Can you deal with that? Also, you must
be content to do what is to be done without seeking
specific results or rewards. Can you do that? You
must be content to love all without expectation of
being understood or loved or respected in return.
You must be as content to give as to receive, to lose
as to gain, to live in the awareness that nothing can
ever be taken from you or added to you. In other
words, "Be ye perfect as your Father in heaven is
perfect." For the truth is, that's who you are.
There's no one else here. Don't imagine you are
something else, and suffer imaginary lack and succumb
to unhappiness. Give up all that stands in the way
of perfect peace, freedom, joy. Unburden yourself of
the thoughts and anxieties that make for stress and
unhappiness. What have you to do with the body, the
work, the results, the future attainments? You are
always the same -- ever-free, ever-filled with bliss.

Listen to what a great saint of the 20th century
said. His name is Swami Rama Tirth. He came
from India and taught in America and around the
world near the turn of the century, and died at the

age of thirty-three. He said:

> Don't think that it's your duty to win
> anybody's love, to make anybody happy or to
> achieve this worldly aim or that.   Discard
> these aims and objectives. Make it your profess-
> ion, your business, your trade, occupation,
> vocation, and the aim of your life, to keep
> your own Self always peaceful and happy,
> independent of all surrounding circumstances,
> irrespective of gain or loss. Your highest duty
> in the world, laid upon your shoulders by God
> is to keep yourself joyful.   Your social duty,
> the demand of your neighbors, is to keep
> yourself well pleased, peaceful.   The duty
> having the greatest claim on you from the
> standpoint of domestic harmony also is to
> keep yourself cheerful; and your duty to your-
> self demands of you again to keep yourself
> happy in all states.   Be true to yourself and
> never mind anything else in the world.   All
> other things are bound to bow down to you
> when you are true to yourself; yet, what does
> it matter to you whether they bow down or
> not. You are happy by yourself!
>
> To be dejected and gloomy is a religious,
> social, political and domestic crime; and this
> is the only crime you can commit -- this is
> the only crime which is at the root of all
> other crimes, falls, or sins. Be full of serenity
> and dispassionate tranquility and you will find
> that all your surroundings and environments
> will, of course, adjust themselves aright.   It is
> not your duty to worry or hurry about any
> business.   Your only occupation or duty is to
> keep yourself Self-contained, Self-poised and
> Self-pleased. [1]

The lotus retains its beauty, its nobility, by standing above the murky waters -- remaining pure and
unstained. Let us learn to do this also. Make the
clarity of your own inner light and the calm happiness
of your own heart your first concern, your primary
duty; and you'll find that the love and joy that you
experience will spill out as God's Glory to all   with

whom you meet, and inspire them with a desire for
God.   What greater benefit could you confer upon
humanity even if you were to feed all the hungry
and clothe all the poor?

Therefore, let this be your highest resolve, your
first priority, to love your Self, to love the peace,
clarity and joy of God within you; and to set that
pursuit above all other so-called "duties" or "obligations" which you have imposed upon yourself.   That
joy is your birthright.   Do what you must to claim
it.

Reflection

The things we touch and see and hold in our
hands are sometimes so lovely or so useful that we
are able to give them up only reluctantly, even when
more beautiful or more useful items have already
taken their place.   But how much more difficult it is
to give up the subtler things; the habits, the memories
of what has been, the wish for what is yet to be --
the stuff by which we bind ourselves to a narrow life
of empty dreams.

A life is made of such subtle mind-productions;
they make a soul, and hem it in within its own self-
limiting confines.   'Fear-for-self' is the watchman
who assures that the ego's borders shall stand firm,
secure; unsuspecting that those prison walls are made
of dreams -- no more than gossamer strands of
mind-spun dreams.

If only once the watchman of the mind could
glimpse his utter freedom, and throw off fear and
need for walls, those mind-walls would come tumbling
down; and silent peace, unending peace, would stand
where dream-walls stood before.

Let go the past!   Be free of memory's dictates:
realize that you create what is, what was, and what
is to be.   Cart out those memories, habits, dreams:
examine them in the light of day; and if they hold
no promise of attaining Truth and Freedom and the
Peace of God, then let them go.   Cast them in the
Goodwill box, and let them go.   Stand free, and let
them go.

*   *   *

THE OX-HERD PICTURES

There is a set of ten picture-drawings in the Chinese (*Ch'an*) Buddhist tradition, called "The Ox-Herd Pictures", which tell the story of the spiritual journey in a parable form. They were originally eight pictures, created by some nameless artist of the Taoist tradition many centuries prior to the establishment of Buddhism in China around the 6th century C.E. The eight pictures were extended to ten by a 12th century Chinese Buddhist named Kakuan, who also wrote verses to go with each picture.

We can easily understand the meaning of these cryptic pictures and verses from our perspective based on the Vedantic teachings which have been explained in previous chapters. Bear in mind that there are not many teachings represented by the many different religious traditions, but only one. They are all the same teaching. It is true that the teaching of the knowledge of the ultimate Unity experienced directly through interior realization had its early expression in India; the Upanishads form one of the earliest known expressions of that knowledge. But, of course, the experience is universal; men and women everywhere experienced the unitive Self, and spoke of it in their own language and in their own way. And this knowledge spread, along with the various ways of talking about it.

Buddhism had its growth from Vedanta -- just as Christianity was a descendent of Judaism, insofar as its concepts and terminology were derived from a pre-existent Judaic culture. The Buddha, who grew up in a Vedantic culture, simply phrased his knowledge of Unity in a new and unique manner; but it was not a new Truth he taught. As the teachings of the Buddha spread to Tibet, China, Japan, they took on the character of the cultural and linguistic traditions of those countries. Chinese Buddhism is therefore unlike its Indian counterpart in its style and manner, but not in its essence. The Truth to which Ch'an points is the same Truth to which the Buddha pointed, the same Truth to which the Upanishads pointed. The Reality experienced is the same for all, but there is room for immense diversity in the expression of it.   Each path, though unique, leads to the same, single, destination.

This will become more clear when we talk about these ten Ox-Herding pictures of the Ch'an Buddhists. The language and style of Vedanta is somewhat different, but we will see that the message is the same for all.

(1)   The first picture, "The Search For The Oxen", shows a young man searching through the woods for the oxen.   He's standing by a river-bank, wondering which way he should go.   The verse of Kakuan which accompanies this picture reads:

> In the pasture of this world, I endlessly push aside the tall grasses in search of the oxen. Following unnamed rivers, lost upon the interpenetrating paths of distant mountains, my strength failing and my vitality exhausted, I cannot find the oxen.   I hear nothing but the locusts chirring through the forest at night.

Comment: First of all, what is this oxen the young man is searching for?   The oxen represents ultimate knowledge.   It is this we are all seeking. Whether we call it "God", "Brahman", the "Tao", the "universal Mind", or simply the "Truth", we possess an inherent longing for it in our hearts.   And, beyond the obscuring "tall grasses" of this world, we are seeking to catch a glimpse of the Truth of existence. This is the elusive oxen of our young man's search. And in his long search, he has followed endless philosophies, labyrinthine twists of speculation and logic, and he has only become more confused, more desperate, more weary of the search; and he hasn't a clue as to which way to turn.   He has heard no guiding voice of God in the wilderness; he hears only the mocking sounds of the crickets and locusts in the darkness.

(2)   The second picture, called "Discovering The Footprints," shows the young man running alongside the hoofprints of the oxen which lead off into the distance.   He carries a rope and a whip with which to capture his prey.   The verse accompanying this picture reads:

Along the riverbank under the trees, I discover footprints! Even under the fragrant grass I see his prints. Deep in remote mountains they are found. These traces no more can be hidden than can one's nose, when looking heavenward.

Comment: Only in the remote mountains, far from the activities of common men and common pursuits; only on the high peaks of thought and yearning, does one find traces of the Eternal. Then, His signs are evident even in a blade of grass. When the eyes are cleared, His traces are evident everywhere we look, planer than the nose on our face! But note that, in the parable, the young man is objectifying the Truth (the oxen), imagining it to be something 'other' than himself. He is still immersed in duality, still seeing from the standpoint of a limited "I" who is seeking a "Thou" out there.

(3)   The third picture, entitled, "Perceiving The Oxen," shows the young man having found the oxen, getting ready to capture it with his rope made into a halter. The verse accompanying it states:

I hear the song of the nightingale. The Sun is warm, the wind is mild, willows are green along the shore. Here, no ox can hide! But what artist can draw that massive head, those majestic horns?

Comment: Now that he has comprehended the Divine, Its beauty and glory is evident in the pleasant sensations of the world. Our young man feels the closeness of God, and feels he is on the verge of capturing his prize. It is almost within his grasp. The Truth is now self-evident! How could It hide from the man of clear vision! And yet, It is beyond description or conception; It is so great, so vast; who could do It justice by description or art? But note: so long as the Truth which the young man conceives remains 'other' than himself, so long is his Truth a mere mirage, a product of his own thought.

(4)   In the fourth picture, entitled "Catching The Oxen," we see the young man, having gotten his rope around the hind leg of the ox, holding on for dear life, as the oxen struggles to get away. The verse says:

I seize him with a terrific struggle. His great will and power are inexhaustible. He charges to the high plateau far above the cloud-mists, or he goes to stand in an impenetrable ravine.

Comment: Now it has become clear that this "Truth" which our young man has got hold of is not ultimate Truth at all, but hs own mind's creation. It is only thought that he as roped; he is chasing only his own mind! It takes him up to the heavens on the subtlest perception, only to careen into the lowest, animal, depths. It drags him up and down, around and around. Who has ensnared who? This "terrific struggle" is the *sadhana* of taming one's own mind. But the mind has an inexhaustibly powerful will. It tosses him about like the wind, while he hangs on for dear life.

(5)   The fifth picture, called "Taming The Oxen," shows the young man leading the oxen along the road peacefully by the rope in his hand, with his whip in the other. The verse states:

The whip and rope are necessary, else he (the ox) might stray off down some dusty road. Being well-trained, he becomes naturally gentle. Then, even when unfettered, he obeys his master.

Comment: The whip is the prodding of the will; the rope is the *mantra*, or name, by which one keeps a firm grip on the wayward mind. The mind untamed will surely dart off down every impure path; but, once kept under tight control, it learns to be quiet and pure, peaceful and gentle, attentive to its master, even when the controls are relaxed. This reminds us of the teaching of the *Bhagavad Gita*, wherein Arjuna complains to Krishna: "O Krishna, the mind is inconstant; in its restlessness, I cannot find any rest. This mind is restless, impetuous, self-willed, hard to train; to master the mind seems to me as difficult as to master the mighty winds."

To which, Krishna answers: "The mind is indeed restless, Arjuna; it is indeed hard to train. But by constant practice and by freedom from passions the mind can, in truth, be trained. When the mind is not

in harmony, Divine communion is hard to attain; but
the man whose mind is in harmony attains it, if he
has knowledge and persistence." [1]

(6) The sixth picture, "Riding The Oxen Home,"
shows the young man astride the oxen, riding along
peacefully, playing his flute. And the verse which
accompanies it states:

> Mounting the ox, slowly I return homeward.
> The voice of my flute intones through the even-
> ing. Measuring with hand-beats the pulsating
> harmony, I direct the endless rhythm. Whoever
> hears this melody will join me.

Comment: This is a very interesting verse. The
young man is doing his *sadhana*, his practices, meditating with a quiet mind (oxen), and progressing toward
his true home in the Self. The sound of his flute is
heard through the night. There are frequent allusions
in the literature of yoga to the stage of *sadhana* in
which one begins to hear inner sounds emanating from
within. The sound of the flute is one of the most
common referred to. It is mentioned not only in the
yogic tradition of India, but also in the ancient Taoist
tradition of China. Yogis speak of this inner music
as *nada*. In the Sikh tradition, it is spoken of as
naam, or *shabd*. In the yogic texts, this unstruck
sound (*anahat nada*) is spoken of as a spontaneous
occurrance which fills the inner ear with music of
different kinds, seemingly produced by different instruments, such as the flute, the vina, the mrdung. It is
appparently to this that our poet refers. He says,
"Whoever hears this melody will join me;" meaning,
they will be on a par with him, and like him, will
reach the Destination. For it is said that this *nada*
is like the rosy color before the dawn; one who listens
to it with concentration will be led to the ultimate
experience of Unity.

(7) The seventh picture, "The Transcendence Of
The Oxen," is, of course, the transcendence of the
mind. It shows the young man sitting all alone by his
hut peacefully. the oxen is nowhere in sight. The
verse states:

> Astride the oxen, I reach home. I am serene.

The oxen too can rest.   The dawn has come.
In blissful repose, within my thatched dwelling
I have abandoned the whip and the rope.

Comment: "Astride the oxen, I reach home;"
mastering his mind, he has attained his final destination.
He has conquered the unconquerable mind; "the oxen
too can rest now."   No more need of whip and rope.
No more discipline, such as mantra-japa, or prayer, or
worship.   The mind is silenced; it does not show itself.
All ignorance has disappeared. Note too that it is not
the oxen -- the original "object" of the quest -- who
remains alone; but it is the "subject" only who is
left.   The object has proven illusory.
   (8)   The eighth picture, the final one in the Taoist
version, is called "Both Oxen and Self Transcended."
In this picture, there is nothing at all.   It is blank.
Nothing.   The verse beneath states:

Whip, rope, person, and oxen -- all are
merged in the Featureless.   This heaven is so
vast no message can stain it.   How may a
snowflake exist in a raging fire?   Here are the
footprints of the patriarchs.

Comment: Here is portrayed the fact that, without
an object, the subject also disappears; and what is
left is the Formless.   The process of bifurcation has
been transcended in *nirvana*, in *samadhi*.   Just as a salt-
doll cannot exist when immersed in the ocean, or a
snowflake cannot exist in a raging fire, neither can
an imaginary individuality exist in the ocean of Oneness.
Neither is there any trace (footprints) of those who
have passed before.   Here, there is no other reality
but the One, the Featureless Ground.   This is the so-
called "union of the soul and God," "the mystical
marriage," "the experience of Unity."
   (9)   The ninth picture, which was added by Kakuan
along with the tenth, shows a nature scene: a willow-
tree bending over a babbling brook wherein fishes play
and above which the hummingbirds hover.   Leaves fall
from the tree into the stream, indicating the changing
of the seasons.   The verse reads:

Too many steps have been taken returning
to the root and source.   Better to have been

blind and deaf from the beginning! Dwelling in one's true abode, unconcerned with what is without -- the river flows tranquilly on and the flowers are red.

Comment: The Taoist who originally framed this little story stopped at the eighth picture. All was reduced to the transcendent One; the division of subject and object was no more. But the Buddhist, Kakuan, found more to say and added two more pictures. From the viewpoint of Ch'an or Zen Buddhism, it was essential to do so. These down-to-earth Buddhists do not care for the apparent world-negating of the Indian and Taoist metaphysics; nor even for the "Emptiness" of their own Buddhist tradition as it was taught elsewhere. The seers of both the Chinese and Japanese Buddhist tradition seem extremely interested in bringing the realization of Unity to its practical conclusion in the world which must continue to be. Here in this verse, the poet says, "It would have been better if I had been born blind and deaf, instead of having to go through all the world-negating I went through to reach the awareness of the Absolute. But, now that I have realized the eternal Truth, I know that, while I transcend the world of form, still I am here watching the river flow serenly by, and I am seeing the redness of the roses."

The poet is alert to the fact that he is both free from and contained in the world; that he is both the transcendent One and the immanent manifold appearance; that (in the words of Vedanta) he is both Brahman and Maya, both Shiva and Shakti. After all, if a small cell within the body of a man realized that it had no separate identity, but was in reality the whole man who contained in himself billions of cells; still, he would have to continue to live and function as a separate cell. Only by living and acting within his larger self in a way appropriate to the needs of a cell would he be able to benefit his larger self. In the case of the Self-realized sage, the knowledge of his universal Identity makes him free; yet he must continue to live and act in a meaningful way as a limited entity. He lives in the world, and is at the same time above it, as the transcendent Self.

(10)   The tenth picture, "In The World," shows
the young man, now grown older, mingling in the
marketplace with the fruit-sellers, as a wizened old
sage, staff in hand, looking like a fat, jolly, Buddha.
The verse with it states:

> Barefooted and bare-breasted, I mingle with
> the people of the world.   My clothes are ragged
> and dust-laden, yet I am ever-blissful.   I possess
> no magic to extend life; yet, before me, the
> dead trees put forth blossoms.

Comment: The young man is now older and wiser.
He looks like a poor fool, yet he is eternally blissful.
The world around him appears as a shimmering lake
of jewels.   All is alive with Consciousness, and the
energy of his Consciousness enlivens all about him.
He is free of all worldly endeavor, yet he wanders
about joyfully, finding happiness everywhere.   This is
the familiar picture of the Avadhut, the blissful sage
of the Vedantic tradition, who has completed his
sadhana and has nothing further to accomplish.   We
meet with him in the *Avadhut Gita*, where he is depict-
ed in this way:

> A patched rag from the roadside serves as a
>   wrap
> To the Avadhut, who has no sense of pride or
>   shame.
> Naked, he sits in an empty shack,
> Immersed in the pure, stainless, bliss of the
>   Self.
> Free from bondage to the fetters of hope,
> Free from the yoke of acceptable conduct,
> Free from everything, he has thus attained
>   peace.
> He is the stainless One, the pure Absolute.
> For him, where is the question of being embodied
>   or bodiless?
> Where is the question of attachment or non-
>   attachment?
> Pure and unpartitioned as the infinite sky,
> He is, himself, the Reality in Its natural state.
> As a yogi, he is beyond union and separation;
> As a worldly enjoyer, he is beyond enjoyment
>   and non-enjoyment.

Thus, he wanders leisurely, leisurely,
While in his mind arises the natural bliss of
the Self.[2]

Listen also to the way the Maharashtran saint,
Jnaneshvar, spoke in the 13th century about the state
of one who has reached final liberation:

One who has attained this wisdom may say
whatever he likes; the silence of his contemplation remains undisturbed. His state of action-
lessness remains unaffected, even though he
performs countless actions. ... Even one who
has attained wisdom may appear to enjoy the
sense-objects before him, but we do not really
know what his enjoyment is like. If the moon
gathers moonlight, what is gathered by who?
It is only a fruitless and meaningless dream.
...Sweeter even than the bliss of liberation is
the enjoyment of sense-objects to one who has
attained wisdom. In the house of devotion that
lover and his God experience their sweet union.
Whether he walks in the streets or remains
sitting quietly, he is always in his own home.
He may perform actions, but he has no goal to
attain. Do not imagine that if he did nothing,
he would miss his goal. ... His rule of conduct
is his own sweet will. His meditation is whatever
he happens to be doing. The glory of liberation
serves as a seat-cushion to one is such a state.
No matter where he goes, that sage is making
pilgrimage to God. And if he attains to God,
that attainment is non-attainment. How amazing!
That in such a state, moving about on foot and
remaining seated in one place are the same.
No matter what his eyes fall upon at any time,
he always enjoys the vision of God.[3]

All the great Enlightenment traditions speak of
this synthesis of the Eternal and the temporal, the
Divine and the mundane, as the final liberation. Such
a sage is known as a *jivanmukta*, one who is free while
living. He lives in the world; but the knowledge of
his eternal Self has freed him from identification with
the apparent limitations of embodiment. He is free.

We too can attain such a state. Most of us are still
at one stage or another along the way to perfect
freedom, perfect awareness. We keep on learning
and practicing and doing what we must to tame our
unruly minds. In this way, we lift our consciousness
to greater and greater heights, till finally we know
our boundless, joyful freedom. May we all, this very
day, begin to taste a little of the bliss of our true,
care-free and omnipresent Self.

Reflection

Now, while there's still time, call on God with a
yearning heart! How swiftly passes this busy life of
occupations and obligations! Too soon, the day is
lost to inconsequential chores; too soon the months,
the years, are lost to scattered aims and fruitless
schemes. Suddenly we awake one morning, and we're
old and feeble, unable to make any effort at all.

And who knows when the end will come? You
may be certain it will come one day; perhaps without
warning, unannounced. Perhaps while you walk, or
sleep, or play; or in between the syllables of a word
you start to say.

And when it comes, will your heart leap up and
cry, "O glorious day!" Or will you beg for just a
little time to set things right, the way you'd always
hoped they'd be?

O friend, make now your heart to be as you would
have it then. O now, my friend, while there's still
time, call on God with a yearning heart! Lead your
soul to Him who is your true and everlasting home!
He is your joy unlimited, your boundless satisfaction;
your Lord, your Goal, your life, your Self.

*   *   *

AS A MAN THINKS

The great Greek philosopher and mystic, Heraclitus, who lived over 500 years before the Christian era, expressed a profound truth in just three words. He said: "Character is destiny." The meaning, of course, is that we become what we become because of our good or bad qualities. Our lives are simply manifestations of our inner soul, and reflect either the beauty or the ugliness of our character. In other words, we are what we think; this is a truth that has been expressed througout the centuries; and it is a truth that has been elaborately treated in one particular Upanishad, the *Maitri Upanishad.* This Upanishad deals very thoroughly with this subject, and explains also the nature of the soul and the means of its progress toward Self-realization. I'd like to share with you a few excerpts from this Upanishad in order to shed some light on the teachings of Vedanta regarding these issues.

The *Maitri Upanishad,* like many others, is composed in the form of a dialogue. Now it should be clear that, if you're going to have a didactic dialogue, there must be one participant who is ignorant, and asks all the questions; and there must be one who is wise, to give all the answers to the questions. This dialogue is no different; it is between the wise god, Prajapati, and the ignorant, though sincere, angels who ask Prajapati:

O Master, this body, without consciousness, is but a chariot without a driver. Who, then, is the Spirit by whose power it becomes conscious? Who, in other words, is the driver of the chariot?

And Prajapati answers:

There is a Spirit who exists within the things of the world, and yet who is beyond the things of this world. He is pure Consciousness; He dwells in serenity as the Infinite, the Eternal. He is beyond the life of the body and the mind. He was never born, He never dies; He is

everlasting, ever-one, and self-sustaining.   He is
the Spirit whose power gives consciousness to
the body.   He is the driver of the chariot.

Prajapati continues:

That infinite Consciousness becomes the
finite consciousness of man, possessing the power
of discrimination and understanding, and also
erroneous conceptions.   He is, in truth, the
great Lord, the Source of creation, and the
universal Self of all.   This Spirit is Consciousness
and gives consciousness to the body.   He is the
driver of the chariot.

What Prajapati says in answer to the questioning
angels is not at all apparent to everyone.   There are
so many questions that arise in one's mind about the
nature of existence, consciousness, the hereafter, etc.
The Spirit is invisible, so how can one know that it
even exists?   By what means did the author of this
Upanishad come by this knowledge?   He cannot be
seen, but He can be known by man, His own manifestation, when He is sought within one's own consciousness.   Prajapati explains to his listeners:

Those sages who have known Him say that
it is He who wanders on this earth from body
to body, free from the good and bad effects of
actions.   He is free because He is free from
the sense of 'I', and He is invisible, incomprehensible, concealed in His own mystery.

He seems to act, but He does not act.   He
seems not even to exist; but He is Existence
itself.   He exists in His own being, pure, never-
changing, never-moving, unstainable; and, in
peace, beyond desires, He watches the drama
of the universe.   He is hidden behind the veil
of the universal appearance; but He is ever One
in His own Bliss.

The supreme Spirit is immeasurable, inappre-
hensible, beyond conception, never-born, beyond
reasoning, beyond thought.   His vastness is the
vastness of space.   At the end of the worlds,
while all things sleep, He alone is awake in
eternity.   Then, from His infinity, new worlds

arise and awake, a universe which is an immensity of thought. The universe exists in the Consciousness of Brahman, and unto Him it returns.

This is an authentic recapitulation of the Truth as It is seen in the mystical vision. All that Prajapati says here is correct and absolutely true; I add my verification to these declarations as one who has also realized their truth for himself. In the mystical experience of unity, one experiences, from the vantagepoint of that eternal unity, the outflowing and returning of the universal manifestation in a recurring cycle. It is similar to the inhalation and exhalation of a breath which we, as humans, experience. This is the truth. One may search through all the accounts of all the mystics and find this same description given.

Apparently, the angels were completely satisfied with what Prajapati said about the supreme Spirit, for now they changed the subject, and questioned him about the individualized soul: "Master," the angel-spokesman said,

> you have spoken to us of the greatness of the Self (*Atman*), but what is the soul (*jiva*) who is bound by the good or bad effects of actions, and who, born again from these good or bad actions (*karmas*), rises or falls in its wanderings, under the sway of duality?

Prajapati replies:

> Yes, there is indeed a soul composed of the elements who is bound by the good or bad effects of actions, and who, born again from good or bad effects, rises or falls in its wanderings under the sway of duality. This human soul is under the power of Nature (*Prakrti*) and its conditions, and thus it falls into confusion. Because of this confusion, the soul cannot become conscious of the God who dwells within, and whose power gives us the power to act. The soul is thus whirled along the rushing, muddy, stream of Nature, and becomes unsteady and uncertain. It is filled with confusion and full of desires, without concentration, and agitated with pride. Whenever the soul has thoughts of

'I' and 'mine', it binds itself to a limited
sense of selfhood, a limited identity, just as a
bird is bound in the net of a snare.

Prajapati is saying that, in other words, as the one
Spirit is self-limited in an individual form, It loses
the sense of Its all-pervasiveness, Its infinity, and
becomes identified with that particular human form.
Swayed by the conditions of Nature in which It finds
Itself immersed, It imagines needs and desires, and
becomes lost in imaginary justifications for Its actions.
Having lost all sense of Its untarnished Divinity, It
feels enslaved and bound by the Nature which is truly
Its own manifestation. Prajapati goes on to say:

> The mind of man is of two kinds: pure and
> impure. It is impure when in the bondage of
> desire, and pure when free from [worldly] desire.
> ... This entire world-illusion (*samsara*) takes
> place in one's own mind. Let one therefore
> keep the mind pure, for *as a man thinks, so he
> becomes.* This is the eternal mystery.

There is a very old story which is meant to illustrate this proclivity of the Divine Self to place Itself
in an imaginary bondage; it involves the god, Indra,
and the god, Shiva. It seems that one day Indra
became bored with all the pleasures afforded him in
heaven, and decided to experience life on earth in the
body of a pig. He found himself a large mud-hole,
and began snorting and cavorting in the mud as a pig.
And he found so much pleasure in this pig-life that
he mated with a sow, and fathered a large litter of
piglets. His life was very happy; he had his cool mud
to lie in, and he had a mate and a lot of squealing
piglets to fondly care for, and he was quite content.

Now, the other gods became upset when they
learned that Indra had let all the affairs of heaven
falll by the wayside while he enjoyed life as a pig on
earth. So they sent Shiva to persuade Indra to return
to his rightful place in heaven. Indra refused, however;
and told Shiva to mind his own business, that he was
very happy where he was, thank you. Shiva tried
again and again, with the same result. Finally, Shiva,
in desperation, took his trident and split the pig-body

of Indra from one end to the other, releasing Indra from his pitiful delusion. Immediately, Indra let out a sigh of joyful relief that he had been freed from bondage to the simple desires and satisfactions of his pig-life; and he expressed his gratitude to Shiva and the other gods for bringing him out of that pitiable state.

We too, Prajapati is telling us, are God; we are the Divine Self of the universe. But we have become deluded into believing that we are poor, limited, and finite forms whose only satisfaction is in the pitiable pleasures of the flesh. We are in the same condition as Indra in the story. Our minds keep on having dreams and fantasies without end. No matter how many times a desire is fulfilled, the mind goes on increasing desires instead of diminishing them. The mind causes you to forget your true nature, and makes you think you're something else; but you must not be fooled. The mind may go on creating universes upon universes; so what? Let it! Continue to remain in serenity, witnessing it. For those who have no understanding, it is the devil. But, for one who understands the nature of the mind, it is only the creative effulgence, the unceasing play, of the Divine Energy. This is what Prajapati says:

The mind is indeed the source of bondage; but it is also the source of liberation. To be bound to the things of this world: this is bondage. To be free from them: this is liberation. Indeed, if men thought of God as much as they think of the world, who would not attain liberation?

After this, Prajapati explained to the angels how to meditate on the Self:

When a wise man has withdrawn his mind from all external things, and when he is no longer attentive even to inner sensations, let him rest in peace, free from the movements of will and desire. Since the soul has come from That which is greater than itself, let it surrender to its Source. For it has been said, 'There is something beyond our mind which abides in

silence within our mind.   It is the supreme
Mystery beyond thought.'   Let one's mind and
one's subtle body rest upon that and not rest
on anything else.

When the mind is silent, beyond weakness
or distraction, then it can enter into a world
which is far beyond the mind; that is the
highest state.   ... As a fire without fuel finds
peace in its source, when thoughts become
silent, the soul finds peace in its own Source.
And when a mind which longs for Truth finds
the peace of its own Source, then those false
inclinations cease which were the result of
former actions done in the delusion of the
senses.   A quiet mind overcomes both good
and evil actions; in quietude, the soul is one
with the Self.   Then one knows the joy of
eternity.   As water becomes one with water,
fire with fire, and air with air, so the mind
becomes one with the infinite Mind, and thus
attains final freedom.

This is the teaching of all the scriptures and all
the seers of God.   See how similar, for example, is
the teaching of the *Bhagavad Gita* on this subject:

When all desires are in peace, and the
mind, gathering all the wayward senses, turns
them within, then, with reason armed with a
strong will, let the seeker quietly lead the
mind into the Self, and let all his thoughts be
stilled.   And whenever the unsteady and restless
mind strays away from the Self, let him always
lead it again and again to the Self.   Supreme
joy thereby comes to the yogi whose heart is
stilled, whose passions are quieted, who is
pure from sin; for he becomes one with Brahman. [1]

Prajapati says:

Words cannot describe the joy of the soul
whose impurities are cleansed away in deep
contemplation, who is one with the *Atman*, his
own Self.   Only those who experience this joy
know what it is.

That is the end of Prajapati's speech, and the end of the *Maitri Upanishad*. Its message, though, has continued through the centuries, and is reflected in countless scriptures and scriptural treatises. Listen, for example, to this affirmation of its message from the *Ashtavakra samhita*, in which Ashtavakra tells his disciple, king Janaka:

> You are neither earth, nor water, nor fire, nor air, nor ether; these are but the elements of which all created forms are made. In order to attain liberation, know the Self as the witness of all these; you are Consciousness itself. If you detach your identification from the body, and rest in Consciousness, you will at once be happy, peaceful and free from bondage. You are the one observer of all and you are always liberated. In fact, it is only your imagining yourself to be other than the one observer that constitutes your bondage. One who considers himself free is, in fact, free; and one who considers himself bound remains bound. '*As one thinks, so one becomes*' is a popular saying in this world -- and it is very true. The Self is all-pervading, perfect, pure Consciousness; It is One, free, actionless, unattached, desireless and quiet. It is the Witness. It is only through delusion that it appears to be an individual entity. [2]

Reflection

When the storm-clouds of oppression and darkness loom all around you, and the gathering winds sweep the contents of your mind into a swirling chaos of confusion, do not be afraid -- be firm, be confident! For after the storm, the Sun will reappear, and calm will reign over all, and there will shine forth on you the clearest and most pleasant weather.

And when the melancholy of autumn turns into the bleak, cold, harshness of winter, and all seems empty, dreary, and void of life; and when your soul cries out in agony for some sign that the Spirit of God still lives and loves, do not loose your hold on faith -- be

firm, be confident! For after the winter comes the
spring, and life that seemed long-dead revives with
all the exuberance of a rekindled love or a newborn
child, and life's joy reawakens to fill the earth once
more with song.

And when night's shadows fall across the landscape
of your heart, and, though straining to see, your eyes
can find no glimmer of light, nor even the slightest
movement of hope within the darkness of your mind,
but only the shadowy spectre of fear that somewhere
close, unseen, lies the pit of unremitting despair;
don't be afraid -- be firm, be confident! For after
the night comes the dawn, and the bright clarity of
day, wherein is seen the truth that you are free as
air, and never touched by night or day, or foul or
fair weather, or the changing of the seasons; but, as
they come and go in their unceasing rounds, you
remain, the one pure Sky, the unblinking Eye of
Consciousness, who watches light and shadow alternate
in this, your own spectacular play.

*   *   *

THE NATURE OF THE MIND

It is said in various scriptures that the Self is beyond thought, beyond the intellect, beyond imagination. All these are activities of the mind, and not the mind itself. The Self is the universal Mind, the absolute Consciousness, and It is experienced only through the individual mind, the human consciousness, when it becomes pure. This is what *sadhana*, or spiritual endeavor, is all about: the purification of the mind. It is not to purify the Self; the Self is always pure. *Sadhana* is for the sake of the mind. Listen to what is said in this regard by Dattatreya in the *Tripura rahasya*:

Realization of the Self requires absolute purity of mind. The only impurity of mind is thought. To make it thought-free is to keep it pure. Then, how could the Self not be found gleaming in a pure mind? All the injunctions of the scriptures are directed toward this end alone, because the one supreme Consciousness, the Self, is revealed only in the pure mind.[1]

Everyone recognizes that it is the mind that is the key to whether we are happy or unhappy, wise or foolish, enlightened or unenlightened. So, it would seem reasonable to give some real attention to just what the mind is and then perhaps we can determine how one can best attain happiness, wisdom and enlightenment through it. A doctor cannot prescribe a remedy for an illness until he knows what the illness is; likewise, one cannot prescribe a remedy for the mind unless one first knows what the mind is. That is the first step in an intelligent approach to molding and shaping the mind the way we want it to be. We have to ask ourselves, "What, exactly, is this mind?" "What is it made of?" "How does it come into existence?" "What is its purpose?" "How can it be made pure?" It is essential to find the answers to these questions if we are going to succeed in our *sadhana*.

We can find some excellent clues in the writings of the authentic seers and sages of the past. For it is they who have realized the Self who, having transcended the individual mind, are in a unique position to take an overview of the mind and its functioning, and to most clearly determine its nature. Here, for example, in the opening portion of the *Pratyabijnahridayam*, a scripture of the Kashmir Shaivites, it is stated that, "Consciousness (*Chiti*) Itself, descending from Its universal state, becomes the individual mind (*chitta*) through the process of contraction."

The remarkable idea presented here is that it is the one pure Consciousness, God Himself, who manifests as that conscious mind which you regard as you. This very mind, by which you are conscious of these words before you, is the one pure Consciousness, the Self, in a contracted, or limited, form. This is why, when that mind is made pure and clear, it is possible to experience one's Self as the ultimate Reality, as the One. For, if such a thing is true -- that God is manifesting as us, then the realization of the truth about our own nature would naturally reveal that "I" and "the Father" are one.

When we speak of "the mind," however, we must be clear about what we mean. We may mean by the word either that conscious awareness which is the background of knowing, or we may mean the activity of thought that takes place against that background consciousness. This ambiguity often results in some confusion when trying to understand what is meant by "the mind." However, in the Sanskrit tradition this confusion is avoided by the use of two different words for these two aspects: the conscious awareness with which we identify our being is *chitta*; and the activity of thoughts, imagination, etc. which arises out of the *chitta* is called *manas*, the active mind. For example, in the *Yoga Vashishta*, king Shikhidwaja asks his wife, Chudala, who is an enlightened sage, the question, "What is this mind?" And his wife answers, "The mind is nothing but a bundle of thoughts!" In this case, the word, "mind" is translated from the Sanskrit word, *manas*. However, in the statement, "The mind is nothing but God," the word, "mind," is a translation of *chitta*.

And so we must be careful to understand just what we mean by the word, "mind"; for it has these two aspects: as *chitta*, it signifies that individualized consciousness which has no characteristics of its own, but which gives rise to all characteristics and every imaginable form; and, as *manas*, signifies the activity of thoughts, images, etc., which play on the surface of consciousness. *Manas* refers more to an activity, an occurrance of movement, than to an actual entity that exists in and of itself. For this reason, it is often said that the Self is revealed when the mind (*manas*) is silenced.

This activity, called *manas*, has also been likened to the ripples on a lake or ocean. The ripples, or thought-waves, are called, in Sanskrit, *vrittis*. In the very first Sutra of Patanjali's *Yoga Sutras*, he states, "Yoga [the realization of the Self] results from the stilling of the waves (*vrittis*) of the mind (*chitta*)."[2] In other words, in order to realize that one pure Consciousness, which is the universal Self, first and foremost one must calm the stormy waves upon the surface of the mind; then one is able to concentrate on the true nature of the mind, and come to the clear realization that one's own mind is the universal Mind, that one's self is the universal Self.

If we examine the activity of the *chitta-vrittis*, we realize that this activity operates on three subtle levels: the unconscious, the subconscious, and the conscious levels. Remember, thoughts are nothing but *vrittis*, or waves, on the *chitta*; and *chitta* is really only a contracted form of *Chiti*, or pure Consciousness. These waves, or *vrittis*, which manifest as thoughts or images, have their beginning at the unconscious level, rise up through the subconscious level, and finally become evident as thoughts or images to the conscious awareness.

At the unconscious level, there is the faintest stir of a *vritti* in the *chitta* at the causal level of thought. Then, as this subtle vibration becomes more gross, it reaches the subconscious level, and then finally it enters our awareness on the grossest conscious level. It is at this point that we actually hear the thought or see the image within. All conceptualization and all expression of thought is dependent upon that initial process of manifestation at the unconscious level. The last stage of this thought-manifestation is, of course, the spoken or written word; and usually we are not even aware of from whence this speech or writing came.   But all thought-manifestation begins with the initiation of activity by the power inherent in one's own Divine Self.   No other Self exists but that one, even though we may imagine that we are independent entities with independent power to do or think or say what we wish.

All of the subtle impressions of countless lifetimes remain in the unconscious level of the *chitta*, in a seed form.   We have no access to them so long as they remain there.   They may be accessed by a particularly deep meditation, or those impressions may filter up to the subconscious, where we come in touch with them in dreams, reveries, or in deep inquiry or thought as disjointed images from the past, or as fragments of thought in a hazy momentary flash of vision within.

What I wish to get across to you is that it's the one pure Consciousness that, by Its own inherent Power, manifests as your mind and your inner and outer worlds.   You, the perceiver, are in fact, the one pure Consciousness; and all that you perceive, both subtle and gross, both within and without, is your own manifestation.   Really, there is nothing here but the one Self.   The *manas*, or *chitta-vritti*, you perceive is the activity of your Divine Self.   In other words, if you should get to know the nature of your own mind, you will get to know God.   Once the mind becomes still at the subtlest level, what is left is God; it is just as, when the waves on the ocean become stilled, what is left is the ocean.

Ordinarily, instead of stilling the many waves which are constantly arising on the *chitta*, we feed them with desire and identify completely with their tumultuous activity.   This is our great mistake.   If, instead of identifying with the waves arising on the ocean of consciousness, we were to identify with the ocean itself, we should be able to remain unmoved and unscathed by the tumult of the raging storms which frequently arise on the ocean of consciousness.

Let the mind think whatever it wants -- but, at the same time, be clearly aware that you are not the thoughts of the mind.   You are the witness of the mind; in other words, you are the *chitta*, and are not affected by the *vrittis*. You are the observer, the spectator, who is watching the activity of the mind. Simply because your mind has become agitated and turbulent, you mustn't think, "I have become agitated and upset." Just watch the agitation of the mind from a distance and observe all its endless creations.

If we truly understand the nature of our mind, the things that it does won't bother us so much. The mystery will go out of its babbling, and we won't be interested in paying it very much attention. You see, the mind (*manas*) is only the vibration of the *chitta*; and, like all vibrations, it is polarized in the form of a peak and a trough. For example, when you produce the thought of "up", you create at the very same time, in the very same motion, the thought, "down"; because one cannot exist without the other. They are an inseparable pair, for they give meaning to each other. Or, when you feel an attraction, a liking -- along with this creation of attraction, you have unavoidably, inescapably, created a repulsion, a dislike. Newton's law that for every action there is an equal and opposite reaction hold just as true on the subtle level as on the gross. Every feeling, every emotion, every thought, begets its opposite. Knowing this, one is not so apt to be dismayed if suddenly the mind comes up with a wave of disgust for one whom you most love, or an evil thought disrupts your thoughts of goodness. For, by its very nature, the mind throws up a continual display of opposites, complementary polarities.

Here are some more examples: consider; if you experience the deepest peace, be sure that you are bound also to experience the profoundest unrest -- for you can't have the one without the other. If you accept the one, you must accept the other. Why be dismayed? It is only natural and to be ex-pected. They are inseparable twins. If you have pleasure, look for pain around the next corner. You welcomed the one; why all this fuss when the twin shows up? Have you ever heard of birth without death? Youth without old age? Happiness without sorrow? Beauty without ugliness? Good without evil? Night without day? No.

So, just as we don't get attached to just the

in-breath and refuse the out-breath, we must learn
also to remain unattached to the waves of thought
and feeling as well.   For so long as this world of
manifestation exists, every positive will bring in its
train a negative.   The world, as has often been observed, is made of duality.   It is nothing but the
play of duality.   And it is only by remaining aware
as the dispassionate witness to all these ups and
downs of the mind that we can transcend the mind
and remain aware of our true Self, which is utterly
unchanging and stable.

My teacher was once asked the question, "Why
does the mind play such tricks on us?"   And he
replied: "The mind plays its tricks on you because
you have become friends with the mind, because you
have become a slave to the mind.   If you become
centered in the Self, if you become free, the mind
will just lie there quietly.   ... A mind free from
thought is a mind in meditation.   A mind free from
external occupations and steady in all circumstances,
is a mind in meditation.   Only in a mind which is
inward-turned and free from change does love bloom
in its fullness."

Meditation is the practice of identification with
the eternal Joy.   It is not thinking; it is being.   The
truth is, we are that eternal Joy, that eternal Being.
It is the mind that thinks.   We are not the mind; we
are not the ephemeral body.   We are the witness of
these, our manifestations.   Our Self, our true Identity,
is the eternal Witness.   It continues throughout all
the various states of the mind: waking, dreaming, and
deep sleep.   Our true Self is pure, blissful, Awareness,
free of all motion or activity.   To become aware of
That, to experience It, is the purpose of human life.
It is liberation from the trammels of thought and
worry.   It is freedom from all limitation.   It is absolute Freedom.   Absolute Peace.   Absolute Happiness.

Reflection

Let all voices be silenced, and do Thou only,
Lord, speak to me in my soul.   Let all the clamor
of thoughts, stirred up in my restless mind, be stilled;
and let my anxious heart find rest in surrender at

Thy feet.

Do Thou with me, Lord, as it pleases Thee to do, and let no care for my own wellbeing arise to trouble my heart; for Thy wisdom and Thy love shall always suffice to guide me day by day.

Dear God, Bestower of grace, lift up my mind to Thee -- above all worldly thoughts and concerns, above all reservations and doubt, and let my heart pour forth loving praise in showers of golden song to Thee. Thy will hast always led me in times past through all my troubles, and why should I turn now to my own devices?

Let Thy joy fill my heart and my soul, and lift me, Lord, on wings of longing, buoyed by the breeze of Thy grace, into Thy perfect stillness, into Thy fatherly embrace.

* * *

THE PURIFICATION OF THE MIND

Because it is the mind through which the universal Self is realized, the nature of the mind is a frequent topic of those who have realized the Self. Now, we all have minds, and equal access to them; but we don't all equally understand our minds. One needs to go beyond the individual mind in order to understand it fully. So long as we identify with the individual mind, we cannot get any realistic perspective on it. We need to go beyond the identification with the contents of the mind.

When I experienced my eternal Self, I realized the universal Mind; and in this experience, the nature of my previously limited mind was clearly revealed. Now, many years later, I can still speak with unwavering certainty about the nature of the mind. What I realized is this: There are not many minds, but only one Mind. This very mind is the universal Mind. We carry around with us the false sense of our difference and separation from one another, but the truth is that there is no one here but the one Mind, the one Self.

This mind, limited by thought and false identification, is man. This same mind, enlightened, quiescent, free from thought, is God. If you get to know the mind, you will know God; and vice versa. This limitation of our mind, which we regard as an individual ego, is the result of God's veiling power, His *Maya*, as Vedantist say. In the Bible, the apostle, Paul, says, "We see now as through a glass darkly, but *then* (meaning when we are enlightened by the grace of God), we shall see as face to face."[1] He was speaking of that veiling power which obscures from us our true, unlimited, Identity as the one Mind. In the act of creation, as God presents before Himself an object of perception, the perceiving subject also comes into existence. It is this God-created illusion of duality, this bifurcation of subject and object out of His indivisible Unity, that constitutes the illusion of *Maya*. It is this *apparent* duality which constitutes the bondage of worldly illusion.

The illusion of duality is God's play. But He also

*ie Mind = Consciousness

reveals the true Unity of subject and object to those who seek to know the true nature of Reality.   This experience of Unity is termed "Yoga"; and it's attainment is elaborately described in an ancient Sanskrit text by Patanjali entitled, *The Yoga Sutras*.   In the very first Sutra, he states: *yogas chitta-vritti nirodha.*   This, translated, means:

Yoga (the experience of Unity) results from the stilling of the waves of the mind.

That is what Yoga is: the reabsorption of the ego into the universal Self, the reabsorption of the soul into God.   It is likened to the reabsorption of a wave into the ocean, as the winds subside.

This "stilling" is not the mere pause of silence in the mind which all of us may experience from time to time while sitting quietly, but is rather the cessation of the subject-object idea which occurs in the profoundest depths of the soul.   It is only in dying (to individual existence) that we are born to eternal life, said the meek Saint Francis, who had experienced this death of the ego-idea.   Such a dying of the individuality and the concommitant awakening to Identity as the one Existence is not an everyday occurrance; it is, in fact, a very extraordinary occurrance -- despite its being so glibly spoken of in popular literature dealing with 'spirituality'.

Those who do experience the Godhead as Identity, who realize the supreme Self, do so only once in a lifetime normally, during an extraordinary period of intense preoccupation with the Divine Reality.   Such a period invariably coincides with a rare set of planetary circumstances in the heavens insofar as their positions relate strongly and distinctly to the planetary configurations existing at the time of the individual's birth. This fact may be surprising to some, but it can be easily verified; and should not actually be so surprising if one considers the inseparability of the universe and God.   All things, after all, move together of one accord.   Assent is given throughout the universe to every falling grain; and the Mind of God is reflected in every part of the living universe.

In the Shaivite scripture, *Pratyabijnahridayam*, it is

said: "*Chiti* (pure Consciousness), descending from Its universal state, becomes *chitta* (the individual consciousness, or mind-stuff) through the process of contraction. In other words, you, in the form of your own manifestory Power, appear not only as a world, but as innumerable individual minds. You, the perceiver, are in fact the one pure Consciousness, the universal Mind; and all that you perceive, both subtle and gross, both within and without, is your manifestation. Really, there is nothing here but you! The thought-activity of the mind is also an object of your perception, and it is produced out of your own consciousness, your Self.

This same treatise states further that, "By becoming deluded by one's own Power of manifestation, one thereby becomes a soul bound on the wheel of transmigration." And this is truly what we do: we become deluded by our own power to create thought. We identify with the creative Power, and forget who we really are. In this way, we come under the sway of our own mental creations. What, then, is to be done? What is the secret knowledge that liberates a man or woman from the wicked devices of the mind? It is the secret of all the wise seers and sages of every land in every time. You'll find this secret in the sacred scriptures of the Hindus, the Buddhists, the Jews, the Muslims, and in the teachings of Jesus. It is this: You are the eternal Self, the Source and Witness of the thoughts. That is who you really are. But, because you are not aware of it, you identify with the mental activity and the transient worldly forms, and forgetting your real Identity, you become swept away in the agitated currents of the mind. It is just this false identification which is the source of all your woes and unhappiness.

With the aim of learning how to break this bondage to duality, and the identification with the false ego, let us turn once more to Patanjali's *Yoga Sutras*, to see if we can obtain some illumination:

After he states that "Yoga results from the stilling of the waves of the mind," Patanjali adds,

Then man abides in his own [true] nature.
Otherwise (i.e., when the mind is *not* controlled),

there is identification with the waves (*vrittis*).

Then he begins to teach us how the waves of the mind may be controlled. "The *vrittis*," he says, "are controlled by means of practice (*abhyasa*) and non-attachment (*vairagya*)." And, in defining these two, he states,

Practice (*abhyasa*) is effort toward steadiness in the consciousness of the Self. Continuous effort for a long time, with earnest dedication, is the means. Non-attachment (*vairagya*) is freedom from desire for what is seen or heard. When, through knowledge of the Self, one ceases to desire the manifestations of God's creative Power (*Prakrti*), that is the highest non-attachment.

But he does not wish to give the impression that the endeavor toward Self-knowledge is a breeze, and so he points out the fact that there are obstacles to be met with on this journey. "The obstacles to Self-knowledge," says Patanjali,

are sickness, mental laziness, doubt, lack of enthusiasm, sloth, craving for sense-pleasures, false perception, despair, and unsteadiness of concentration. [But] these obstacles can be overcome by concentration on the one Truth.

But what about the normal relations with others in the course of one's daily life? Patanjali has some beautiful advice to give in this regard also. He says:

Calmness of mind is attained through friendliness toward the cheerful, compassion for the cheerless, delight in the virtuous, and indifference toward the wicked.

In his endeavor to cover all the means of calming and controlling the mind, Patanjali does not omit to mention the relationship between the mind and the breath, and the fact that, by controlling one, the other is also controlled. "The mind may also be made calm," he says, "by the [rhythmic] expulsion and retention of breath." The *prana*, or subtle breath, nourishes and regulates the activity of the mind and

the nervous system and is linked closely with the
physical breath. Thus, the control of the breath has
a corresponding effect on the *prana* and the mind.

Then, he lists some of the other ways one might
calm and concentrate the mind. "Concentration," he
says, "may be attained by fixing the mind on the
inner light." And for those who may not experience
any light within, he adds: "Or by meditating on one
who has overcome passions and attachments."

The meaning of this idea is that your mind reflects
the object on which you meditate, and takes on the
qualities of that object. If you think about a teacher
whom you admire, who has overcome the distractions
of the mind, and is unattached to the world, then, by
concentrating on that individual, you will take on
those same qualities. "Or," says Patanjali, you can
obtain the same effect by "fixing your mind on any
Divine form or symbol that appeals to you." Here,
he is pointing out the fact that devotion may be
aroused by any form or symbol that awakes in you
the thought of God. In India, as elsewhere, we may
find many such symbols in use to serve as the means
to arouse devotion to God.

In the second chapter of the *Yoga Sutras,* Patanjali
becomes a bit more systematic. He begins categoriz-
ing and listing the various ways and practices required
of the yogi to attain Self-realization:

> The preliminary steps to Yoga are austerity
> (*tapas*), study (*svadhyaya*), and the dedication   of
> the fruits of one's work to God.

Austerity is the natural outcome of a mind disciplined to focus in one direction; study is a great help-
mate in that discipline; and the dedication of the
fruits of one's work to God is the means to be free
of any self-serving tendencies or egotistical ambitions
which only serve to fortify the false sense of ego.

Again, he adds a warning to the unwary that the
path to Self-realization is not a pursuit without obstacles and difficulties. "The obstacles to enlightenment,"
says Patanjali, "are ignorance   (which he defines as
regarding the non-eternal, impure and painful as eternal,
pure and blissful), egoism (which he defines as identifying consciousness with that which merely reflects

consciousness), attachment (to the pleasurable), aversion (to the painful), and clinging to life."

The subject of egoism, the identification of consciousness with that which merely reflects consciousness, then becomes a point of departure for Patanjali. "The seer," he says, "is pure Consciousness; but, though pure, it appears as the [activity of the] mind." This mental activity is then the object of perception for the seer; it is "the seen." Patanjali goes on to say:

> The seen exists only for the sake of the seer; the seer is identified with the seen only so that the seer may experience itself.

You see, he is speaking of that illusory duality of subject-object of which I spoke earlier. It is all the play of the Self; it is He who becomes the thought-forms, and it is He who is their witness. This is true both on the cosmic and on the individual levels.

> The seen (i.e., the thoughts, images, etc.) exists only when the seer (i.e., the pure Witness, the Self) becomes incognizant of his own nature. And the seer regains His independent and free state when that ignorance is dissolved. The means to dispel that ignorance is the uninterrupted practice of the awareness of the Self.

Here we are back again to *abhyasa*! -- the practice of the awareness of the Self! This is the recurring injunction of all the scriptures and all the sages. Shankaracharya, for example, spoke frequently of the practice of Self-knowledge (*jnan-abhyasa*). This is the real purification of the mind: to know yourself as God's own manifestation, and to retain that awareness in all circumstances. It is this truth we must practice, if we are to know the freedom and peace and happiness of our true nature, our eternal Self.

Patanjali then introduces his "eight limbs" of yoga, which detail the prerequisites to Self-realization. These include such moral precepts as non-violence, non-lying, non-stealing, non-violence, etc.; and such practices as breath-control (*pranayama*), proper posture (*asana*), leading to concentration (*dharana*), meditation (*dhyana*), and absorption (*samadhi*). "Then," says Patanjali, comes cessation of ignorance, the cause of suffering, and freedom from the effects of actions. Then, the whole universe, with all its objects of sense-perception, becomes as nothing compared to the infinite perception which is free from all obstructions and impurities. This is liberation. The Self shines forth in its own pristine nature, as pure Consciousness.

We turn to such spiritual texts as Patanjali's *Yoga Sutras* because we wish to find peace in understanding and to discover the path to true knowledge of the Self. We require some guidelines by which to journey on the path, and such texts as this can provide them. In essence, however, all such guidelines may be reduced to a very few basic principles of conduct:

(1) *Understand the nature of the mind.* It produces thoughts as the ocean produces waves. Witness them, but do not identify with them. Withdraw your attention from the incessant clamor of thoughts and become aware of who is watching and listening to the thoughts. Identify with that clear consciousness; because that's the only real you there is. Thoughts are the product of temporal influences; they have a beginning and an end. But you, the Self, are eternal.

(2) *Practice Self-awareness.* Give less attention to thinking, and more attention to your Self. Find joy in silence. And if you can't attain to perfect inner silence, take a word, such as a name for God, or a sound that corresponds to the sound of your breath, to help you to return again and again to the awareness that is you, beyond thoughts, beyond the chattering mind. It is a practice that may be done in absolute secrecy; no one need know. Return again and again to this practice; you'll find an imperturbable confidence and peace that is much more satisfying than anything else you could think or say or do.

(3) *Meditate regularly.* Find time in the early mornings and in the evenings to meditate, to 're-collect' your mind and focus it on your Self without the distractions of the active world. It is this time alone which must become your most valued treasure. Then, during the busyness of your day, carry out your duties in the clarity obtained during those times of meditation,

secure in the knowledge that all before your eyes
and behind them is Divine, is your very own Self.

No longer is the Divinity thought of as something
other than oneself, but is realized at all times to be
the very soul and substance of one's conscious existence.   Such a person, whose mind is completely
purified, no longer recognizes anything but God.   His
thoughts are God, his images are God and even his
agitation is God.   His acts are God, as well as their
consequences; and every object that is perceived
before his eyes is recognized as his own Divine sport.
Above all, he never loses sight of his own identity,
and never ceases to experience the calm certainty
and sweet bliss of his own eternal Self.   May this
perfect state of purity, which all are destined to
enjoy, be yours today.

Reflection

What is it that keeps me from being all I can
be?   Ah, it is the long-established habits of my
mind!   The habits of indolence, the habits of forgetfulness!   Habits can be broken, to be sure; and yet I
know full well that it is only I, and no one else,
who can lift my mind to wakefulness, and keep me
ever alert to Truth.   And I know that no one else
but I, myself, stands guard to prevent my wayward
mind from slipping downward into the dark fantasies
of delusion.

Then let me resolve this moment to awake!   And,
though I fall asleep at my post again and again, let
me rouse myself again and again; until, by my very
persistence and determination, I train this mind to
cling to wakefulness, and learn to retain my nature
as purity and clarity and light, consistently and uninter-
ruptedly.

O mind, you are the clear blue sky of peace and
bliss!   You are already perfect and free, unblemished,
and full to the brim with light.   Do not identify
with the clouds that float by in the breeze.   Let the
light from the Sun of Knowledge, rising high, disperse
those clouds; and see, with sight unimpaired, your
infinite Self, your conscious and blissful Self, stretch-
ing, boundlessly, everywhere.

*   *   *

THE PATH OF DIVINE LOVE

Whenever the question arises of how one is to become more aware of one's own Divine Self so as to enjoy the bliss and freedom of an expanded awareness, then we discover that there are two separate and distinct paths vying for our allegiance. One says, "Since the eternal Self is your true and lasting Identity, why don't you identify with That, and not with the ephemeral appearance of the ego-mind and body. Remain always identified with that pure Consciousness which is the witness of the mind and body, and be free." This is the call to the path of knowledge, or *jnan*.

But there is another point of view which also asks to be heard; this is the view of those who extol the path of Divine Love, or *bhakti*. Those who follow this devotional path say: "Oh, it's true all right that your real Identity is the eternal Self, but how can you hope to become aware of that pure and perfect Self without first making your heart and mind pure? First you must foster in your heart the habit of love, and then you may become aware of the One who is unconditional Love. Foster in your mind the thought of oneness with all beings; then you may become aware of the One who is Unity itself. Your separative ego, your sense of individuality keeps you apart from the awareness of the one Self; therefore humble your ego before the Self in the manner of a servant before his master, or a child before a parent, or a lover before her beloved. Then you will be prepared and able to experience the Infinite, the eternal Self."

Which of these two approaches to Self-realization is correct then? The path of knowledge or the path of love? The knower says, "There is but One; identify with That, for in truth you *are* That!" The lover says, "That may be so, but so long as there is the appearance of a separate self, make it subservient to the universal Self, until it is merged in and dissolved in the Divine." Clearly, they are both true, both correct, both valid and proper paths for the sincere aspirant.

There is a saying that the path of devotion and

the path of knowledge are like two men, one blind and the other lame. Neither are able to get about on their own. The devotee without discrimination can't see where he's going; and the man of knowledge without love is unable to progress due to a lack of mobility. However, if we put the two of them together, they are able to manage very well; for then, the man of knowledge rides on the shoulders of the devotee, and the devotee becomes his legs, while he serves as the devotee's eyes. So this is what we also must do with the two complementary sides of our own nature; we must unite the two; that way we have the benefit of both knowledge and devotion.

Oftentimes, the faculty of devotional love is characterized as being akin to the feminine side of our nature; and the sober, discriminative intellect is thought of as being a masculine trait. It is the feminine side of us which is capable of tenderness, compassion, emotional love, self-effacement through service, etc. And it is the masculine side of ourselves which allows us to be coldly analytical, logical, dispassionate, unattached, etc. But, clearly, both of these "aspects" present in everyone to some degree, are necessary to our progress in the spiritual life.

If we were to examine the lives and characteristics of the saints and sages of all the various religious traditions whom we have known, we would no doubt find that some were more devotional, some more discriminative. However, I am certain that, in all cases of genuine spiritual greatness, we would find that the intellect and the heart played equally essential parts; for, like the blind man and the lame man, the heart and the intellect are helpless without the other.

The heart without discrimination falls into the pit of sentimentality and sensuality; the intellect without the sweetness of the heart remains a dried-up cripple, unable to enjoy life in the world. It is my considered opinion that if a person is to reach the highest perfection possible to man, there must be a balance of heart and mind. There must be both the knowledge of the Self, and at the same time, the love of God.

All the great scriptures of all the world's religions extol in one way or another the focusing of the mind on God. This is what is known as "devotion." Listen to how two different sages have defined it: Narada, who was the epitome of the devotee of God, defines devotion in his *Bhakti Sutras* as "the constant flow of love towards the Lord, without any selfish desire." Shankaracharya, who was chief among the followers of the path of knowledge, says in his *Viveka-chudamani,* "Devotion is continuous meditation on one's own true Self."   It will be evident to the intelligent person that whether we focus our minds on God or on the Self, it is the same; that devotion to God is nothing else but meditation on the Self.   In either case, we must transcend the individual ego, the false sense of selfhood.

Whether we regard ourselves as the worshipper or the worshipped, there is nothing here but the One, playing both of these roles.   Whether we call our intrinsic nature by the name of "Bliss" or "Love", its taste remains the same.   We may call the Eternal by whatever name we like; we may sing it out to our heart's content.   Whether we are gamboling in the streets or sitting quietly in our meditation room, we are always God playing within God.   To remember Him is our only happiness; to forget Him our only sorrow.

In the Upanishads, we find a description of how the universe came into being: "This world," it says, "arose from Bliss, lives in Bliss, and will eventually merge back into Bliss."[1]   This word, "Bliss," is synonymous with the word, "Love."   Love is God.   And Love is the universe.   The supreme Lord has manifested Himself as this world out of Love.   Existence is nothing but the loving throb of the Divine.   Man, therefore, is nothing but a flame of Love.   Within us is the Divine Love that is God.   However, if we are not experiencing that Divine Love, we must ask ourselves how we may discover, experience, and manifest that Love, that Bliss.   Those who know, say that Love is attained by loving.

For some, this path, the path of *bhakti*, is considered to be a lower path, a path for beginners, or emotionalists; but the fact is, the path of Divine Love is the highest path of all.   Why?   Because it is the path of immediate joy; it is the quickest and easiest path to God-realization.   It is also the most natural and therefore the most available path to all. But also because, since supreme Love is the highest state, your final goal, then it makes sense to make love your practice as well.   There is no doubt that love is the most gratifying and effective means of God-realiization.   Any discipline lacking love can never lead one to the soul's Bliss.

We must understand that Love is nothing else but the Divine in us.   It reveals Itself when our hearts *Grace* are pure enough to receive It.   Not by our doing, but by Its own doing is It revealed; that is why It is referred to as grace.   Grace cannot be explained.   If it was something that could be explained in terms of cause and effect, then it wouldn't be grace.   Grace means something freely given, without cause or desert. You can't earn grace; but, on the other hand, grace is never withheld from those who seek it with a pure heart.   That Divine grace manifests in many different ways, but is always leading the individual to the path of spiritual realization.   The truth is that it is God's grace that is the only cause of Self-realization; and it is entirely independent of human effort.

All of the great sages of the past have come to the conclusion that grace is absolutely undetermined and unconditioned.   What may, at first, appear to be a condition of grace, turns out upon closer inspection to be a consequence of grace.   For example, perhaps an inspirational book awakens your spiritual aspirations, and your soul is stirred to great heights.   You may say it was the reading of that book which was the condition required for the grace you experienced; but consider, was it not God's grace that brought that book into your hands and opened your mind to receive it?

Another question may arise: If Divine grace has no regard for the merit or demerit of the recipients, does it not amount to an act of partiality on the part of God?   How is it that He favors some individuals by bestowing His grace and disfavors others by keeping it from them?   And the answer is that grace is always operating in all individuals.   The difference in the descent of grace is really in the differences of receptivity in each individual.   Also, we have to consider that, since it is only God Himself who appears as the bound soul, and then becomes liberated, all according to His own free will, He cannot be accused of partiality, as it is only Himself whom He favors or rejects.

Also, we must recognize that grace visits us with different intensities and in different forms at different times.   Each person's individual destiny according to their soul-evolution is on a separate "schedule", so to speak.   There is a time for the dawning of under- standing, and there is a time for worldly accomplish- ments, a time for solitude, and a time for sharing love with others, and so forth.

In fact, it is possible to tell something of the nature of the life-cycle or particular focus operating in a person's life at a given time by the examination of the planetary movements in relation to their posi- tions at that person's birth.   This is so because the universe is one whole, and each part reflects the other. We may think of the cosmos as a huge clock, which when referred to each individual soul, tells the life-time of each.   Those who can read the configur- ations of the planets can tell us something of the kind of life-experiences apt to occur during any given period.

But do not misunderstand!   Do not imagine that grace is dependent upon the positions of the planets and can only operate when everything is lined up appropriately.   This is thinking backwards.   The fact that the whole universe is coordinated does not mean that grace is fixed, determined.   No.   It is God who creates this universe of His own free will.   The events of our life may seem determined from our perspective, but God is creating everything of His own free will.   He is the One who determines when you will be feeling devotion, when you will need to struggle to overcome old tendencies, when you will suddenly experience the Love, the Unity, of God.   It is all His play.   And His sense of time is quite differ- ent from ours.   For Him, an entire lifetime is scarcely an instant.   But one thing we may be sure of: all of us must eventually be brought to perfect clarity in the Unity of God.

Meanwhile, we experience His grace in many different ways; and we should recognize that it is

God's grace that is working through us.   Perhaps the first grace, the first taste we have of God's presence in our life, is the grace of aspiration, the desire to understand the nature of our own existence.   This grace may occur to us while we are still children, or it may occur when we are older, and have already put behind us all other desires.   Such grace may involve the pain of severance from old ties and allegiances; but it is grace nonetheless, and it is drawing us toward the light of our true, eternal Self.

Then comes the dawning of the light of understanding.   This is a very special time, a great gift of grace.   The mind is suddenly filled with a new and wonderful understanding which had hitherto been hidden from it.   All becomes clear, and all one's past life is seen to have been leading inexorably toward this present clarity of mind, this new awareness of the unity of Existence.

But this dawning of light is but the beginning.   It comes only to whet our appetite.   And along with this little bit of light, He also puts before us some obstacles to the keeping of that light, so we might come to understand what those obstacles are that pull the mind away from the clarity of vision.   So we learn to practice patience and to make greater effort to remember Him.   He nurses us along in His infinite wisdom, knowing precisely what is needed for each of us to inch us along toward perfection.   And there will be many inches gained and then lost, only to be regained.

Even in times of great trouble, God's grace is there.   His grace comes to us in two ways: (1) In fulfilling our needs, both spiritual and worldly; and (2) in placing obstacles before us, so that we can grow strong in faith and strong in perseverance.   He brings us occasions of trial and dryness so that we may have the victory over all adversities, and thereby become confident in the power and goodness of God within us.

Then there is the grace of devotion, the grace of Love.   It is a very special gift of grace, and is sought by all the saints who've ever lived.   It is the one thing needed to wend one's way to God Himself.   And so to win this great gift is something much to

be prized and prayed for.   This is how Krishna, speaking as the incarnation of God, advised his disciple in
the *Bhagavad Gita*:

> Give Me your mind and give Me your heart;
> give Me your offerings and your adoration; and
> thus, with your soul in harmony, and making
> Me your supreme goal, you shall truly come to
> Me. [2]

And again:

> Only by love can men see Me, and know
> Me, and come unto Me.   He who works for Me,
> who loves Me, who regards Me alone as his
> supreme goal, who is free from attachment to
> all things, and with love for all creation, he in
> truth comes to Me. [3]

In my own case, the grace of love for God came
upon me very suddenly and spontaneously.   And the
more I read of the lives of the saints, the more surely
I was convinced that I had no other goal in my life
but God, and day by day the grace of love increased
in me.   For me, there is no doubt that it was God's
grace which drew me lovingly to Himself, and made
me to know my oneness with Him.   Listen also to
what some other Western seers have said about the
power of God's grace:

Philo Judaeus:

> Without Divine grace, it is impossible to
> leave the ranks of mortality; [but] when grace
> fills the soul, it is possessed and inspired, ...
> and hastens to that most glorious and loveliest
> of visions, the vision of the Uncreated. [4]
> ... The soul, stirred to its depth and maddened
> by heavenward yearning, [is] drawn by the truly
> existent Being and pulled upward by Him. [5]

Plotinus:

> When the Divine in us stirs us, then the soul
> becomes filled with a holy ecstasy; stung by
> desire, it becomes love.   ... When there enters
> into it a glow from the Divine, the soul gathers
> strength, spreads true wings, and, however dis-
> tracted by its proximate environment, speeds its

buoyant way to something greater; it's very
nature bears it upwards, lifted by the Giver of
that love.   Surely we need not wonder that It
possesses the power to draw the soul to Itself,
calling it back from every wandering to rest
before It; [for] from It came everything; nothing
is mightier. [6]

St. John of the Cross:
   Desire for God is the preparation for union
with Him.   If a person is seeking God, his
Beloved is seeking him much more.   And if a
soul directs to God its loving desires, God
sends forth His fragrance by which He draws
it and makes it run after Him. [7]

In a time known only to Him, God sends His
grace of revelation; He reveals Himself to His lover.
And the lover then knows that God is his own Self.
He reveals that there never was anything other than
God; that nothing at all exists but Himself.   The
lover who obtains this grace knows full well that it
was God's grace and nothing else that brought to
him this vision.   All who have obtained it declare to
all the world that they realized God by His grace
alone.   Listen to what some seers from the East
have had to say about it:

Dattatreya:
   Truly, it is by the grace of God that the
knowledge of Unity arises within.   Then a man
is released at last from the great fear of life
and death. [8]

Shankaracharya:
   Teachers and scriptures can stimulate spiritual awareness.   But the wise disciple crosses
the ocean of ignorance by direct illumination,
through the grace of God. [9]

Sri Ramakrishna:
   You may try thousands of times, but nothing
can be achieved without God's grace.   One
cannnot see God without His grace.   But God
can be seen the moment His grace descends.

He is the Sun of knowledge.   One single ray of
His has illumined the world with the light of
knowledge.   This is how we are able to see one
another and acquire various kinds of knowledge.
One can see God only if He turns His light
towards Himself.[10]

Yet even this, the vision of God, is not the end of
His graces to His devotees.   After this, He bestows
many wonderful graces, leading Jesus of Nazareth to
say, "Seek ye first the kingdom of God, then all the
rest shall be added unto ye."   All that follows upon
the grace of vision is just so many lessons on how to
live in absolute freedom; in other words, how to be
one with God while eating, sleeping, walking, sitting,
while giving, while receiving, while enjoying, and while
suffering.   This is the grace of freedom, of unity, of
perfect contentment.   Such continuously ongoing peace
and happiness cannot be had without much grace.
That grace comes from the Self, from God within us.
There is no final grace; it just goes on giving forever.

The author of the *Svetasvatara Upanishad* said it well
when he said:

He is indeed the Lord supreme whose grace
moves the hearts of men.   He leads us unto
His own Joy and to the glory of His Light. [11]

Reflection

The love of God is sweet, O friend!   Please do
have a taste of it.   Call on Him, your compassionate
Father, with a true and yearning heart, and He will
fill your body and your mind with the nectar of love.

Look up and reach to Him; beg for His embrace.
Can a father refuse to draw his child to his breast?
Cry for Him, and He will certainly lift you to His
heart.

Turn your attention upward; it is there He lives.
Call to Him, and feel the rapture He bestows upon
your soul.   Delicious caresses He bestows upon the
yearning heart!   The spine tingles with the uprushing
joy that flows upward toward Him.   O friend, the
love of God is sweet!   It is nectar to the thirsty soul.

Please don't hesitate; the cup is brimming full.   O
friend, the love of God is sweet!

*   *   *

THE PATH OF DIVINE LOVE
PART II

Let us assume that Divine Love has awakened in your heart, by the grace of God.   Still, there is much to learn in order to retain that Love, and to continue along the path to God-realization.   There are many guides to help us along that path, and one often accepted as an unfailing authority is the book called *The Bhakti Sutras*, attributed to the legendary sage, Narada.   It is this book which will serve as a framework for the following discussion of the nature and practice of devotion.

Narada begins his book by defining *bhakti*:

Bhakti is the constant flow of love towards the Lord, without any selfish desire.   This bhakti is the nectar of immortality (*amrit*).

When God's love awakes in the heart it fills the mind and body with a nectarean joy.   As one thinks of God, thrills flood the body, and one's hair stands on end, as thought inwardly caressed by the hand of God, or as though bathed in the dissolving warmth of His glance.   Truly, this Love is nectar; it transforms one from an ordinary blind and bound soul dedicated to selfish aims into a devout and blissful child of God, dedicated to His love and service.

Here's what the medieval Christian saint, Thomas a Kempis, had to say about this love:

Love is a great and goodly thing, and alone makes heavy burdens light, and bears equally all things, pleasant and unpleasant.   It bears a heavy burden and feels it not, and makes bitter things to be savory and sweet.   The noble love of God perfectly printed in the soul makes a man to do great things, and stirs him always to desire perfection, growing more and more in grace and goodness.

Love will always have his mind upward to God and will not be occupied with love of the world.   Love will also be free from all worldly affections, that the inward sight of the soul be not darkened or hindered, nor that his affection for heavenly things be put aside willingly because of the inordinate winning or losing of worldly things.   Nothing, therefore, is more sweet than Love, nothing higher, nothing mightier, nothing greater, nothing more joyful, nothing fuller, nor anything better in heaven or in earth; for Love descends from God, and may not rest finally in anything but God.[1]

Narada then goes on to say:

Attaining this Love, one becomes perfect, Divine and contented; attaining this Love, one has no more desires.

In other words, one who experiences Divine Love feels that he is totally fulfilled, totally satisfied. He does not worry about his family, his job or the future.   Although he no longer has any desires, by God's grace and the power of devotion, everything comes easily to him; he lacks nothing.   He is filled with joy and sweetness, because God Himself is Bliss.

And, having attained Divine Love, one becomes intoxicated and enthralled, and becomes continually immersed in the Bliss of the Self. This Love isn't the same as lust; it's very essence is renunciation.

The desires for worldly satisfaction are painful distractions to the soul whose mind is drawn to God through prayer and contemplation.   To know that clarity, that eternal Bliss, he gladly renounces the lusty desires for what he recognizes to be mere images.   To know and experience God, he gladly surrenders God's world of illusion.

By "renunciation" is meant the dedication of all one's actions to God.   That renunciation brings union with God, and indifference toward everything else.

The need to renounce all worldly desire in order to attain God was often spoken of also by the great Sufi poet-saint, Kabir.   "Love based on desire for

gain," said Kabir, "is valueless!   God is desireless.
How, then, could one with desire attain the Desireless?
... Very subtle is the path of Love!   There, one loses
one's self at His feet; there, one is immersed in the
joy of the seeking, and plunged in the depths of Love
as a fish in the depths of the water.   The lover is
never slow in offering his head for his Lord's service.
Kabir declares the secret of Love."

'How strange,' one might think; 'must I really
offer my life, be willing to give up my head in order
to attain God?'   It is not one's actual death that is
necessary, of course, but the death of the ego-self.
The identity of the individual soul is to be sublimated
into the greater Identity of the one all-pervading
Self, in a continual surrendering of the separative
mind to the universal Mind, and an offering of the
individual self in the service of the universal Self.

This is the recurring theme among the devotional
poets of all traditions.   The poet, Kabir, whom we
already cited, asks of the devotee: "Are you ready to
cut off your head and place your foot on it?   If so,
come!   Love awaits you!   Love is not grown in a
garden, nor sold in the market-place.   Whether you
are a king or a subject, the price is your head and
nothing else.   The payment for the cup of Love is
your head!   O miser, do you flinch?   It is *cheap* at
that price!   Give up all expectation of gain.   Be like
one who has died, alive only to the service of God.
Then God will run after you crying, 'Wait!   Wait!
I'm coming!' "

Back to Narada:

Narada holds that bhakti is distinguished by
the dedication of all activities to God, complete
surrender to Him, and extreme anguish in the
event of forgetting Him.

We see evidenced in many writings of the poets
and lovers of God the extreme anguish that's felt
when the remembrance of God has slipped away through
lack of attentiveness.   The mind that is drawn by the
Love of God suffers greatly by the distractions of
everyday thoughts and rambling images that normally
course through the mind.

Love, the supreme Love, is superior to dedicated service, knowledge, or meditation, for it is the fruit of all of these. Also, because the Lord dislikes conceit or egoism, and likes the quality of longing, bhakti is best.

Service to mankind as service to God is a means to awaken love for God; this is true of knowledge and meditation as well. It is the Love, the bliss of devotion, that we seek; that is what our heart and soul desires. For that Love is a taste of God Himself; it is the sweetness of His supernatural presence, the gracious uplifting of the soul to His embrace. The longing of the heart for God is the signal of Love's approach.

Many other devotees of God have commented on the quality of longing or yearning as essential to the realization of God; here, for example, is what Kabir had to say on this theme:

O man, if you don't know your own Lord, what are you so proud of? Put your cleverness away; mere words can never unite you to Him. Do not deceive yourself with [merely reading or repeating] the words of the scriptures; Love is something other than this. He who has yearned for God knows what it is.

This yearning for God has been described by His devotees over the centuries as the thirst of a man whose throat is parched from lack of water, or like the suffering of a fish cast out upon the bank, or in a number of other ways. Sri Ramakrishna, the 19th century saint of Bengal, was once asked by a devotee how it is possible to develop Divine Love; and Ramakrishna said:

Through restlessness -- the restlessness a child feels for his mother. The child feels bewildered when it is separated from its mother, and weeps longingly for her. If a man can weep like that for God, he will see Him. At the approach of dawn, the eastern horizon becomes red. Then one knows it will soon be sunrise. Likewise, if you see a person restless for God, you can be pretty certain that he hasn't long to wait for His vision.

Then Sri Ramakrishna told this story:

> A disciple once asked his teacher, "Sir,
> please tell me how I can see God." "Come
> with me," said the Guru, "and I will show
> you." Then he took the disciple to a lake,
> and both of them got into the water. Suddenly
> the teacher pressed the disciples's head under
> the water. After a few moments he released
> him and the disciple raised his head and stood
> up, gasping for air. The Guru asked him,
> "How did you feel?" The disciple said, "Oh, I
> thought I would die! I was longing for a
> breath of air!" The teacher said, "When you
> feel like that for God, then you will know you
> haven't long to wait for His vision." [2]

> Narada: Some teachers think that knowledge
> alone is the means to attain bhakti; others
> think these two are mutually interdependent;
> but Narada thinks that the fruit is of the
> same kind as the tree.

In other words, Love comes from loving; knowledge
cannot produce it.

When we speak of the knowledge of the Self, we
must differentiate between that Knowledge which is
identical with Self-realization and that knowledge
which is a mere intellectual formulation of that
perfect Knowledge. Intellectual, conceptual, knowledge
of the Self is a wonderful thing, but it is only preparatory to the true, perfect, Knowledge -- the Knowledge which is synonymous with Enlightenment.
Conceptual knowledge we must certainly go beyond.
To do so, it is necessary to utilize the heart. Devotion leads the mind beyond mere intellectual knowledge to the experience of the blissful Self, which is
the true Knowledge.

Listen to this song, often sung by Sri Ramakrishna:

> How are you trying, O my mind, to know the
>   nature of God?
> You are groping like a madman locked in a
>   dark room.

He is grasped through ecstatic Love; how can
you fathom Him without it?
For that Love the mighty yogis practice yoga
from age to age.
Then, when Love awakes, the Lord, like a magnet,
draws to Him the soul.
It is in Love's elixer only that He delights, O
mind!
He dwells in the body's inmost depths, in everlasting Joy. [3]

The attainment of God, the attainment of the Bliss
associated with God-awareness, is not had by engaging
the mind in trying to figure out the nature of God.
This has its place, no doubt; but the Bliss of God-
awareness, Self-awareness, is attained through devotion.

Devotion requires a complete surrender of pride in
one's intellect; instead, one must supplicate God as a
child supplicates its mother.   One must cultivate an
awareness of one's utter dependency upon God for
everything, and the inward gaze of one's mind must be
upturned to the Source of all mind and all vision.

We engage our minds so often in circuitous analysis
and repetitive thought-patterns.   Far better would it
be if we could build into our minds the thought-pattern
of calling on God for our succor and support.   He is
capable of filling the mind and body with ecstasy and
light, of answering all our questions and setting our
minds in perfect peace.   All that's required is a pure
and innocent heart, and a simple and steady regard to
Him for all our satisfaction and reward.

As the mind becomes steady and one-pointed on
God, all questions will become answered automatically.
A mind at peace is a mind illumined by Truth.   Let
there be duality between you and your Lord!   But keep
on trying to close the gap through love.   Talk to Him.
Pray to Him.   Give all your life and love to Him.
And the God within you will manifest the more as you
become engrossed in Him.   You become what you
meditate on; so meditate on God.   Regard Him as the
only Reality, and become as a moth dancing about His
flame.   Yearn to be immersed in His perfect Light,
His perfect Love, and He will draw you into Himself
and make you one with Him.

Sri Ramakrishna became, at one time, so full of desire for God, whom he called "Mother," that people began to fear for him when they saw him weeping for his Mother to come to him, and singing:

O Mother, make me mad with Thy Love!
What need have I of knowledge or reason?
Make me drunk with Thy Love's wine;
O Thou who stealest thy lover's heart,
Drown me deep in the sea of Thy Love!
Here in this world, this madhouse of Thine,
Some laugh, some weep, some dance for joy.
Jesus, Buddha, Moses, Gauranga,
All are drunk with the wine of Thy Love.
O Mother, when shall I be blessed
By joining their blissful company? [4]

Such total abandon, such complete disregard for one's own reputation, status, future welfare, is typical of those who, in the end, attain to God.

Therefore, bhakti is the means that is worthy of acceptance by all seekers after liberation.

Bhakti, says Narada, is the goal; and bhakti is the means of attaining the goal.

Various teachers sing of the means to attain that Divine Love, and say that one may attain it right now by withdrawing one's attachment from the world; by continuous loving service; or by hearing and singing the glories of the Lord even while engaged in the ordinary activities of the world. But mainly, it is attained through the grace of God, or the grace of a great soul.

That grace is always there, and always seeking ways and means and opportunities to lift us up. That grace is the grace of our own inner Self, and so it has no trouble reaching us, so long as we are open and receptive to it. As Sri Ramakrishna often said, "The breeze of God's grace is always blowing, but we must set our sail for it."

The path of knowledge, with all its austerity, its renunciation, is really very difficult; so practice devotion to the Lord. This is really the easiest and best path. Just remember God all the time; focus your mind entirely on Him. All other thoughts will be swept away in your mind's eager rush to be fixed on Him alone. Truly, he is very fortunate indeed who has been gifted with a spark of Divine Love, and whose heart yearns for God and God alone. He speeds along the path to God-realization while the yogi is wearily practicing his dry exercises.

It is impossible to precisely describe the intrinsic nature of Divine Love; one is in the same predicament as a voiceless person asked to describe the taste of sugar.

That Love may manifest at any time or place in one who is fit to receive it. It has no distinctive characteristics, except that it is free of selfish motive. It is an extremely subtle inner experience of all-pervading Unity. Attaining That, one sees That alone, one hears That alone, one speaks of That alone, and one contemplates That alone.

Divine Love is easily recognized; it is not dependent upon any proof outside of itself; it is its own proof, because it takes the form of mental peace and supreme joy. One who has attained it has no anxiety about the miseries of the world; he has completely surrendered himself and the world to the Lord.

One who has dedicated all his activities to the Lord also dedicates such feelings as desire, anger, pride, and so forth to Him alone. That Love should be practiced which expresses itself as constant loving service, like that of a devoted servant or a loving wife.

The desire for God, for His grace, and His service, is the only legitimate desire for the purified ego, the servant-ego. To commune with God, to maintain that communion, and to become one with Him, becoming the instrument of His will, completely surrendered to His Love -- that is the only desire of the purified ego. That ego, which has been transformed into the servant of God, is no longer an obstacle to God-realization, but is rather a means toward the realization of God. You see, even though we may realize that the ego is false, that it is merely a mirage, still that is only an intellectual realization. The ego still remains. The sense of selfhood which identifies with the body and the mind and one's individual circumstances is still very much alive.

The ego is not gotten rid of so easily; in fact, even after God-realization, the ego, the sense of separation, returns again. Then, however, it is merely an appearance. It is like a chalk-drawing that has been erased. You can still see the trace of where it was, but it scarcely exists. The truth is, one cannot function at all without a little of a sense of connection with the mind and body; so we keep a little ego. It's alright. So long as we regard ourselves as the children, the lovers, the servants of God, that kind of ego is okay. It doesn't have the ability to hurt anyone, or to create attachment. It is only an appearance; it is engaged solely in the worship of God -- regardless of the circumstances in which it finds itself. It remains conscious of the presence of God in all places, and in all beings; and thinks only of how it can awaken the Love, the Bliss, of God in all others.

For devotion, we require some ego, as devotion is a dualistic practice; that is to say that, for devotion, there must be two: the devotee and the object of devotion. We know, of course, that there's only One; but the apparent duality of the soul and God exists so long as we do not directly experience that Unity. So, in the practice of devotion, we utilize that apparent duality, that sense of separateness, to make and strengthen our bond to the One. Then, instead of operating as randomly self-indulgent persons, we become servants of God, thinking always in every circumstance of surrendering to His will.

His will is Love; His will is our Joy. How to keep alive that Love, that Joy, is the task of life. We say that we "follow His will," or that we "surrender to His will;" but it is the Love that is our own essential nature that we wish to follow, to which we wish to surrender. In our make-believe duality between ourselves and God, we make of ourselves the servants of Love, following the ways of Love, until we become established in Love. That Love is our

very nature; but, because we have encrusted our
hearts and minds with so many wrong concepts and
habits, we must make our way back to our true
nature by conforming to what seems to be something
other than, and greater than, our limited selves.   As
we learn to be more and more attentive to God, to
God's Love within us, we are actually becoming more
and more attuned to our own true nature.   As we do
so, that Love, which is our own nature, becomes
more and more manifest in us as a natural exhilaration,
an imperturbable peace, a thrilling sense of the Divine,
which leads us ever upward toward mergence in the
absolute Unity.

Sri Ramakrishna, the modern-day saint of India,
knew how persistent is this false sense of ego.   For
this reason, he taught not the denial of this ego, but
surrender of the transformed ego in devotion and
service to God.   "The devotee," he said, "feels 'O
God, Thou art the Lord and I am Thy servant.'   This
is the ego of devotion.   Why does such a lover of
God retain the 'ego of devotion?'   There is a reason.
The ego cannot be gotten rid of; so let the rascal
remain as the servant of God, the devotee of God."

You see, Sri Ramakrishna understood that, so long
as this universe exists, the *apparent* duality of soul
and God continues to exist.   Both of these are real
-- until such time as God merges the soul into Himself.   Our identity consists of both the absolute Consciousness and the relative phenomena, both the universal Self and the individualized self.   It is foolish
not to acknowledge both sides of our nature.   To do
so only leads us into great conflicts and difficulties.
We are the manifestation of the universal Mind as
well as that Mind Itself.   We are a wave on the
Ocean as well as the Ocean itself.   We mustn't deny
and neglect the existence of the soul, and assert
only, "I am pure Consciousness."   The active soul
will rise up and make you acknowledge its presence.
The only way to lead the soul to the experience of
its all-pervasiveness is to teach it love.   If the soul
goes on expanding its power to love, it will be transformed into love, and merge finally into the absolute
Love.

No amount of acquired knowledge will merge the

soul into God; nor can the soul be dissolved into God
by force or the power of the will.   It will only become   more   frustrated,   agitated,   and   antagonistic.
Instead of trying to punish or force the soul, lead it
into meditation by the power of love.   Soak the cloth
of your soul in the dye of love; then it will become
the color of love, and merge into the sweetness of
God.

   Those devotees are the greatest who feel
one-pointed love for the Lord for His own sake.
Conversing with one another with choking voices,
hair standing on end, and tears in their eyes,
they purify not only their own families but the
entire earth.   They make holy places holy; they
lend goodness to good deeds, and authority to
the scriptures, for they are filled with His
Spirit.   Their ancestors rejoice, the gods dance
with joy, and the earth feels it has a savior.
Among such beings there is no distinction based
on caste, learning, beauty, family, wealth, pro-
fession, and so forth, because they recognize
everything as belonging to Him.

   Philosophical disputes are not to be entered
into, as there is room for diversity in viewpoints,
and no single viewpoint is exclusively correct.
One should reflect upon scriptural teachings on
devotion, and one should practice that which
awakens devotion.   The blessed Lord alone is to
be adored and worshipped at all times with a
mind free from care.   He quickly manifests and
reveals Himself to those devotees who thus
glorify Him.

The essence of Narada's message -- and all the
saints have echoed it -- is that in order to experience
the highest state of God's Love, one must (1) remember Him constantly, (2) see Him only at all times,
and (3) give oneself completely in His service.

   About remembering Him constantly: One of the
easiest ways to do this is to repeat the name of God
continually in your heart.   This is the practice recommended by all the saints of all religious traditions.   It
is the nectar on which all the saints are drunk.   Let
His name be sung aloud or silently; cling to it as a

drowning man clings to a log floating on the sea.
And at night, when you go to bed, repeat His name
with love and pray that He will wake you in the
morning with His name on your lips.

We remember Him by the singing of His name,
but we draw near to Him through prayer.   Now,
what is prayer?   It is a dialogue with God, with
your real Self. but, more than that, it is an intensi-
fication of the focus of one's attention upon the
Eternal within.   The important thing is that we look
entreatingly to God for help.   His compassion is
well-known. and why should He not be compassionate
to one who is a manifestation of Himself?   Have
faith in that truth: that you are a manifestation of
the highest Lord.   And continually commune inwardly
with Him.   Instead of allowing the mind to wander
incessantly in dead-end alleyways, engage it purposely
in searching out God.   Beseech Him to draw you
nearer and nearer to Him, to lift up your soul into
His Light.   Have no other thought for as long as you
can sustain it.   Focus your attention so deliberately,
so entreatingly, that He cannot resist the urgency of
your call.

Show Him your tears, and your bare heart.   He
will caress you with His tender touch.   Concentrate
on the thought that this very body in which you sit
is the light-body of God.   It is only a quivering mass
of Energy, vibrating at frequencies which give the
appearance of form.   What is this Energy?   It is the
one Light.   He alone fills all this universe.   Know
that you are nothing but That.   What else could you
possibly be?   Be filled with Divine Joy, and never
cease your prayer that you may live and act as His
instrument on earth.   Prayer is the tender thread by
which you retain contact with that highest Self; it is
nothing else but a concentrated focus of consciousness
upon itself.   As much as you are able, keep that
contact alive by calling inwardly His name during the
course of your active life.

And, of course, when you are able to cease your
involvement in worldly affairs, then leave everything
else aside, and be free to give your whole mind to
Him.   Keep as your special time for communing
freely with your Lord at least one hour in the early

morning; and at night also, break away from your
recreation, and sit in your special and private place,
so you can return to the peace and silence of your
eternal Self. That's where you will find your strength,
your rest, your invigoration, your inspiration, your
solace, your greatest joy. And it will carry over into
all your life and all your relationships and all your
activities in the world.

It is devotion, it is the continual obsession with
God, and the long upward climb to Him, calling out
His name, and pleading for His grace and light, that
will bring you slowly but surely to that state of self-
negation in which you will be capable of merging into
the state of contemplation of God. Devotion merges
into contemplation and contemplation merges into
devotion. They are closely related, and it's really not
difficult to mix the two. Devotion and contemplation
flow one into the other like water into water; the
one does not disturb the other. In fact, the more
bliss you feel in contemplation, the more it becomes
transformed into the tender love for God which we
call devotion.

Love for the absolute, eternal Truth is the
greatest path. Indeed, Divine Love is the highest.
Whoever has faith in these teachings of Narada
and who practices them, attains Love and realizes
his beloved Lord. Truly, he attains that Lord
whom everyone adores.

Reflection

Lord of the universe, watch over me and guide me
in this, my time on earth. Shed on me the light of
true understanding that I may see the way that Thou
hast ordained for my life. And lift me from my
weakness to Thy strength that I may serve as Thy
vessel of Truth in this world of Thy children.

God of all peoples, great Mind of the universe,
gentle Father, tender Mother, fill me with Thy song
of joy, and let the sound of Thy sweet love reverberate
through all the earth. Make me worthy to uphold
Thy banner, and worthy to receive Thy blessing, that
the fragrance of Thy sweetness may be wafted from

this heart to fill the whole world with the heavenly nectar of love's bouquet.

*   *   *

JAPA: THE REMEMBRANCE OF GOD

One who has been granted the "vision" of the ultimate Reality, who has realized the absolute Truth, God Himself, knows without the least doubt that everything that exists is nothing but God. He has no more need of philosophical theories about the nature of reality; he has seen that it is God who exists as the very consciousness that lives and experiences as 'I', and it is God who exists as every perceivable form. In other words, He is, in every case, the subject; and He is, in every case, the object.

Naturally, those people who have not been graced with the realization of this truth, identify solely with the individual perspective which they possess as perceiver, and regard all that they perceive as something 'other' than themselves. But, say the seers, the expounders of Vedanta, it is the one eternal Consciousness who is manifesting as the subject, and it is that same Consciousness who is manifesting as the phenomena that we perceive as the 'objective' world. Everything is God -- both the subject and the object. It is He who is the witness of the universal play, and it is He who provides that universal drama from His own creative imagination. He projects Himself as Energy-in-form, and then lives within His creation as the many individual subjects who experience that world of forms through their senses.

The subject-object relationship is most evident to us in our perception of objects in the external world, but it is just as operative, though in a subtler way, in our perception of internal phenomena -- such as thoughts, images, reveries, etc. Ordinarily, we do not think of such phenomena as "objective" occurrances because they are so ephemeral and insubstantial. Also, because they occur within our minds, we tend to view them as part of the "subjective" reality. Strictly speaking, however, the subjective "I", the witness-Self, is pure, unqualified Consciousness; clear, unblemished Awareness. Thoughts, images, dreams, etc., as they arise, are projected from that pure Consciousness and appear upon that conscious Screen as "objective" phenomena. Thus, on this subtle, mind-level, the witness-Self, which is the true subject, experiences mental phenomena as the "objects" of perception.

The pure Consciousness, or witness-Self, is the only subject; and all that is perceived, both on the subtle and on the gross sensual level, is the object. This apparent duality of subject and object constitutes all experience. Without this apparent separation between the two, no experience would be possible. However, we must never lose sight of the fact that this duality is *apparent* only; and that God and the world, the experiencing Self and the experienced phenomena is a Unity still. This is the ever-recurring theme of Vedanta, also known as the philosophy of *Advaita*, or "Non-Dualism." For, while it admits to an apparent duality existing between the immortal Self and the world-appearance, as between the individual awareness and the activity of the mind, it does not acknowledge an actual duality. There is nothing that is not God: this is the watchword of Vedanta. From this, it clearly follows that *tat tuam asi*, "That thou art!"

However, even though we may know with certainty that this is true, we may continue to identify with our own unique perspective from the standpoint of our own embodied soul. To explain what the soul is, we may compare it with a wave on the ocean which identifies with its wave-form and not with the entire ocean. From its isolated perspective, it is, of course, a unique wave, separate from all other waves; but when that wave comes to know its own nature, it will realize that it is only a manifestation of the ocean, which has never really divided its identity into separate waves. We too, like waves on the ocean, continue to identify with our separate make-believe identities, even though we know intellectually that there is no one here but God. That make-believe identity is the "soul". When true realization comes, it will know that it was never anything but God, and that no "soul" ever existed. Nonetheless, while it has the semblance of existence, it cries out in longing for God, and seeks Him as though instead of being the subject, He were an object to be attained.

The truth is that, whether we seek Him as the

ever-present subject, "I", or as the ever-present object, "Thou", we must seek Him beyond the puny ego of individual personality, in the silence of a keen and clear intelligence. For it is only in the upper reaches of concentrated intelligence, in the rarefied atmosphere reached only by a soaring mind, uplifted on the draft of Grace, that He is found. In truth, He is both subject and object; it is He who plays both of these parts. It is He who calls out to Himself, and it is He who answers, "See, I have always been here as you!"

The man of knowledge, identifying with the One, speaks of being aware of the Self; and the man of devotion, identifying with the soul, speaks of remembering God. But the pure sky of Consciousness whom the man of knowledge calls the Self is the same eternal Consciousness whom the devotee calls God. One identifies himself with that pure Consciousness and calls it "I"; the other regards It as other than himself, and calls It "Thou". But both are setting their eyes toward the same eternal One.

And though the man of knowledge may speak of being aware of the Self, there is no awareness of the Self, for the Self is Awareness. Can Awareness be aware of Itself?   Yes; but only in the unitive "vision". And the devotee who speaks of remembering God is likewise defeated, for God is quite beyond the comprehension of the intellect or the conception of the imagination or the vision of memory. It is possible, however, to lift the individual soul to the awareness of God in the unitive vision through an intense aspiration which utilizes "reminders" as rungs on the ladder leading to mental clarity and higher consciousness. Such reminders may take the form of prayer, the reading of devotional works, the singing of hymns of love, or the mental repetition of a name which brings to the mind of the individual the awareness of God. These lift the consciousness from its limited individual perspective to a Divine perspective from which all is seen as it truly is, as God.

The mental repetition of the name of God is the highest form of prayer; it is prayer reduced to its essence. It is concentrated aspiration and love-longing minus all the self-serving guile of petitionary prayer.

A mind focused on a *mantra*, a single word-symbol for God, is a mind reduced to one-pointedness. It is just such fervent single-mindedness which is capable of supplanting the normally scattered flow of worldly thoughts, leaving in its stead a calm and focused awareness, empty of thought, full of peace and bliss.

And because it is so simple and so effective a method of emptying the mind of its contents, and directing the flow of awareness inward upon itself, it is one which has been highly recommended by numerous sages and saints over the centuries.

There is, of course, no end to the number of names that may be given to God, who is the absolute Existence in which we live. And each one has the power to focus the mind upon its conscious Source. All that is needed is a sweet fondness for that particular name and a true and sincere love for Him whom that name signifies. There are those who have extolled the name of "Rama," or "Krishna," or "Karim," or "Adonai;" all these names are holy, for it is the same One who is signified by each.

In the following Song in praise of the practice of reciting the Name of God, the name used is "Hari". As a familiar appelation for Vishnu, or His manifestation, Krishna, it refers to God as the adorable Beloved, "the stealer of hearts". Here in this Song of 25 verses, Eknath Maharaj extols the practice of singing the name of Hari, and elaborates upon its benefits. However, before the Song itself, I'd like to tell you just a little about its author, Eknath Maharaj.

Eknath lived from 1548 to 1609. When he was still a young boy, he heard a voice speaking to him in his meditation which said, "Go to Devgiri Fort!" Now, in the 13th and 14th centuries, this Fort had been a glorious castle, the center of a great kingdom, but now it was merely a ruins. And when Eknath went there and searched among the ruins, he found living there the man who was to become his Guru, whose name was Janardan Swami. Under the tutelege of Janardan, Eknath became a great yogi, and later wrote many wonderful works.

One day, during his adult years, while he was meditating, Eknath saw in his meditation a vision of Jnaneshvar, a great saint who had lived three centuries

before him in the same region.   Jnaneshvar, who had
entered his tomb alive at the age of twenty-five, was
seen in this vision sitting in his tomb at Alandi, where
a root from a nearby tree had encircled his neck and
was choking off the prana in his still-living body.
Acting on this meditative vision, Eknath dug into the
tomb and found Jnaneshvar just as he had envisualized
him.   He loosened the root and removed it from
around the saint's throat.   And while he was in the
tomb, he took the manuscript of Jnaneshvar's famous
book, *Jnaneshvari*, which had been buried with him,
and brought the book back to the light of day.   In
Eknath's time, the words of this great book had been
corrupted by various transcribers, and so Eknath brought
forth the authentic *Jnaneshvari* to serve as the authority.   This is a true story.

Eknath went on to write some wonderful books on
the true realization of God; this little book of Songs
written by him is called *Haripatha*, or "Sing The Name
Of God".   Others before him, including Jnaneshvar
himself, had written such a collection of verses with
the same title; here, then, is Eknath's version of the
oft-repeated call to remember God by singing His
name continually within the heart:

Haripatha
("Sing The Name Of God")

1.

In the eyes of Hari's servant, God is everywhere;
We can see Him by our love and faith.
To put an end to all distress,
Sing Hari's name, and be released from birth and
    death.
Rebirth results from clinging to the world;
The devotees of Hari cling to Him alone.
Dissolved in Hari, they lose the sense of "I";
Where only One remains, both "I" and "Thou" are
    gone.
Says Eknath, "Remember Hari; meditate on Him!
Always be aware of Hari; sing aloud His name."

2.

Sing Hari's name, or else be still;
Don't chatter and gossip -- give up your pride.
Find joy in surender of "I" and "Thou";
Your joy will then bring peace to all,
And lead the lost to the righteous path.
He who walks God's path with love and faith
Will not be caught in the snare of the world.
Says Eknath, "I have unmistakably seen the Lord;
He's everywhere before my eyes.
I see Him when I'm in a crowd as well as when I'm
    alone."

5.

That mouth is a rat-hole which does not sing the
    name [of God];
That tongue is a viper that lives therein.
That unscented speech is the shriek of a witch;
That life is accursed. In hell suffering awaits.
Not wife, wealth, or children, but only Hari, can save
    you;
In your final journey, you'll travel alone.
Therefore, while living, seek the company of the
    saints;
Through such company, you'll at last be united with
    God.
Says Eknath, "These two syllables, 'Ha' and 'ri',
Have saved millions; it is this I continually sing."

6.

Blessed is that mother whose child loves the name
    [of God];
Such love is the fruit of good deeds in past lives.
In a life without God, what good fruit can there be?
The whole essence of Vedanta is in 'Ha' and 'ri'.
This song of God's name is sufficient to man;
Not yoga, nor yajna, nor puja does he need.
The cream of sadhana is the singing of the name;
Says Eknath, "All is accomplished by singing "Hari!"
He who sings the name is ever free, a knower of
    Brahman;
Therefore, sing Hari, Hari.

7.

Your human body is the reward of good deeds,
But unless it's used to increase love for God,
Alas, O man, it will totter to doom.
O fool, learn the secret of extinguishing all karma,
And thus hasten the dawn of your unending good.
Your fervent desire to sing the Divine name
Is the reward you have earned from your countless
    past lives.
Whether a king or a beggar, a prince or a thief,
He who does not fill his mouth with the name [of
    God] fills it with dust.
Says Eknath, "Sing Hari; Liberation will come!"

8.

One who sips Divine nectar by singing the name
Will view Liberation as a very small thing.
That home where the sound of the Divine name is
    heard
Is the city of Kashi, the holiest ground.
Even Varanasi must crumble one day,
But the name of God will forever resound.
Thousands of creatures come and go in a wink;
The Lord's devotees enjoy watching this play.
Says Eknath, "So many have lived and died in this
    world;
But he alone is blessed who resorts to the name.

11.

To learn the true knowledge, to unlearn what is
    false,
The true Teacher's guidance and grace is required.
The lovers of God's form then attain to the Formless;
Do not doubt this, O man; your tongue may fall out.
When an actor, disguised as a beggar, receives alms,
It's the actor who receives what the beggar is given.
In the same way, the love which is offered to the
    form
Is received by the Formless, the God-beyond-form.
Says Eknath, "I've perceived that both the form and
    the Formless
Are the play of the Lord."

12.

Can one who's seen Hari and enthroned Him within
Ever be touched by sorrow or pain?
Though that lover may have had an unsavory past,
By singing the Divine name, his life is made pure.
One who sings every day the holy name of God,
Brings blessings upon his parents and family as well.
But those whose minds are reeking of lust, anger and
    greed
Cannot reap the full fruit of singing the name.
Says Eknath, "The singing of the name [of God] is
    my secret:
I've revealed it to you; now please sing Hari's name!

13.

Sing Hari when you give, and Hari when you get;
Sing Hari when you're happy, and Hari when you
    play.
Sing Hari when you're chanting, while you eat, and
    while you work;
Sing Hari when you're by yourself; sing Hari in a
    crowd.
Sing loudly Hari's name when you find you're in a
    brawl;
When your life is giving out, sing Hari's name aloud.
Sing Hari when you're pounding grain,
When you sit, and when you rise.
Says Eknath, "In the forest, or in the marketplace --
Wherever you may be, keep singing Hari's name."

14.

The universe is made of three, five, twenty-five,
Or even thirty-six Principles, they say.
How many branches, I don't know; but Hari is the
    root!
"The soul is only Shiva's Maya;" so they say.
These too are only wavelets on the ocean of Hari!
Oyster-shell appears as silver, a rope seems to be a
    snake;
Yet 'silver' and 'snake' are illusions;
Both the subject and the object are Hari.
Says Eknath, "The crown of wisdom is bestowed
On the one who sings loudly the name of Hari."

15.

By the power of his imagination, a   man   creates
    goals;
Then, seeking to attain them, he forgets his Lord.
He may attain those goals on which his heart dwells,
Yet attaining those goals can never bring peace.
Yearn for a goal that's nearby: Hari's feet!
Then Hari will grant you whatever you wish.
Until   the   knot   of   imagination   is   untied,
Hari will stay away; birth and death will go on.
Says Eknath, "I've found it -- the secret of Hari:
Even my imagination has become one with Him."

16.

Can an impotent man appreciate the charms of a
    girl?
Can a woman who's barren appreciate what childbirth
    is like?
A lamp to a blind man,
Or fragrant sandal-paste to a mule,
Or milk to a serpent;
All these have no use.
What good is a lecture to an angry, faithless man?
It's just a tiring exertion of speech!
The company of the mean is not good; it is harmful.
Says Eknath, "Shun the widked and cherish the good."

19.

Take refuge in the name; it will lead you to Hari.
Why resort to the needless activities of the world?
Take refuge in That which will free you from agony
At the hands of Yama in the kingdom of death --
In That which will free you from the pain of rebirth.
The name of Hari is the essence of all sadhanas,
The seed of all mantras, the means to the Self.
The singing of Hari is worth thousands of yajnas;
Says Eknath, "Sing Hari, live as Hari Himself --
You'll become one with Hari; it's certain, beyond
    doubt."

20.

The sun and the moon in their circular course
Are ignorant of Hari; hence their unceasing whirl.
The thousand-headed serpent [in the story of Creation]
Joyously attempted to sing His praises,
But became exhausted in the end.
The Vedas, in hopes of describing Him, failed;
How, then, shall you know Him with no effort at all?
Accumulate merit, always sing the name [of God];
Serve the true Teacher faithfully; then you'll realize
    Him.
Says Eknath, "Even fools become wise by singing His
    name;
So I urge you all to sing Hari's name aloud."

21.

Both the world outside and the world within
Will delude you, unless you see Hari in them.
Yajnavalkya, Shuka, Datta, and Kapila
Attained knowledge of Hari, and remained united
    with Him,
Dear ones, come close: cling fast to Hari's name;
His name is the boat to cross over this sea.
There's no need for fear! By resorting to the name,
Countless saints have drowned in bliss, and thus were
    fulfilled.
Says Eknath, "I've opened a market that's unique:
My entire stock I offer you, and everything is free."

22.

Take refuge in Hari's name; sing it with faith.
Then Hari, Himself, will keep you in His care;
He'll take up the burden of your worldly life.
Don't languish and worry; our Lord knows your plight.
He protects every soul; He'll protect you as well.
Did you think only you would be unloved and forgot?
Accept this life in which you're now placed;
Witness the play your past karma has made.
Says Eknath, "It's only by Shri Hari's grace
That the store of past karma is finally erased."

23.

When a poor girl marries a rich man's son,
All of her poverty vanishes at once.
The same is true of a devotee
On whom smiles Shri Hari's grace.
Then God and His devotee are no longer apart,
But one, as they were at the start;
Like the lump of camphor on the arati-tray,
Consumed in, and united with, the fire.
Says Eknath, "See even your attachments as Hari;
Then you'll live as Hari, you'll live as the Self."

24.

Sing Hari as you talk, and as you move about;
Sing Hari while you play as a child.
Sing the name of Hari; all your wishes will come
true --
You'll hold Brahman, like a fruit, in your palm.
Sing Hari when you're standing, and when you're
sitting down;
Sing Hari as you witness the game Existence plays.
Sing Hari when you're in your chair, and when you're
in your bed;
With every single bite of food, keep singing Hari's
name.
Sing Hari at the end of day, and Hari in the morning;
Sing Hari when you march to war, and Hari when
you're alone.
Sing Hari when you're in trouble; cling to Him with
love.
Sing Hari when you're wandering, or when you're
doing chores.
Sing Hari when you're giving, and Hari when you
seek;
Sing Hari as you move along, with every single step.
Sing Hari in your homeland, and when you're far
away;
Sing Hari in the day and night, and always be awake.
Sing Hari in your loneliness, and in the crowded
streets;
Sing Hari when your last breath leaves -- sing Hari,
and be free.
Performing duties, taking pleasure, or while you're

earning wealth,

Sing Hari's name, and all desires will surely be fulfilled.

Sing Hari for your own delight, and for the good of
all;

Sing Hari to reach Brahman, even when you feel no
love.

O sing the name of Hari; Liberation will be assured.

"Hari is my only treasure!" Remember this, and sing.

Sing "Hari! Hari!" joyfully; He's the origin of all
bliss.

Says Eknath, "Please sing Hari, whether in a crowd
or in the woods;

Within you and without -- no matter where you are,

There's no one else but Hari! He's sporting everywhere!"

This song of fourteen stanzas is, indeed, the sacred
Gaya [mantra];

Those who sing it save themselves, and their ancestors
as well.

25.

Yogis try to see the Self through exertions and through
strain,

But that Self, whom I call Hari, I see without their
pain.

Hari, whom my ears have heard, has also filled my
eyes;

Everywhere I see Hari, only Hari, everywhere.

The celebrated paths to God: bhakti, karma, and
jnan,

Are outlined in this song of Hari; it's the essence of
all paths.

Whoever sings this song with love for God

Will be blessed with Hari's grace.

Says Eknath, "My Hari-song has reached its end;

So please sing "Hari! Hari! I urge you all once
again."

Reflection

In this storm-tossed ocean of the mind, your fragile boat is carried up and down, from side to side. You have but one anchor in this chaotic storm: the name of Hari. Fix it deep in the bedrock of this ocean's floor, and cling tenaciously to the anchor-line; above the sound, above the frightful threat, hear only Hari! Hari! Hari! Hari! Then watch the turbulent waves subside, and see the dawning Sun, triumphant, rise reflected on a tranquil sea.

In times of raging storm, His name is your unfailing anchor; in the calm beauty of the day, the name is the Sun that fills your day with light, and illumines the path ahead. At night, when navigating darkened seas, that same name will be the pole-star leading you home.

Hari! Hari! No other creature, place, or thing exists but Thee. Then, let me name all that appears before my outer or my inner eye as Thee, seeing Thee alone; for there's nothing else but Thee!

Oh, what marvellous beauty, what delicious joy, what wondrous vision of content, arises, like perfume, from the nectar of the name! O friends, let me not be the only one who enjoys such good fortune as this. This nectar is incomparably sweet, and it costs nothing! It's free! Just taste it: in the secret chamber of your mind, say "Hari!" Again, call "Hari!" Soon you'll be a Hari-junky, addicted to His name, like me!

*   *   *

IN PRAISE OF GOD

I

Let us now, for our own heart's joy, give praise
to God. He is the Refuge of the troubled mind and
the Bringer of peace to the troubled heart. As a
cold drink of water to a thirsty man, so is the name
of God to the wearied soul. He is the cool Cave of
the heart, wherein the soul finds quiet sanctuary
from the darting demons of egotistical thought. He
makes the passionate will to be stilled in silence,
and dispels all the incriminations of the wounded
heart. O let us rest in that silent, bliss-filled Cave,
hidden away from the clamor of the world; and drink
from the fountain of the nectar of His name.

O mind, scratch His name on the cave-wall of
your heart, and never let your eyes be without the
sight of His name. Sing His name softly in that
heart-sanctuary, that your ears may never be without
the sound. And give praise to Him who alone is
worthy of praise; for all that is done is done by
Him, and every gift that comes is a gift from His
hand.

O my heart, praise Him with words, and praise
Him in acts of love. No sin has ever touched so
much as a hair on the head of one who is busied
with the praise and remembrance of God. If you
wish to do some good in this world, O my soul,
never stray from His dwelling-place in the heart.
For, as the moon sheds the light of the Sun only
when its face is turned to the Sun, so may we be
bathed in and reflect His gentle Love only when
we're turned in love to Him.

II

We gather to give praise to God, not that we
might please Him with our devotion, nor to make a
show to others of our holy ways. Why, then, should
we find pleasure in singing His praise? Is it not out
of a pure love that springs from God Himself and
wells up to overflowing from within us? Is it not
His own heart's Love that made us, and that fills
our every fibre with a sweet desire? And is it not
His inward flame of Love round which we, moth-like,

dance, yearning to be extinguished in His unifying
light?

He is the Love and He is the Light that draws us
to Himself. From His gentle Light we have emerged,
and to Him we shall return. May we learn, in this
fragile life, to walk always in His Love, and to keenly
sense in every moment His all-pervading Light. May
we breathe His joy, and taste His sweetness, and
shed His mercy on everyone we meet.

It is this for which we gather, for which we give
Him praise. For, as the summer flowers blossom
forth the exuberant joy and beauty of God on earth,
so do our hearts blossom forth His Love in songs of
praise; and mercifully shower on ourselves the fullness
of His Light.

III

How, Lord, may I praise Thee? My soul yearns
to flood the world with Thy praise, yet when I open
my mouth to speak, there are no words to say. My
heart leaps up to sing, but the sound is stillborn in
bewildered silence. My arms lift up thousands of
bouquets of multihued flowers to lay at Thy feet, but
fall helpless in realization that these flowers already
belonged to Thee, were indeed Thy glory and Thy
gift.

How may I praise Thee, Lord, who art the singer,
the praise, and the instigator of the desire to praise?
What words are worthy to speak of Thee? What gift
is not Thine own? What song is not Thy sound?

O God, who dost fill my heart with the desire to
praise Thee, let Thy song of love cascade from this
heart which is also Thine own, and enchant the world
with its joyful melody. Let all hearts be awakened
to see Thy spreading light. Let knowledge of Thee
spring up like a clear spring of water to quench the
thirst of every mind, and satisfy every soul with
certainty and peace.

O God, Thou dost praise Thyself in the countless
hearts of countless creatures fountained forth from
Thine own effulgent Will. If it be Thy Will, let this
life which Thou hast imaged into being become an
instrument of Thy praise, whether in song or in silence.
Let Thy love, Thy grace, Thy boundless joy release

itself and flow through this projected form of Thine
and flood the world with Thine own light and Thine
own song to lift all souls to Thee.

IV

Lord, when I look within me, I see Thy light and
I know Thy peace, and I am guided by Thy sweet
words of wisdom.   And when I look about me, I see
only Thee in all Thy splendorous forms.   It has been
said that man is like an empty bottle floating in the
sea of God; water flows within and water flows
without; everywhere there is only the vast ocean of
God.   Thus, Lord, I am immersed in Thy ocean of
Consciousness and Light, and I know Thee both within
and without.

But, O God, what of this 'bottle', this "me",
which separates the within from the without?   What
is this "I" that stands apart and speaks to Thee of
within and without?   O my Lord, even this body is
Thine own!   It is a form composed of consciousness
and Light, composed of Thyself; it is a shimmering
mass of Energy projected from Thee, and can never
be separate from Thee.

Who, then, is this "I" that speaks of "I and Thou",
and thus sets up a division between my soul and
Thee?   Truly, there is none else but thee; there is
none but the one Life that is manifest as all this
vast cosmos in all its variety of color and form.
And, though I sometimes imagine I am far from
Thee, and I seek Thee in the darkness and turbulence
of my mind, truly I can never be separate from
Thee.

Therefore, let me ever remember my oneness, my
identity, with Thee.   For the lover, the Beloved, and
the love itself, all are one.   And I know: "I am the
Soul of all; I am the Light that illumines the world.
I am as pure and vast as the infinite blue sky.   I am
the Self of all.   I am the Self of all."

V

I know, my Lord, that, in essence, I am Thine
and ever one with Thee.   Yet, so long as there is in
me this errant and rebellious mind, let it learn to be
ever-ready at Thy service -- the service of my eternal

Self.   How, then, may I serve my greater Self, my
God?   Only by letting Thee live through me.   By
loving what Thou lovest.   By desiring what Thou desir-
est.   By seeing with Thine eye of equal vision, and
loving all as Thou dost love and sustain all.

Let me, then, be perfect in love, O God, as Thou
art perfect, that I may be fit to serve as Thy instrument.   All of us are helplessly driven to action in
this world by the forces of Nature; therefore, let all
my actions be done in the joyful remembrance of the
Self who lives as me.   And may the darkness of
illusion be so dispelled in me that Thy light shines
forth clearly in all I say or do.

Let me see no other in this world but the one
Self whose dance of joy fills all this immense universe;
let me offer my work as well as my heart's love to
Thee in all Thy many forms.   And, lastly, may my
heart's good intent so move Thee that Thou dost
consent to listen to my prayer, and lift up my mind
to greater likeness with Thyself, till I am merged and
melted into Thee, and know first-hand my oneness
with my Lord.

VI

O my Lord, remove from me all confusion and
dullness of mind, and open my heart to the sweetness
of Thy Love; for I have no other goal but Thee.

It is Thy most wondrous grace to me that, when I
am sunk in the greyness of my own misery, Thou
dost cast a sunbeam of Light into my heart and
awaken in me Thy Love.   O Lord, I have no other
goal but Thee.

And so I ask of Thee, O God, lift up my soul to
Thee, that has so long been locked in a self-created
dungeon of darkness and despair.   Lift me into the
clarity and freedom of Thy Light!   For I have no
other goal but Thee.

O Father, grant me this grace of Thine; light up
my soul with the gladness of Thy joyful presence, and
fill my heart with song.   For I have no other goal
but Thee, O Lord.

Thy Love is the food I crave; increase in me Thy
bounty and let me feast on Thy sweetness.   For Thy
grace of Love is my only treasure, my sole desire.   I

have no other goal but Thee, O Lord.

Assuage, then, O God, the pain of darkness which I so often bear, and open my eyes and my heart to Thee. Reveal to me that Thou art all that appears before me, and that Thou art my very soul, my life, my light, my joy. Dear Lord, I have no other goal but Thee.

VII

Once, when this soul was meditating on her Lord, she became aware of the presence and nearness of God, and she earnestly entreated Him, saying, "Dear Lord, so many in this world of Thine suffer needlessly because of their ignorance of Thee and do not know the joy of devotion to Thee. What may I say or do to open their eyes to Thy truth and Thy joy?"

And the Lord replied to her,

My child, give your love to all, but give sparingly of your words. I am within others also, and I shall reveal Myself to them in My time. Therefore, take no thought of others, how they might be shown the way to Me; for, if I would teach others through you, I wll do so only after you have subdued yourself, so that I might shine freely from your eyes as a beacon for all. I am Love, and am best taught by loving.

This soul, receiving that inner revelation, suddenly realized that her God was the Soul of her soul, the heart of her heart, and manifested through her as the joy of love. And then and there she vowed her allegiance to the God of her heart, proclaiming:

Thou art Love, and I shall follow all Thy ways.
I shall have no care, for Love cares only to love.
I shall have no fear, for Love is fearless;
Nor shall I frighten any, for Love comes sweetly and meek.
I shall keep no violence within me, neither in thought nor in deed,
For Love comes peacefully.
I shall bear no shield or sword, for the defense

of Love is love.
I shall seek Thee in the eyes of men, for Love
seeks Thee always.
I shall keep silence before Thine enemies,
And lift to them Thy countenance, for all are
powerless before Thee.
I shall keep Thee in my heart with precious
care,
Lest Thy Light be extinguished by the winds;
For without Thy Light, I am in darkness.
I shall go free in the world with Thee --
Free of all bondage to anything but Thee --
For Thou art my God, the sole father of my
being,
The sweet breath of Love that lives in my
heart;
And I shall follow Thee, and live with Thee,
And lean on Thee 'til the end of my days.

And, after pledging her life to God's Love, this
soul felt such inner rapture that her heart was overcome with sweetness and light from within; and with
great humility she asked, "How, O Lord, may I subdue
my own selfish desires so that Thy perfect Love may
shine through me upon all Thy children?"
And the Lord said to her:

Keep your mind on Me, and self shall be
overcome. Your thoughts are with that which
you love, and lead you to the object of your
desire. If you love the pleasures and favors of
the world, your thoughts will be with the
world, and you shall obtain your desire. But
if you love Me, your thoughts will be with Me
and you shall live as My beloved child, and I
shall lead you to your end in Me.

And the soul was so filled with love and gratitude
that she cried out, "O Lord, Thou art my joy and
my sole desire!" And, so saying, she lifted up her
mind to God, and kept it there in focused concentration, till all the wispy clouds of thought dissolved
away, leaving her mind clear, free, and full of light.
And then, from the stillness deep within this soul,
came the heavenly desire to be merged in and one

with God.   "Dear God," she whispered, "let me be
one with Thee -- not that I might glory in Thy Love,
but that I might speak out in Thy praise and to Thy
glory, for the benefit of all Thy children!"   And, in
that very moment, the veil of separation fell away,
and she exclaimed:

O my God, even this body is Thine own!
Though I call to hee and seek Thee amidst
chaos,
Even I, who seemed an unclean pitcher amidst
Thy waters,
Even I am Thine own.

Does a wave cease to be of the ocean?
Do the mountains and the gulfs cease to be of
the earth?
Or does a pebble cease to be stone?
How can I escape Thee?
Thou art even That which thinks of escape!

Even now, I speak the word, "Thou", and create
duality;
I love, and create hatred;
I am in peace, and am fashioning chaos;
Standing on the peak, I necessitate the depths.

But now, weeping and laughing are gone;
Night is become day.
Music and silence are heard as one;
My ears are all the universe.

All motion has ceased;
Everything continues.
Life and death no longer stand apart.
No I, no thou;
No now, or then.
Unless I move, there is no stillness.

Nothing to lament, nothing to vanquish,
Nothing to pride oneself on;
All is accomplished in an instant.
All may now be told without effort;
Where is there a question?
Where is the "temple?"
Which the Imperishable, which the abode?

I am the pulse of the turtle;
I am the clanging bells of joy.
I bring the dust of blindness;
I am the fire of song.
I am in the clouds and in the gritty soil;
In pools of clear water my image is found.

I am the dust on the feet of the wretched,
The toothless beggars of every land.
I have given sweets that decay to those who
crave them;
I have given my wealth unto the poor and lonely.
My hands are open; nothing is concealed.

All things move together of one accord;
Assent is given throughout the universe to every
falling grain.
The Sun stirs the waters of my heart,
And the vapor of my love flies to the four
corners of the world;
The moon stills me, and the cold darkness is
my bed.

I have but breathed, and everything is rearranged
And set in order once again.
A million worlds begin and end in every breath,
And, in this breathing, all things are sustained.

Reflection

The great Sufi mystic and poet, Jalaluddin Rumi, said: "The religion of love is distinct from all others; the lovers of God have a religion and a faith all their own."

What is this religion of love? It has no name. Neither does it have any nationality. It is beginningless, and without end. It originates in the heart, and can only be mimicked in speech. It is the cry of the heart for God's mercy and grace. Yet, even this heartfelt pain is His grace; for this yearning is but the drawing of His comfort and solace.

Love calls, and Love responds. In both instances, that Love is accompanied by tears. Yet, even this calling, though painful, is sweet; for it is *His* Love that burns in the heart. And when He responds, the heart's cup is filled with much more than it can hold. No eyes have seen this filling; no words have ever told of its taste. Yet, in countless hearts, throughout the universe, this religion lives, and supplies the world with Love.

*   *   *

About The Author

The author of *The Wisdom Of Vedanta* was born Stan Trout in Indianapolis, Indiana on August 14, 1938. After service in the Navy, he settled in northern California, where he pursued his studies in philosophy and literature. At the age of twenty-eight, he became acquainted with the philosophy of Vedanta, and experienced a strong desire to realize God. Abandoning all other pursuits, he retired to a solitary life in a cabin hermitage in the mountain forests near Santa Cruz, California, where he devoted himself, for the next five years, to the realization of the Self.

In the autumn of 1966, he became enlightened by the grace of God, and realized the great unity. This experience formed the hub round which all his future activities were to revolve. In 1971, he journeyed to India to live and study at the Ashram of Swami Muktananda of Ganeshpuri; and in 1978 he was initiated by his master into the ancient Order of *sannyasa*, and given the monastic name of Swami Abhayananda -- a Sanskrit name, which means "the bliss of fearlessness."

Since that time, Swami Abhayananda has taught the philosophy of Vedanta and the art of meditation in a number of major cities throughout the U.S., and has lectured at numerous colleges and universities. He presently resides in the Olympia area of Washington state, where he continues to teach, write, and publish his works on the knowledge of the Self.

*   *   *

NOTES

Preface

1. Jnaneshvar, *Amritanubhav*, *5:66*; Abhayananda, S.,
    *Jnaneshvar: The Life & Works Of The Celebrated
    13th Century Indian Mystic-Poet*; p. 152

1. Introduction To Vedanta

1. Shankara, *Vivekachudamani*; Prabhavananda, Swami
    and Isherwood, C., *Shankara's Crest-Jewel Of Dis-
    crimination*; pp. 112–113

2. *Kena Upanishad, I:4–6*

3. *Kaushitaki Upanishad, III:8*

4. *Svetasvatara Upanishad, II:14*

5. *Ibid., I:11*

6. *Isha Upanishad, I:7*

7. *Brihad–Aranyaka Upanishad,*

8. Shankara, *Vivekachudamani;* Prabhavananda, Swami
    and Isherwood, C., *Ibid.,* p. 64

9. *Vedanta Sutras, I:1:5;* Thibaut, George (trans.),
    The Vedanta Sutras Of Badarayana, Vol. I, p. 51

10. *Vedanta Sutras, III:2:37;* Thibaut, G., *Ibid.,* Vol. II,
    p. 174

11. *Vedanta Sutras;* Thibaut, G., *Ibid.,* Vol. II, p. 173

12. *Svetasvatara Upanishad, I:12*

13. *Ibid., III:19*

14. *Ibid., I:11*

15. *Ibid., II:17*

2.   The Perennial Philosophy

1.   *Matthew, Gospel of, 23:36-39*

2.   *Udana, 8*

3.   Dadu, *Bani 190, 191;* Orr, W.G., *A Sixteenth Century Indian Mystic;* pp. 93-94

4.   Dattatreya, *Avadhut Gita, I:39;* Abhayananda, S., *Dattatreya: The Song Of The Avadhut;* p. 33

5.   *Ibid., I:42;* Abhayananda, S., *Ibid.,* p. 35

6.   *Ibid., I:55;* Abhayananda, S., *Ibid.,* p. 41

7.   *Ibid., I:56;* Abhayananda, S., *Ibid.,* p. 41

3.   The Supreme Self

1.   Bohm, David, "On The Intuitive Understanding Of Non-Locality As Implied By Quantum Theory", *Foundations Of Physics, Vol. V (1975);* p. 96, 102

2.   Zukov, Gary, *The Dancing Wu Li Masters;* p.

3.   Jnaneshvar, *Amritanubhav: Chapt. 7:233, 240, 135, 143, 144, 146, 162, 163;* Abhayananda, S., *Jnaneshvar: The Life & Works, etc.;* pp. 193, 194, 183, 184, 186

4.   Oneness

1.   Jnaneshvar, *Amritanubhav, I:21-24, 41, 42;* Abhayananda, S., *Jnaneshvar: The Life & Works, etc.;* p. 116

2.   Shankara, *Vivekachudamani, III:7;* Prabhavananda, Swami & Isherwood, C., *Op. Cit.;* p. 49

3.   Jnaneshvar, *Amritanubhav, 7: 165, 233, 235, 237, 244;* Abhayananda, S., *Op. Cit.,* pp. 186, 193-195

4.   Jnaneshvar, *Changadev Pasashti, 25;* Abhayananda, S., *Jnaneshvar: The Life & Works, etc.;* p. 240

5. Maya

1. *Bhagavad Gita,* 18:61

2. Shankara, *Vivekachudamani, III:7;* Prabhavananda, S. and Isherwood, C., *Shankara's Crest-Jewel Of Discrimination*; pp. 51-52

3. Plato, *Republic, Book VII*

4. *Bhagavad Gita, 7:14*

5. Vidyaranya, *Panchadashi, 6:236;* Shastri, H.P. (trans.), *Panchadashi*; p. 161

6. The Quest For Joy

1. *Taittiriya Upanishad, 3:1-6*

2. *Maitri Upanishad, 6:24*

3. Vidyaranya, *Panchadashi, 14:41, 58-64;* Shastri, H.P., *Op Cit.;* pp. 459-465

4. Jnaneshvar, *Amritanubhav, 5:66;* Abhayananda, S., *Jnaneshvar: The Life & Works, etc.;* p. 152

7. The Wisdom Of The Svetasvatara Upanishad

1. *Svetasvatara Upanishad, I:1-3, 6*

2. *Ibid., I:7-10; II:15*

3. *Ibid., II:16; III:2*

4. *Ibid., III:3, 16-17*

5. *Ibid., III:7-8*

6. *Ibid., II:7-9; II:2; II:14*

7. *Ibid., IV:1-6, 15, 17, 10*

8.   The Wisdom Of The Svetasvatara Upan. -- Part II

1.   *Svetasvatara Upanishad, V:6-13*

2.   Plotinus, *Enneads, 27:4:2-5;* Turnbull, G.H.; p. 118

3.   Shankara, *Vivekachudamani, III:13;* Prabhavananda, S., p. 64

4.   Shankara, *Commentaries On The Vedanta Sutras;* Thibaut, G. (trans.), *The Vedanta Sutras Of Bad-arayana;* Vol. II, p. 173; Vol. I, p. 51; Vol. II, p. 174

5.   Meister Eckhart, *Sermon 6;* Colledge, E. & McGinn, B. (trans.), *Meister Eckhart: The Essential Sermons, etc.;* p. 188; *Sermon 23;* Blackney, R.B., *Meister Eckhart: A Modern Translation;* p. 206

6.   Shankara, *Atma Bodha, 2*

7.   Shankara, *Vivekachudamani, I:7, 12;* Prabhavananda, Swami & Isherwood, C., *Op. Cit.;* pp. 33, 34

8.   *Svetasvatara Upanishad, V:12-14, 16*

9.   *Ibid., V:17-20*

9.   Vedanta -- Christian Style

1.   Meister Eckhart, *Sermon 6;* Colledge, E. & McGinn B. (trans.), *Meister Eckhart: The Essential Sermons, etc.;* p. 188

2.   Meister Eckhart, *Sermon 18;* Blackney, R.B., *Meister Eckhart: A Modern Translation;* p. 181

3.   Nicholas of Cusa, *De Visio Dei, XXV;* Salter, E.G., *The Vision Of God;* p. 129

4.   *Ibid., XVI;* p. 78

5.   *Ibid., XII;* p. 56

6.   *Ibid., XVII;* pp. 81-82

7.   *Ibid., XIV;* p. 66

8.   Juan de la Cruz, *Spiritual Canticle,26:4;* Kavanaugh, K. & Rodriguez, O. (trans.), *The Collected Works Of John Of The Cross;* p. 512

9.   *Ibid., 22:3-4;* p. 497

10.   *Ibid., Living Flame Of Love, III:78;* p. 641

11.   *John, Gospel of, 13:40*

12.   *Matthew, Gospel of, 5:43-48*

13.   *Ibid., 6:24-25, 31-33*

14.   Dionysius, *Mystical Theology, I;* Editors Of The Shrine Of Wisdom, *Mystical Theology, etc.;* p. 10

15.   *Ibid., V;* p. 16

16.   *Ibid., I;* p. 10

17.   Juan de la Cruz, *The Ascent Of Mount Carmel, I:5:6;* Kavanaugh & Rodriguez, *Op. Cit.;* p. 83

18.   *Ibid., I:15:2;* p. 106

19.   Thomas à Kempis, *De Imitatio Christi, III:9;* Abhayananda, S., *Thomas à Kempis: On The Love Of God;* pp. 109-110

20.   *Ibid., III:3;* p. 90

21.   *Ibid., II:5;* p. 70

22.   *Ibid., III:4;* pp. 95-96

10.   Non-Dualism In The Teachings Of Jesus

1.   *John, Gospel of, 13:40*

2.   *Ibid., 17:25*

3.   *Ibid., 8:54*

4.   *Thomas, Gospel of, 114;* Robinson, James M.(trans.),
     The Nag Hammadi Library; pp. 118–130

5.   *Ibid., 51*

6.   *Luke, Gospel of, 17:20*

7.   *Thomas, Gospel of, 3;* Robinson, J.M., *Op. Cit.*

8.   *Ibid., #83*

9.   *Ibid., #24*

10. *John, Gospel of, 1:1*

11. *Thomas, Gospel of, #50*

12. *Ibid., #77*

13. *Matthew, Gospel of, 5:14–16*

14. *Mark, Gospel of, 9:1*

15. *Thomas, Gospel of, #111;* Robinson, J.M., *Op. Cit.*

16. *Ibid., #59*

17. *Ibid., #70*

18. *Ibid., #17*

19. *Luke, Gospel of, 18:18*

20. *Luke, Gospel of, 18:18–30; Matthew, 19:16*

21. *Matthew, Gospel of, 5:17*

22. *Thomas, Gospel of, #105*

23. *Ibid., #28*

1.   Plotinus, *Enneads, I:9;* Turnbull, G.H., *Op Cit.,* p. 49

2.   Shankara, *Vivekachudamani, III:10;* Prabhavananda, S.,
      & Isherwood, C., *Op. Cit.,* p. 58

12.   Beyond Learned Ignorance

1.   Vidyaranya, *Panchadashi, 6:16;* Shastri, H.P. (trans.),
      Op. Cit., p. 97

2.   *Kena Upanishad, II:1*

3.   *Kena Upanishad, I:5*

4.   *Kaushitaki Upanishad, 3:8*

5.   *Katha Upanishad, II:24*

6.   *Katha Upanishad, II:23; Mundaka Upanishad, II:3*

7.   Nicholas of Cusa, *De venatione sapientiae,* Ch. xii;
      Beck, L.W., *Early German Philosophy,* p. 64

8.   Nicholas of Cusa, *De docta ignorantia, I:3;* Heron, G.
      (trans.), p.

9.   Nicholas of Cusa, *De sapientia, I;* Dolan, J.P. (ed.),
      *Unity And Reform: Selected Writings of Nicholas
      of Cusa;* p. 107

10.   *Ibid.;* pp. 115–116

13.   How To Meditate On The Self

1.   Jnaneshvar, *Amritanubhav, 9:20–21;* Abhayananda, S.,
      Op. Cit., p. 207

2.   *Ibid., 9:31, 34;* p. 208

3.   *Ibid., 9: 38–41;* p. 209

4.   *Ibid., 9:35–36;* pp. 208–209

5.   *Svetasvatara Upanishad, 3:12*

15. The Wisdom Of The Katha Upanishad

1. *Mundaka Upanishad, III:1:1-2; Svetasvatara Upanishad, 4:6-7*

17. The Spiritual Life

1. Thomas à Kempis, *De Imitatio Christi,* Abhayananda, S. *Thomas à Kempis: On The Love Of God, Bk. I; Chapt. XV;* p. 33

2. Meister Eckhart, *Sermon 23;* Blackney, *Op. Cit.,* p. 206

19. Shankaracharya: The Man And His Message

1. Shankara, *Vivekachudamani, III:8;* Prabhavananda, S. & Isherwood, C., *Shankara's Crest-Jewel Of Discrimination;* p. 52

2. *Ibid., III:9;* p. 58

3. *Ibid., III:12;* pp. 64-65

4. *Ibid., III:15;* p. 69

5. *Ibid., III:19;* p. 77

6. *Ibid., III:21;* p. 83

7. Shankara, *Atma Bodha, 34, 35, 37*

20. Self-Knowledge

1. *Mundaka Upanishad, 1:2:10*

21. Self-Knowledge -- Part II

1. *Taittiriya Upanishad, 2:7*

2. Patanjali, *Yoga Sutras, 2:26*

23.   **Philosophy Of Recognition**

1.   Shankara, *Vivekachudamani, III:16;* Prabhavananda,
      S. & Isherwood, C., *Op. Cit.;* pp. 70–71

2.   Jnaneshvar, *Amritanubhav, 7:165, 166;* Abhayananda,
      S., *Jnaneshvar: The Life & Works, etc.;* p. 186

3.   *Ibid., 7:170, 171;* p. 187

4.   *Ibid, 7:235–237, 240;* pp. 193–194

24.   **Philosophy Of Recognition –– Part II**

1.   *Luke, Gospel of, 18:18; Matthew, 19:16*

25.   **The Physical, The Mental, And The Spiritual**

1.   *Vijnana Bhairava, 155*

2.   *Ibid., 24*

3.   *Ibid., 25*

4.   *Ibid., 51*

5.   *Ibid., 64*

6.   *Ibid., 26*

7.   *Ibid., 74*

8.   *Ibid., 92*

9.   *Ibid., 104*

10.   *Ibid., 110*

11.   *Ibid. 63*

12.   *Ibid., 65*

13.   *Ibid., 96*

14.   *Ibid., 97*

15.   *Ibid., 98*

16.   *Ibid., 100*

17.   *Ibid., 101*

18.   *Ibid., 102*

19.   *Ibid., 107*

20.   *Ibid., 108*

21.   *Ibid., 118*

22.   *Ibid., 127*

23.   *Ibid., 132*

24.   Jnaneshvar,
      Amritanubhav,
      9:20,21; 31, 34
      Abhayananda,
      Op. Cit., pp. 2
      208

26.   Vedanta And Buddhism

1.   Buddha, *Udana, 8*

2.   *Ibid.*

3.   Buddha, *The Sermon at The Deer Park, in Benares*

4.   *Ibid.*

5.   *Ibid.*

6.   *Ibid.*

7.   Buddha, *The Dhammapada, I*

8.   *Ibid., XX*

27.   The Meaning Of Renunciation

1.   Swami Rama Tirtha, *In Woods Of God-Realization, Vol. II;* pp. 323-324

28.   The Ox-Herd Pictures

1.   *Bhagavad Gita, 6:33-36*

2.   Dattatreya, *Avadhut Gita, VII:1,3,4,9;* Abhayananda, S., *Dattatreya: The Song Of The Avadhut;* pp. 161, 163, 165

3.   Jnaneshvar, *Amritanubhav, 9:20,21,25,30-32,34,53-55;* Abhayananda, S., *Jnaneshvar: The Life & Works, etc.;* pp. 207-211

29.   As A Man Thinks

1.   *Bhagavad Gita, 6:24-31*

2.   *Ashtavakra Samhita*

30.   The Nature Of The Mind

1.   *Tripura Rahasya*

2. *Yoga Sutras, I:1*

31. The Purification Of The Mind

1. *1 Corinthians, 13:12*

33. The Path Of Divine Love

1. *Taittiriya Upanishad, 3:6*

2. *Bhagavad Gita, 9:34*

3. *Ibid., 11:54*

4. Philo Judaeus, *On Drunkeness, 145f.;* Winston, D., *Philo Of alexandria – The Contemplative Life, etc.;* p. 152

5. Philo Judaeus, *Who Is The Heir?, 69f.*

6. Plotinus, *Enneads, 38:6:22–23;* Turnbull, *Op. Cit.;* p. 199

7. John of the Cross, *The Living Flame Of Love, III: 26–28;* Kavanaugh & Rodriguez, *Op. Cit.;* p. 620

8. Dattatreya, *Avadhut Gita, I:1;* Abhayananda, S., *Dattatreya: The Song Of The Avadhut;* p. 15

9. Shankara, *Vivekachudamani, III:37;* Prabhavananda, S. & Isherwood, C., *Shankara's Crest-Jewel Of Discrimination;* p. 112

10. Sri Ramakrishna, from Nikhilananda, Swami (trans.), *The Gospel Of Ramakrishna;* pp. 173–174

11. *Svetasvatara Upanishad, III:12*

BIBLIOGRAPHY

Abhayananda, Swami, *Jnaneshvar: The Life And Works Of The Celebrated Thirteenth Century Indian Mystic-Poet*, Naples, Atma Books, 1989

_____ *History Of Mysticism: The Unchanging Testament (2nd Revised Edition);* Olympia, Atma Books, 1994

_____ *The Supreme Self: A Modern Upanishad;* Fallsburg, Atma Books, 1984

_____ *Dattatreya: The Song Of The Avadhut;* Olympia, Atma Books, 1992

_____ *Thomas à Kempis: On The Love Of God;* Olympia, Atma Books, 1992

Beck, Lewis W., *Early German Philosophy;* Cambridge, Mass., Belknap Press, 1969

Blackney, Raymond B., *Meister Eckhart: A Modern Translation;* N.Y., Harper Torchbooks, 1941

Colledge, E. and McGinn, B. (Trans.), *Meister Eckhart: The Essential Sermons, Commentaries, Treatises, and Defense;* Ramsey, N.J., Paulist Press, 1982

Dolan, John P. (Ed.), *Unity And Reform: Selected Writings of Nicholas of Cusa;* Notre Dame, University of Notre Dame Press, 1962

Editors of The Shrine Of Wisdom (trans.), *Mystical Theology and The Celestial Hierarchy,* Fintry Brook, England, Shrine of Wisdom, 1965

Heron, Germain (trans.), *On Learned Ignorance;* New Haven, Yale University Press, 1954

Kavanaugh, K. and Rodriguez, O. (trans.), *The Collected Works Of John Of The Cross;* Wash. D.C., ICS Publications, 1973

Nikhilananda, Swami (trans.), *The Gospel Of Ramakrishna;* N.Y., Ramakrishna-Vivekananda Center, 1942

Orr, W.G., *A Sixteenth Century Indian Mystic;* Longon, Lutterworth Press, 1947

Prabhavananda, Swami and Isherwood, Christopher, *Shankara's Crest-Jewel Of Discrimination;* Hollywood, Vedanta Press, 1978

Rama Tirtha, Swami, *In Woods Of Cog-Realization (5 vols.);* Lucknow, Rama Tirtha Pratisthan, 1956

Robinson, James M. (Ed.), *The Nag Hammadi Library;* San Francisco, Harper & Row, 1977

Salter, Emma G. (trans.), *The Vision Of God;* New York, Frederick Ungar Publishing Co., 1960

Shastri, H.P. (trans.), *Panchadashi by Vidyaranya;* London, Shanti Sadan, 1965

Thibaut, George (trans.), *The Vedanta Sutras Of Badarayana (2 vols.);* N.Y., Dover Publications, 1962

Turnbull, Grace H. (Ed.), *The Essence Of Plotinus;* N.Y, Oxford University Press, 1934

Winston, David (trans.), *Philo Of Alexandria -- The Contemplative Life, Giants, and Selections;* Ramsey, N.J., Paulist Press, 1981

Zukov, Gary, *The Dancing Wu Li Masters;* N.Y., Bantam Books, 1979

THE BOOKS OF SWAMI ABHAYANANDA

THE SUPREME SELF: A Modern Upanishad by S. Abhayananda
A modern mystic tells the inspiring story of his own spiritual quest and ultimate enlightenment, and reveals the timeless secrets of the undivided Reality which is the universal Self of all. A great introduction to "mysticism" and the concept of Self-realization.
A quality paperback, 180 pp., ISBN 0-914557-01-7 $9.95

HISTORY OF MYSTICISM: The Unchanging Testament by S. Abhayananda
A comprehensive history of the lives and teachings of over forty famous mystics, from the earliest sages of antiquity to the unique saints of modern times, written from the standpoint of a partisan spokesman for the mystical view. An indispensable volume for the library of the student-initiate as well as the informed scholar.
2nd (Revised) Edition. A quality paperback, 460 pp., ISBN 0-914557-03-3 $16.95
hardback, ISBN 0-914557-08-4 $24.95

THE WISDOM OF VEDANTA by S. Abhayananda
The Non-Dual philosophy of Vedanta, originally presented in the ancient Upanishads of India, is elucidated by a seasoned mystic in thirty-six varied and illuminating Talks, including "Non-Dualism In the Teachings Of Jesus", "Vedanta And Buddhism", "The Philosophy Of Recognition", "The Nature Of The Mind", "The Path Of Divine Love", and much more. The best introduction to Vedanta philosophy available.
2nd (Revised) Edition. A quality paperback, 360 pp., ISBN 0-914557-06-8 $14.95

JNANESHVAR: The Life & Works Of The Celebrated 13th Century Indian Mystic-Poet by S. Abhayananda
The life and works of one of the greatest mystics who ever lived, viewed in the context of the exciting historical milieu in which he lived; with complete translations of his greatest works, including *Amritanubhav*, "The Nectar Of Mystical Experience", *Changadev Pasashti*, "Letter To Changadev", and *Haripatha*, "Sing The Name Of God".
A quality paperback, 260 pp., ISBN 0-914557-02-5 $11.95

DATTATREYA: The Song Of The Avadhut by S. Abhayananda
One of the best known mystical treatises of ancient classical Indian literature, *The Avadhuta Gita* or *Song Of The Avadhut* is also one of the most sublime and uncompromising statements ever written on the unitive knowledge obtained through mystical vision. A compellingly eloquent translation, with Sanskrit transliteration on facing pages.
A quality paperback, 180 pp., ISBN 0-914557-07-6 $7.95

THOMAS Á KEMPIS: On The Love Of God by S. Abhayananda
A revised and edited version of the magnificent 15th century English translation of Thomas á Kempis' Christian classic, *The Imitation Of Christ*. Deprived of its sectarian bias, this great work becomes a devotional manual of truly universal application, a handbook of spiritual contemplation relevant to all true seekers of God. Not for the half-hearted.
A quality paperback, 160 pp., ISBN 0-914557-00-9 $7.95

Add $2.00 shipping & handling to: **ATMA BOOKS**
3430 Pacific Ave. SE
Suite A-6144
Olympia, WA 98501

Grace 275, 277   keep yourself joyful! –237

"So-ham" – I am That – 214

The man of knowledge and the man of devotion 298/1
Hari as Japa – 308